SENSEMAKING FOR WRITING PROGRAMS AND WRITING CENTERS

SENSEMAKING FOR WRITING PROGRAMS AND WRITING CENTERS

EDITED BY
RITA MALENCZYK

UTAH STATE UNIVERSITY PRESS
Logan

© 2023 by University Press of Colorado

Published by Utah State University Press
An imprint of University Press of Colorado
1624 Market Street, Suite 226
PMB 39883
Denver, Colorado 80202-1559

All rights reserved

 The University Press of Colorado is a proud member of the Association of University Presses.

The University Press of Colorado is a cooperative publishing enterprise supported, in part, by Adams State University, Colorado State University, Fort Lewis College, Metropolitan State University of Denver, University of Alaska Fairbanks, University of Colorado, University of Denver, University of Northern Colorado, University of Wyoming, Utah State University, and Western Colorado University.

ISBN: 978-1-64642-434-4 (hardcover)
ISBN: 978-1-64642-435-1 (paperback)
ISBN: 978-1-64642-436-8 (ebook)
https://doi.org/10.7330/9781646424368

Cataloging-in-Publication data for this title is available online at the Library of Congress.

Cover painting, "After the Pear Tomatoes," by Rita Malenczyk

For Nick
1999–2019

CONTENTS

Introduction
   Rita Malenczyk   3

PART I: SENSEMAKING WITH TUTORS AND TEACHERS

1. The Medachtic Tutor: Jewish Discourse, Metaphor, and Undergraduate Tutors' Sensemaking of Writing Center Work
   Andrea Rosso Efthymiou   11

2. Beyond the Anecdote: TA Sensemaking as Writing Program Underlife
   Courtney Adams Wooten   23

3. Celebrating Sensemaking Cultures in the Writing Center: Scaffolding Transparent Communication between Tutors and Directors
   Jeanne R. Smith, Shannon McKeehen, Barbara George, and Yvonne R. Lee   42

4. Tutor-to-Tutor: Attending to the Operations of Race and Privilege among Writing Center Staff Members
   Alba Newmann Holmes   62

5. Making Sense of How Things Feel: Attending to Emotional Experiences in Writing Programs
   Bronwyn T. Williams   85

PART II: SENSEMAKING AND INSTITUTIONAL STRUCTURES

6. New Writing Center Ecologies: Challenging Inherited Sensemaking in the Center
   Genie Nicole Giaimo and Joseph Cheatle   109

7. Stories to Support and Sustain a Program: Connections among the Library, WID, and the Writing Center
   Susanmarie Harrington and Sue Dinitz   127

8. Cascading Texts and Cat's Cradles: An Institutional Ethnographic Approach to Understanding the Textual Production of Unionized Labor
   Melissa Nicolas   141

9. Distributed Leadership for WPAs: Making Sense of Leadership Methods
   Christy I. Wenger   158

10. Sensemaking as Antiracist Writing Program Administration: Reappropriating Activity and Actor-Network Theory
    Brian Hendrickson   181

   Afterword: A 2X2 Review of *Sensemaking for Writing Programs and Writing Centers*
   Karen Keaton Jackson   205

   Index   211
   About the Authors   219

SENSEMAKING FOR WRITING PROGRAMS AND WRITING CENTERS

INTRODUCTION

Rita Malenczyk

Over the last two decades, writing studies has been preoccupied with scholarship and research on writing program and center ecologies, the relationship of individual programs and centers to the larger structures—social, institutional, global—in which they function (see, for instance, Reiff et al. 2015). The implication of that scholarship for writing program and center administrators is that centers and programs are not the only means available for writerly development and that the academic structures we create are not the sole means by which students learn to write. Of these extracurricular literacies, Kevin Roozen claims, "coming to terms with the complexity of undergraduates' growth as writers—not just in terms of improving their ability to produce academic prose but also in the kinds of literate activities in which they will participate and for how long and to what extent—has increasingly meant attending to the writing that goes on beyond the temporal and spatial boundaries of the classroom" (2009, 543). Writing program administrators (WPAs) and writing center directors (WCDs) need to be aware, then, that much goes on in peoples' lives and environments that influences their writing and is beyond our control as teachers and administrators—yet, if attended to, might influence how we administer our programs and centers.

In keeping with this awareness, WPAs and WCDs also need to acknowledge that much goes on in the working lives of our tutors and faculty that is also beyond our control yet may affect how writing is taught and delivered. This collection turns from the outside influences contributing to student literacies to the often-unseen interactions within centers and programs that define or make sense of program and center work. Sensemaking, a concept from organizational theory, is used in this collection to explore how to harness those unseen interactions for more effective administration. What might looking inward—"attending," in Roozen's (2009) words, to the microinteractions of faculty, tutors, and others—show us about attitudes and orientations toward program and center work and ultimately about how that work is done? What other sensemaking cultures exist within our programs and centers too? How, for example, are institutional documents constructed in order to help others make sense of WPA and WCD work?

WHAT IS SENSEMAKING?

Sensemaking, a term native to organizational theory, is a process used to make meaning within groups; the term is most frequently applied to organizations and their processes of understanding events that take place within them. Arguably the best-known theorist of sensemaking is Karl Weick, whose 1995 book *Sensemaking in Organizations* stands as one of the most frequently cited works in the field. Like other sensemaking theorists, Weick believes that sensemaking in organizations is "driven by plausibility rather than accuracy" (55); it is inherently social; it is "grounded in identity construction" (17), which takes place through interaction with others and is not a static but an ongoing process; and "the sensemaker is himself or herself an ongoing puzzle undergoing continual redefinition, coincident with presenting some self to others and trying to decide which self is appropriate" (18). Changes in how people make sense of events within organizations—in other words, changes in how they view the organization—may result in "redefining the organizational identity" (18). Sensemaking is, according to Weick, also "retrospective" (24), "enactive of sensible environments" (30), and "focused on and by extracted cues" (29). In other words, sensemaking focuses on things that happened in the past; affects particular places, times, and events; and is based on observation coupled with experience.

Many organizational theorists focus on narrative, on storytelling as a form of sensemaking. Yiannis Gabriel (2000) likens storytelling in organizations to folklore; Brown et al. (2005) attribute storytelling to the fact that "organizations have a lot of people in them" (20) and that people naturally use stories to make sense of their experience. Those stories serve to explain events in organizations; whether or not such explanations are objectively true makes little or no difference for the sense made by them—they must, rather, be true to the storyteller's sense of events (Brown et al. 2005, 43–44). Stories can explain why one person got promoted and one didn't (Brown et al. 2005, 43–44), why a company seems to be in danger of going bankrupt, and why certain people get along and others don't. Some theorists also explore elements of talk—for example, metaphor—that help explain why and how stories told within conversation shape organizational life (see, for instance, Jordan and Mitterhofer 2010; see also Rosso Efthymiou, this volume).

Often these conversations are informal; they are no less influential for that. Narratives, according to these theorists, are also "carriers of behavioral norms. . . . The continuity and endurance of behavioral norms have a great deal to do with stories" (Brown et al. 2005, 2). They can also be used as "tools for change"—stories told about one organization can be applied to another to solve problems (Brown et al. 2005, 97–135).

Other theorists, however, focus on aspects of sensemaking that are either distinct from narrative or emphasize certain aspects of narrative central to how people interpret, or want others to interpret, experience. As mentioned earlier, the use of metaphor (which is, admittedly, often an element of narrative) has been studied by theorists such as Jordan and Mitterhofer (2010, 244–245) as well as others to show how the kind of figurative language used by promoters of organizational change can affect the character of the change itself. Similarly, organizational theorists have employed actor-network theory to understand how organizations function (Hernes 2010; see also Hendrickson, this volume). Others—like Giaimo and Cheatle, as well as Nicolas, both in this volume—have explored how documents function within a network of other documents to create a sense of organizational identity (see also Buckland 2013).

The authors in this collection consider sensemaking in writing programs and centers from a range of perspectives, some grounded in organizational theory, some exploring common and uncommon narratives, and some taking different theoretical approaches. In the first chapter of section 1, "Sensemaking with Tutors and Teachers," Andrea Rosso Efthymiou analyzes the way writing center administrators and scholars have historically used metaphors to make sense of their work (for how this happens within organizations, see Hernes 2010). To disrupt those metaphors, which are particular to the writing center community of scholars, Rosso Efthymiou turns to tutor narratives that can deepen our understanding of the knowledge tutors—as members of discourse communities outside the writing center—can bring to their tutoring practice and thereby enrich the work of the center itself. In chapter 2, Courtney Adams Wooten analyzes the common stories graduate teaching assistants (GTAs) tell about their work—stories that might be easy to dismiss because they're heard so often—in order to explore how those stories shape the GTAs' development of a teacherly identity and how a WPA might assist in that shaping. Chapter 3, "Creating Sensemaking Cultures in the Writing Center," by Jeanne Smith, Shannon McKeehen, Barbara George, and Yvonne Lee, explores how understanding the different types of sensemaking within a center community—sensemaking by tutor practitioners and sensemaking by administrators conducting tutor education programs—can "influence, inform, or complicate" administrators' work and perhaps lead to a more integrated theory and practice within the center. In chapter 4, Alba Newmann Holmes considers her own and tutors' experiences within a culture of white privilege through the lens of scholarship on race and racism in writing centers. Newmann Holmes argues that teachers, WPAs, and WCDs must attend to their own positionality, as well as to what different tutors bring to their experiences of race and racism, in order to begin challenging those structures of privilege in which they and their centers are enmeshed. The section closes with Bronwyn Williams's "Making Sense of How Things Feel: Attending to Emotional Experiences in Writing Programs." In this chapter, Williams turns to theories of learning to consider emotion as a way of meaning-making for students, faculty, and administrators within writing programs.

The second section, "Sensemaking and Institutional Structures," examines which administrative texts and intra-institutional relationships might inform WCD and WPA sensemaking and, possibly, extend its influence. In chapter 6, Genie Nicole Giaimo and Joseph Cheatle return to common writing center documents and practices that have been used over the years to make sense of writing center work. Given competition for resources and the increasing need to justify the importance of our writing centers to university administrators and other stakeholders, Giaimo and Cheatle suggest additional forms of sensemaking that may have more resonance for those administrators and stakeholders. In chapter 7, "Stories to Support and Sustain a Program," Susanmarie Harrington and Sue Dinitz explore how collaborations between a writing-in-the-disciplines (WID) program, a writing center, and a library are maintained by narratives of those collaborations. Chapter 8, by Melissa Nicolas, uses institutional ethnography to understand how the hierarchy of relationships within a university structure that includes unionized labor is maintained. In chapter 9, Christy Wenger employs leadership studies and feminist ecological perspectives to theorize "a way of creating a framework for the unknown . . . and as a way of figuring out what can be." Chapter 10, by Brian Hendrickson, brings together Weick's theories of organizational sensemaking as well as activity theory and actor-network theory to discuss the possibilities and challenges of transforming racist organizational dispositions within universities. In her afterword, Karen Keaton Jackson speculates on the significance of sensemaking for the field of writing studies and calls for inclusion of all voices in our conversations about how we, and students, learn.

In the final analysis, this book aims to deepen and broaden the way writing program and center administrators think about the work they do. Writing centers and programs do, after all, exist within organizations and within even larger structures, and recent scholarship has foregrounded the problems inherent in failing to attend to those organizations and structures. For instance, antiracist work in writing studies (see, for instance, Martinez 2020; Faison and Condon 2022) has shown that without the narratives of those who experience academic life outside the dominant stories told within our educational system, narratives that are not accounted for in the courses we offer and the documents we generate and promulgate, our field is incomplete and our work oppressive.

Finally, I would like to extend my profound and heartfelt thanks to all the contributors, as well as to Rachael Levay of Utah State University Press, for their patience and understanding as *Sensemaking for Writing Programs and Writing Centers* came to fruition. For personal reasons of my own, it was not an easy road, and the contributors' forbearance has meant more to me than they will ever know. The field of writing studies is full of remarkable and generous people, and it's my honor to have worked with those represented in this book.

REFERENCES

Brown, John Seely, Stephen Denning, Katalina Groh, and Laurence Prusak. 2005. *Storytelling in Organizations: Why Storytelling Is Transforming Twenty-First-Century Organizations and Management.* Oxford: Elsevier.

Buckland, Michael. 2013. "Document Theory: An Introduction." In *Records, Archives and Memory: Selected Papers from the Conference and School on Records, Archives and Memory Studies, University of Zadar, Croatia, May 2013,* edited by Mirna Willer, Anne J. Gilliland, and Marijana Tomić, 223–237. Berkeley: University of California. http://people.ischool.berkeley.edu/~buckland/zadardoctheory.pdf.

Faison, Wonderful, and Frankie Condon. 2022. *CounterStories from the Writing Center.* Logan: Utah State University Press.

Gabriel, Yiannis. 2000. *Storytelling in Organizations: Facts, Fictions, and Fantasies.* Oxford: Oxford University Press.

Hernes, Tor. 2010. "Actor-Network Theory, Callon's Scallops, and Process-Based Organization Studies." In *Process, Sensemaking, and Organizing,* edited by Tor Hernes and Sally Maitlis, 161–184. Oxford: Oxford University Press.

Jordan, Silvia, and Hermann Mitterhofer. 2010. "Studying Metaphors-in-Use in their Social and Institutional Context: Sensemaking and Discourse Theory." In *Process, Sensemaking, and Organizing,* edited by Tor Hernes and Sally Maitlis, 242–274. Oxford: Oxford University Press.

Martinez, Aja Y. 2020. *Counterstory: The Rhetoric and Writing of Critical Race Theory.* Urbana: National Council of Teachers of English.

Reiff, Mary Jo, Anis Bawarshi, Michelle Ballif, and Christian Weisser. 2015. *Ecologies of Writing Programs: Program Profiles in Context.* Anderson, SC: Parlor Press.

Roozen, Kevin. 2009. "From Journals to Journalism: Tracing Trajectories of Literate Development." *College Composition and Communication* 60 (3): 541–572.

Weick, Karl. 1995. *Sensemaking in Organizations.* Thousand Oaks, CA: Sage.

PART I

Sensemaking with Tutors and Teachers

1
THE MEDACHTIC TUTOR
Jewish Discourse, Metaphor, and Undergraduate Tutors' Sensemaking of Writing Center Work

Andrea Rosso Efthymiou

Writing center administrators have a knack for metaphor-making as sensemaking. From Lunsford's Burkean parlor to Lerner's laboratory, writing center scholarship has a long history of using metaphors to make sense of our work, spaces, and the people who circulate in our centers (Lunsford 1991; Lerner 2009). Writing center scholarship has often reacted to the metaphors that pervade our field in binary terms, by either embracing or rejecting these metaphors. In *Peripheral Visions for Writing Center Work*, Jackie Grutsch McKinney historicizes the "grand narrative" of our field, demonstrating that writing centers have toggled between embracing the writing-center-as-cozy-home metaphor and rejecting it, saying that such descriptions "are not unique; [happening] so often it has probably become transparent, something we no longer pay attention to" (Grutsch McKinney 2013, 23). Grutsch McKinney's work attempts to dislodge this binary response by identifying "alternative peripheral stories" (Grutsch McKinney 2013, 19) to the metaphors to which we have grown accustomed.

Scholars blur the boundary between accepting and rejecting our field's metaphors by creating new metaphors to revise old ones. In looking at tidy metaphors of writing center work—like a writing process birthed smoothly with the help of a midwife-tutor—Elizabeth H. Boquet pleads, "Where is the noise?"—a proclamation that invites loud narratives, multiple stories of chaos and struggle that our centers engage across institutional stakeholders (Boquet 2002, 19). In *The Everyday Writing Center: A Community of Practice*, Geller et al. offer revised metaphorical representations of writing center work, one popular example being tutors as trickster figures, expanding our field's understanding of tutors' roles and potential for staff development (Geller et al. 2007).

Much of this scholarship on writing center metaphors attempts to parse realities of our work from the perspective of writing program administrators. While the work in many writing centers relies on the labor of undergraduate, graduate, and professional staff, who often do not maintain administrative positions in our centers, scholarship that analyzes writing center pedagogy looks to metaphors constructed *by* administrators to define that pedagogical labor performed by non-administrators. In "Metaphors and Ambivalence: Affective Dimensions in Writing Center Studies," Lawson probes the limited ways our field has understood emotions and analyzes "the prevalence of metaphorical language in discussions of emotion and how that language has framed the way emotion has been conveyed" (Lawson 2015, 20). Lawson examines the archives of *Writing Center Journal* and *WLN* for scholarship representing emotion or affective dimension; of the twenty-seven articles that Lawson coded to understand emotional metaphors in writing center scholarship, only four of those articles were published as "tutor columns" in *WLN*. Lawson's (2015) critique highlights the "binaristic" way scholarship in our field tends to construe emotion as the opposite of reason. Like Lawson, I encourage further disrupting the binaries that have framed the way we make sense of writing center metaphors and take such disruption a step further by turning to undergraduate tutors' metaphors, rather than writing program administrators' language, for how they have characterized writing center work. Focusing on tutors' language attempts to get at knowledge to which administrators may not have immediate access.

To begin addressing the potential of tutors' own metaphor-making, this chapter draws on organizational theory to consider how tutors use metaphors to make sense of the work they do in writing centers and to further understand tutors' agency within our writing centers. As Rita Malenczyk notes in her introduction to this collection, organizational theorists consider how metaphors function as storytelling within institutions, furthering meaning-making about people and activities that are a part of workplace systems. While scholars of organizational theory hail from fields such as management, finance, economics, and risk assessment, much of the language of organizational theory is familiar to writing center and writing program administrators. For example, organizational scholars Cornelissen and Kafouros distinguish between various types of metaphors—specifically, between primary and complex—to identify "the social nature of theorizing" metaphor-making within institutions (Cornelissen and Kafouros 2008, 973). Heracleous and Jacobs further understand that metaphors within organizations are socially constructed and that studying metaphor use lends to "epistemological pluralism" within organizations (Heracleous and Jacobs 2008, 74). Organizational theory values employees' language as a cornerstone of knowledge for how organizations work. While my work here will not offer a one-to-one equivalent between terms in organizational theory and writing center metaphors, this chapter draws upon organizational theory's notion of metaphors-in-use as a sensemaking mechanism in writing centers, particularly from the perspective of those doing the labor of tutoring. I present interview data at one writing center to do work analogous to that of organizational theory and sensemaking: "Sensemaking studies focusing on the use of metaphors in organizations have described *how* and *by whom* certain metaphors were used to give and make sense of events" (emphasis in original, Jordan and Mitterhofer 2010, 243). My data demonstrates that metaphors-in-use, documented in one writing center at an all-women's Jewish college, represent tutors' sensemaking, placing tutors' knowledge and their discursive framework at the forefront of defining writing center work. Looking at writing center metaphors in this way does two things: it gives tutors, and the knowledge they create about their work, more agency within the writing center and offers directors and administrators new possibilities for tutor education and engagement.

METHODS

This chapter looks at interview data collected in an institutional review board (IRB) approved study at a writing center on an all-women's Jewish college campus. At the time of the study, I was associate director of the writing center at the research site and reached out to current and recently graduated tutors, recruiting voluntary participation in data collection toward my dissertation. With informed consent, I interviewed ten women for the study, all of whom were current undergraduate tutors or recent graduates of the college and had tutored at the writing center during their undergraduate careers. Of the ten tutors interviewed, this chapter contains analysis of interview and fieldnote data from two participants, who chose the pseudonyms Shulamit and Tara, and who, at the time of these interviews, had recently graduated and were enrolled in advanced religious studies masters or certificate programs. I note the tutors' postgraduate education to punctuate that Jewish education characterizes these tutors' discourse communities beyond the college, and these religious and educational communities inherently informed the language participants used to describe their lived experience, both in the writing center and outside of the center. Building on Jordan and Mitterhofer's framework for studying metaphors-in-use, I analyze Shulamit's and Tara's metaphors to "focus on the concrete use of conceptual metaphors in a specific setting . . . with regard to power effects, legitimation, and strategies of sensegiving" (Jordan and Mitterhofer 2010, 249). Understanding the way discourse communities of all kinds, not solely religious ones, permeate the lives of undergraduate tutors may help writing program administrators focus on the language our staff uses to give sense to their work, even when that language may seem unfamiliar to us as administrators.

RESPONSIBILITY, INTENTIONALITY, AND TUTORING

Unlike writing program administrators and their professional tutor counterparts, undergraduate tutors may not have access to the same language or sensemaking tools that directors have access to—and indeed are often expected to use as part of their jobs—through writing center scholarship. Even with deliberate attempts to offer staff at all levels access to scholarship, possibly at staff meetings or in pedagogy courses, undergraduate tutors in particular might not have immediate access to the discourse of writing center scholarship as they circulate among, and are novices in, a number of other discourse communities within higher education. While writing center directors certainly see benefits to offering undergraduate staff contact with current conversations in the field, we also have been taken aback by the keen way undergraduate staff make sense of their work without access to the same language and frameworks that we have. This section looks at one tutor's language about her work—language that is distinctly religious—to offer a window into what knowledge a writing center administrator can gain from paying attention to tutors' frameworks for sensemaking alongside writing center administrators' own research-based frameworks.

Informed by her Jewish education, Shulamit uses religious metaphors to describe her work as a tutor. At one moment in our interview, Shulamit's religious metaphors intersect not only with writing center pedagogy but also with a concept foundational to composition pedagogy broadly: the valuing of process over product. After a long conversation about her relationship with Jewish education and her faith, I asked Shulamit if anything she said during our interview related to her life as a writing tutor. Here is Shulamit's response:

> Absolutely! . . . Working in the writing center was the best thing I did in my college experience. And I think that it made me . . . feel a lot more responsible for the kind of writing that I did because I was so . . . I can only

think of, like, the Hebrew word for this: *medachtic*. . . . Medachtic means, like, very careful and particular. With the work my students wrote, I would ask them, "Why did you choose that word?" And I would make them give an answer. And it made me feel much more responsible. . . . In terms of my relationship with language and my relationship with writing, [a concept] that comes up a lot in Jewish prayer [is] *kavanah*, which means intentionality. Yeah, people talk about, "it's really important to have intentionality when you pray." And people ask, "if you're not gonna have intentionality, why would you pray?" . . . And, like, people ask the question, "[is it] better to pray without intentionality [or] better to pray with intentionality?" Maybe lack of intentionality will lead you ultimately to have intentionality.

Shulamit uses metaphors here to make multiple comparisons, some reflecting her undergraduate religious college and some reflecting her writing center pedagogy. In fact, the line between each of these categories is fuzzy at best. Shulamit begins by describing how working in the writing center made her feel more responsible for her writing, a reflection that quickly turned to a description of working with students. Yet Shulamit needed different words to describe her work tutoring; she turned to two Hebrew terms, *medachtic* and *kavanah*, clearly imbuing the latter with religious meaning. While she never articulates an explicit simile (such as, "writing tutoring is like kavanah in prayer because . . ."), Shulamit's language is particularly striking here for the way her metaphors for writing center work extend into her religious identity. Both the writing center, where she worked for three of her undergraduate years, and her Jewish faith are familiar discourses to Shulamit and represent how "institutionalized language and discourse are essential elements of cultural-cognitive institutions, since language mediates certain taken-for-granted meaning and connotations" (Jordan and Mitterhofer 2010, 245). Reading Shulamit's metaphors-in-use, which are clearly situated within the discourse of the religious institution that houses the writing center, acknowledges the central role of institutions in sensemaking.

Much of my conversation with Shulamit proceeded on a path similar to the above interview excerpt; initiated by my question about the writing center, Shulamit's response gently grazed her experiences in the writing center but also wound toward an answer that reflected her own religious practices. For Shulamit, the line between religious discourse and writing center discourse is not quite there, which is telling for me as a writing center administrator. In Shulamit's institutional space, where students' discourse community is distinctly religious, tutors bring their religious discourses—indeed, they bring all of their primary and secondary discourses—into the writing center with them as part of their "identity kit" (Gee 1989, 19). For Shulamit, this means necessarily understanding her tutoring practices through the lens of religion. By extension then, tutors will draw upon any of their discourse communities, whether or not tutors identify as religious, to make sense of the work they do.

As Shulamit develops the connection she makes between the writing center and the concept of kavanah, which she describes as questioning the intent of Jewish prayer, she extends her metaphor by considering the value of having a rigorous process. When Shulamit says that "maybe lack of intentionality will lead you ultimately to have intentionality," she considers the value of a consistent process for a tutoring, writing, or religious practice. By thinking about the line between genuine intent and a perfunctory act, whether those feelings apply to prayer or to a college writing situation, Shulamit shows that the value of intentionality and responsibility is neither in the ultimate representation of prayer nor in the surface appeal of words. She defines that she uses the product a student shows her in the center to get to some keener insight on the student's process of thinking and writing. Likewise, Shulamit's presentation of various ways of understanding the intent of prayer demonstrates that she is not resolved upon a singular way to view prayer as a religious experience.

Shulamit uses discourse specific to her religious community—medachtic and kavanah—to express the responsibility she as a writing tutor feels toward her own writing as well as the responsibility she feels when working with student writers. But Shulamit is not talking about the kind of responsibility that Jennifer Nicklay says tutors sometimes feel when they are caught between directive and nondirective tutoring, the kind of responsibility that inspires feelings of guilt and self-doubt (Nicklay 2012). Rather, Shulamit articulates a kind of responsibility more akin to that which Bobbi Olson writes about when helping multilingual students make rhetorical choices (Olson 2013). Specifically, in the writing center, a tutor can talk to a writer about their meaning, perceived "error," and about intent in any writing situation (and, incidentally, at the writing center where Shulamit tutored, tutors often talked to each other about all of those elements in terms of prayer too). In talking about tutoring, language, and prayer side by side, using the language of one to describe the language of the other, Shulamit is really describing what composition scholars might understand as drafting and writing processes.

Directors and administrators at mission-driven and secular campuses alike should heed this relationship between tutors' discourse communities beyond the center and how that discourse community influences tutors' language for describing their work. Shulamit's sensemaking describes the adage of valuing process over product in writing, which she extends to her tutoring experience and to prayer. But Shulamit's discourse-specific language around tutor-sense here is likely more effective than any attempt an administrator could make at describing writing process to their staff. Shulamit's metaphors employ language that was not immediately available to me as a Christian person working as an administrator in a Jewish space. Had I not taken the time to understand how Shulamit thought about her tutoring through the lens of religion, I would have missed an opportunity to see how Shulamit's religious discourse intersected with ideas very present in writing center scholarship. And, of course, I could have done more work in relation to the opportunity Shulamit presented to me, specifically in terms of tutor engagement. Had I understood Shulamit's thinking at the time of our interview, when I was working as an administrator in this research site, I could have asked Shulamit to present her ideas about tutoring-as-a-representation-of-kavanah to our staff and asked staff to reflect upon that religious notion for describing their work. This would have offered me a meaningful inroad for presenting tutors with writing center scholarship in a staff meeting to complement ways Shulamit was already thinking about tutoring but in tutors' sensemaking terms.

OPENNESS, COMMUNITY, AND SHARED EXPERIENCE

Tutors' sensemaking is a kind of theorizing, and undergraduate tutor discourse *is* writing center discourse. So, while I, as an administrator, rely on sources like *Writing Center Journal*, *WLN*, *Praxis*, and Utah State University Press for theoretical frameworks to help me make sense of my work, tutors use their own discursive frameworks for many of the same concepts. Tara's interview data in this section represents a kind of theorizing around writing center pedagogy and communities of practice, particularly through metaphors around religious identity. Similar to Shulamit's description of tutoring as medachtic and as representing kavanah, the line between religion and the writing center is again fuzzy in the interviews I conducted with Tara. When she worked in the writing center, Tara was the only undergraduate tutor in our center who was married. She was also an education major and an undergraduate tutor who was committed to having "a leadership role in Jewish education."

Tara's commitment to education and to normalizing talk around women's religious experience meant that she often used the space of the writing center to discuss her lived experience as an observant woman in Jewish Modern Orthodoxy. One such tradition that Tara addressed is the Orthodox Jewish practice that some married women perform of covering their natural hair by wearing a wig. My field notes at a staff meeting shortly after Tara was married document that, like Shulamit's earlier, undergraduate tutors' discursive practices move into the center in productive ways. At the onset of that staff meeting, Tara chatted with her peer tutor colleagues about washing her wig, noting that she had two: "Her mother bought her one and her mother-in-law the other." Tara "makes joke about her wig" and "says she wants to write about it" for a blog about Modern Jewish Orthodox women's experiences. During our interview for this study, Tara referenced this staff meeting and her conversation about her wig with our staff when discussing her writing center work:

> When I get to the writing center, everyone finds it hilarious that I'm bitching about the hair. "It's hot. It's itchy. I have so much hair on me right now." It was nice to be able to talk about it. . . . There's an openness [in the writing center]. I don't know what it was. It was just so great to be able to come in and say, "Yes, [covering my hair] is actually really annoying. These are the crazy things that happen because I'm not actually wearing my own hair." That was really great. [The writing center] is also a space that makes you think about things in their broader context. That's the culture of the writing center. That's what we do.

Tara's identity as a religious person and a writing center tutor are intricately bound during her undergraduate life. Tara moves fluidly between describing her experience wearing a wig as a newly married woman to describing the openness of the writing center. This openness describes the freedom that characterizes Tara's workplace, a writing center where she can speak honestly to her tutor-peers in a way that she presumably cannot in other institutional spaces that, while religious, might not allow for disclosing genuine struggle about religious practices like women's hair covering. By using *openness*, a word that denotes physical space, to describe the abstract feeling of freedom, Tara crafts a metaphor that describes the ease she feels expressing herself in the writing center. Tara's metaphor-making tells me that her religious identity and her pedagogy are deeply and thoughtfully parts of her and that she thinks about both "in their broader context."

Tara's reference to our earlier staff meeting, to having come to the center "bitching about the hair" with her tutor-colleagues, is a move that engages tutors' shared religious identity. Discussing this gender-specific religious practice gives sense to Tara's understanding of the writing center as an affective space, while also characterizing her pedagogy as one that is devoted to making student writers feel more at ease in the center. Although the other undergraduate tutors in the writing center at the time when Tara worked there were not married, her fellow tutors certainly understood the tradition of covering one's hair that Tara talks about above. In this way, Tara serves as both a community member and community leader, speaking honestly about a part of her identity that is certainly relevant to her community of Jewish tutors. This metaphor of openness, which represents a network of religious referents, shows how tutors' identities constantly circulate within a community of practice, how contact between identities past, present, and future happen within the space of the writing center (Geller et al. 2007, 56). Consistent with work in literacy studies, Tara's "bitching about the hair" represents findings consistent with Beverly Moss's work in African American churches, as Tara's interview demonstrates "shared knowledge to signal 'in-group' communication, group memberships, [and] community" (Moss 2002, 80). Tara's sensemaking is distinct from anything I could have offered, both as a Christian person and also as an administrator wholly removed from the experience of being married as an undergraduate student. Tara's metaphors-in-use engage her tutor-colleagues in ways I as the WPA in that space was not capable of; Tara had the ability to productively use language to harness her peers' attention at our staff meeting *and* connect that experience to the writing center in our interview.

Tara's interview further demonstrates her sense of herself as part of a community. As Tara goes on to develop her idea of thinking in a "broader context" in relation to writing center work, she circles back to her own identity as a writer:

> I think [the writing center] fosters an environment of thinking about whatever you were thinking about that day more broadly. . . . I think that's great. Why? [Because] people have such a lonely experience. . . . I feel like a majority of my sessions have been . . . trying to get the students to say exactly what they want to write: "just say it!" I think writing can be lonely like that, and just having someone to say, "I've been there" is companionship and shared experience. . . . Having peer tutors . . . say, "Yes, I took that class. I remember, I did that paper." Having someone say that [they] survived it, it's pretty nice.

While the image of the lonely writer is certainly nothing new, I see this characterization of writing as connected to Tara's description of her experience as the only married tutor in the writing center. In Tara's effort to describe thinking "more broadly," she too goes broad with the metaphor for loneliness, pulling strands from women's religious rituals together with the solitude of writing. In describing both moments, Tara suggests that existing in a community of writers is part of the shared experience of writing center work that makes it a supportive space (Geller et al. 2007, 73).

In the wake of Tara's interview, even some years later, I feel that I, as a writing center administrator, missed an opportunity here. If Tara represents one tutor who used her agency in the writing center to address issues relevant and immediate to her identity as a Jewish woman, there may have been other tutors who remained silent. Beneath the surface banter of "bitching about the hair," Tara was getting at the genuine frustration she felt acclimating to women's practices as a part of married life in the Jewish tradition, practices which she was intent on observing for her commitment to her community. Tara's sensemaking, the fact that she embraced talking about these moments of frustration with the staff and with me during our interview makes me think that her writing center community helped her feel more supported as she adopted these practices and transitioned into a new stage in her life. Considering our field's work around supporting racial, sexual, and gender identity in writing centers, Tara's sensemaking in the writing center staff meeting and our subsequent interview could have served as a launching pad for supporting other tutors in this identity-specific space (Greenfield and Rowan 2011; Denny 2010). I know too many tutors who remained closeted about of range of identities during their undergraduate years at the religious institution where this study took place for fear of losing their community; perhaps structuring more time during staff meetings, beyond the happy accident of staff meeting banter, to invite reflections like Tara's could have offered support for tutors in the center dealing with struggles related to various aspects of their identity, particularly as they intersected with tutors' religious observance. As the administrator of the center during the time of this research, I see a missed opportunity here for reflective writing in staff meetings or journaling between sessions that could have served as appropriate spaces for exploring tutoring selves, in Tara's words, "more broadly" within our tutoring community.

IMPLICATIONS FOR TUTOR EDUCATION AND ENGAGEMENT

Inasmuch as this chapter represents tutors' sensemaking through Shulamit's and Tara's metaphors, I hope to offer possibilities for new models of collaboration inspired by tutors' sensemaking. Tara and Shulamit show us that tutor discourse has the potential to name theoretical frameworks that administrators rely on all the time. If we make concerted efforts to point out tutors' sensemaking, both in moments when they happen and as opportunities for later reflection, writing center administrators can place tutors' knowledge as central to the work we do (after all, we can only *do* writing center work *with* tutors). I echo a suggestion that Smith, McKeehen, George, and Lee make in this collection: that WCAs attend to the sensemaking of tutors, "facilitating tutor crosstalk" to forward professional development and a deeper commitment to tutoring pedagogy. Such foregrounding of *tutor-sense* could also empower staff to develop local responses to their work, understanding which language has the most power within unique contexts. Similar to the relevance religious language around prayer and gender-specific practices has at an all-women's Jewish college, there is certainly potential for writing center administrators to do more with tutors' discursive frameworks at mission-driven institutions like Christian colleges, HBCUs, and tribal colleges, where students' shared discourse communities are often built into their choice in college attendance.

Tara's and Shulamit's interviews demonstrate some of what has been substantiated by recent scholarship on tutors' religious identity. Consistent with LeCluyse and Stock's findings, Tara and Shulamit certainly "perceive their religious beliefs and experiences as compatible with or highly relevant to writing center praxis" (LeCluyse and Stock 2018, 3). There is added potential, however, when looking at tutors' language outside of the categories (moral values, missionary work, etc.) that LeCluyse and Stock (2018) identify. By understanding tutors' non-writing-center-discourse as *giving sense* to writing center work, we can invite new frameworks for thinking about the work of tutoring. This has the effect of creating logical spaces for introducing scholarship related to tutors' sensemaking. For example, Shulamit's metaphors about responsibility and intention would have paired well with "Rethinking Our Work with Multilingual Writers: The Ethics and Responsibility of Language Teaching in the Writing Center" (Olson 2013). As a writing center director, I aspire to (and sometimes fail at) helping tutors see their local knowledge-making as having an impact on our center.

Paying closer attention to naming tutors' metaphors for their work may also encourage tutors to pursue research reflecting the connections they make in our centers. Approaching tutor education as an opportunity for tutors' research helps tutors develop as writing teachers as well as offers tutors engagement opportunities within and beyond their centers. This research-based emphasis is foregrounded in more recent approaches to tutor education, such as Fitzgerald and Ianetta's *The Oxford Guide for Writing Tutors* (2016). If I could go back to my time in the writing center with Tara, I can envision a possible research project on community development around Jewish women's religious practices and the work of Jewish women writing center tutors. This imagined potential inspires revisions in my own approach to staff development and mentoring tutor research. Shulamit's and Tara's interviews serve as a constant reminder to listen to the language of tutors, not only in religious spaces but also wherever tutors use discourse specific to their peer groups. My lack of access to tutors' discourse inspires me in ways I imagine student writers are often inspired by our tutors, to ask questions about what something means, to listen to tutors' responses, and to learn perspectives beyond my own.

REFERENCES

Boquet, Elizabeth. 2002. *Noise from the Writing Center*. Logan: Utah State University Press.
Cornelissen, Joep P., and Mario Kafouros. 2008. "The Emergent Organization: Primary and Complex Metaphors in Theorizing about Organizations." *Organization Studies* 29 (7): 957–978.
Denny, Harry. 2010. *Facing the Center: Toward an Identity Politics of One-to-One Mentoring*. Logan: Utah State University Press.
Fitzgerald, Lauren, and Melissa Ianetta. 2016. *The Oxford Guide for Writing Tutors: Practice and Research*. Oxford: Oxford University Press.
Gee, James Paul. 1989. "Literacy, Discourse, and Linguistics: Introduction." *The Journal of Education* 171 (1): 5–176.
Geller, Anne Ellen, Michele Eodice, Frankie Condon, Meg Carroll, and Elizabeth H. Boquet. 2007. *The Everyday Writing Center: A Community of Practice*. Logan: Utah State University Press.
Greenfield, Laura, and Karen Rowan. 2011. *Writing Centers and the New Racism*. Logan: Utah State University Press.
Grutsch McKinney, Jackie. 2013. *Peripheral Visions for Writing Center Work*. Logan: Utah State University Press.
Heracleous, Loizos, and Claus Jacobs. 2008. "Understanding Organizations through Embodied Metaphors." *Organization Studies* 29 (1): 47–78.
Jordan, Silvia, and Hermann Mitterhofer. 2010. "Studying Metaphors-in-Use in their Social and Institutional Contexts: Sensemaking and Discourse Theory." In *Process, Sensemaking, and Organizing*, edited by Tor Hernes and Sally Maitlis, 242–274. Oxford: Oxford University Press.
Lawson, Daniel. 2015. "Metaphors and Ambivalence: Affective Dimensions in Writing Center Studies." *WLN: A Journal of Writing Center Scholarship* 40 (3–4): 20–27.
LeCluyse, Christopher, and David Stock. 2018. "Religious Identity and Writing Center Tutoring: Perceptions from Latter-Day Saint (LDS) Tutors." *WLN: A Journal of Writing Center Scholarship* 45 (5–6): 2–9.
Lerner, Neal. 2009. *The Idea of a Writing Laboratory*. Carbondale: Southern Illinois University Press.
Lunsford, Andrea. 1991. "Collaboration, Control, and the Idea of a Writing Center." *Writing Lab Newsletter* 16 (4–5): 1–5.
Moss, Beverly J. 2002. *A Community Text Arises: A Literate Text and a Literacy Tradition in African-American Churches*. New York: Hampton Press.
Nicklay, Jennifer. 2012. "Got Guilt? Consultant Guilt in the Writing Center Community." *Writing Center Journal* 32 (1): 14–27.
Olson, Bobbi. 2013. "Rethinking Our Work with Multilingual Writers: The Ethics and Responsibility of Language Teaching in the Writing Center." *Praxis: A Writing Center Journal* 10 (2). http://www.praxisuwc.com/olson-102.

2
BEYOND THE ANECDOTE
TA Sensemaking as Writing Program Underlife

Courtney Adams Wooten

> *One of my TAs came into my office panicking because a student had emailed to contest a grade, and he wasn't sure how to handle it.*
>
> *The other day a TA emailed me five times in an hour about a student who was disruptive in her classroom.*
>
> *This TA just shut down when we discussed pedagogical ideas they weren't familiar with. It was as if they were too proud and too stuck in their ways to consider the merit of new teaching ideas.*
>
> *My TAs who identify as young women are always concerned about their authority in the classroom and how they will develop respect from students.*

These types of anecdotes should sound familiar to most WPAs who work with graduate teaching assistants. In the hallways and at conferences, we often share stories about how first-year writing TAs struggle to make sense of the work they are doing and the programs in which they are teaching. When considering the unseen interactions of people working in writing programs, focusing on TAs is particularly important because they are typically newcomers—or outsiders—to the field of rhetoric and composition who are trying to juggle theoretical and practical aspects of teaching writing. They also perform a lot of the work of teaching first-year writing, in some schools teaching almost all of the first-year writing classes offered. Their high involvement in teaching first-year writing means that we need to pay particular attention to how TAs make sense of their work and the programs around them.

Work by scholars such as Betty P. Pytlik and Sarah Liggett (2002), Sidney I. Dobrin (2005), and Jessica Restaino (2012) has brought more attention to what Heidi Estrem and E. Shelley Reid (2012b) call writing pedagogy education (WPE). Such scholarship often revolves around anecdotes or accounts from WPAs about the things that happen with TAs. However, despite the many anecdotes in which WPAs often recognize common narratives about TAs, few studies have been done to articulate exactly how TAs themselves use often-unseen or -unheard rhetorical processes to narrate their work and what these narratives mean for the WPAs who train and supervise them. This chapter brings some of these sensemaking practices to light by examining written reflections by TAs who are teaching for the first time and by identifying rhetorical strategies they use to make sense of the teaching they are doing.

One reason to pay attention to such sensemaking is, of course, to better understand first-year writing TAs and how they try to process their identities as teachers in writing programs. However, another reason to pay attention is because TA sensemaking contributes to a writing program's underlife. Robert Brooke (1987) proposes that underlife refers to "those behaviors which undercut the roles expected of participants in a situation" (141). While he discusses underlife in relation to student behaviors in writing classes, this concept is equally helpful in considerations of how TAs push against the expectations set up for them as teachers of writing. Underlife in this context is about TA identities and the games TAs play to go beyond the roles ascribed to them and assert more complex identities. As Brooke points out, composition as a field is invested in fostering student underlife so that the educational system can be questioned, particularly in the way it limits identities to singular, restrictive roles. Because TAs function as both graduate students and teachers in our programs, WPAs need to also consider the ways that we can help them juggle both their roles as teachers in institutions with particular expectations of them and their complex identities that exist outside of institutional structures.

TAs' sensemaking processes can reveal some of the ways that they try to balance this tension and help WPAs consider ways to help TAs negotiate their identities as they come into contact with the expected role of teacher. Like Brooke (1987), I see both TAs and WPAs working against common educational narratives to construct new identities for writing programs and those within them. TAs' sensemaking processes, therefore, can offer WPAs new ways to consider the work we are doing as well and how we work with TAs to identify the constraints of their institutional roles and to negotiate these productively. Doing this work allows our writing programs to become more open to productive disruption and change from the inside out rather than from the top down. In this chapter, I discuss WPE scholarship about TAs and how this intersects with theories of sensemaking narratives. Then, I provide the results of a study of TA reflections at one university to explain the sensemaking narratives they use to think about their work. Finally, I offer suggestions for how WPAs can take advantage of the underlife TAs experience as they foster their roles as composition instructors.

SENSEMAKING NARRATIVES AND WPE

Increasingly common in composition studies are pieces written directly to TAs about the work they are doing and how to approach it, as well as advice for WPAs who work with TAs (see Dobrin 2005; Pytlik and Liggett 2002; Reid 2017; Saur and Palmeri 2017). These pieces are framed in different ways, sometimes as letters, sometimes as advice columns, and sometimes as academic essays. However, they all acknowledge the difficult position many first-year writing TAs find themselves in: being asked to teach writing classes that they are often unfamiliar with that are built out of a discipline they sometimes are disconnected from, while receiving limited training before this work begins. The complexity of this situation has led to work such as a new edited collection by William J. Macauley Jr. (2021) *Standing at the Threshold: Working through Liminality in the Composition and Rhetoric TAship*. This collection theorizes the position of rhetoric and composition TAs and offers varying pieces of advice about how WPAs can help those who are teaching first-year writing while simultaneously completing graduate studies.

In WPE scholarship, while many common issues such as training, TA preparation, curricular decisions, and so on are discussed, TA voices are less often heard. Two recent pieces, Reid's (2017) "On Learning to Teach: Letter to a New TA" and Elizabeth Saur and Jason Palmeri's (2017) "Letter to a New TA: Affect Addendum," directly address TAs and offer advice to them about their work, but these do not tell us what TAs think and why. Instead, such advice is largely based on assumptions WPAs make about the things they observe happening and have experienced with their TAs. While valuable, a more comprehensive understanding of how TAs themselves experience their journey as new writing instructors can help TAs collectively better understand their positioning and assist WPAs as they try to strengthen their programs, including support structures for TAs.

The need for more work focused around TAs themselves ties into scholarship about sensemaking. Karl E. Weick, Kathleen M. Sutcliffe, and David Obstfeld (2005) begin their essay "Organizing and the Process of Sensemaking" with an extended explanation of what sensemaking entails: "Sensemaking involves the ongoing retrospective development of plausible images that rationalize what people are doing. Viewed as a significant process of organizing, sensemaking unfolds as a sequence in which people concerned with identity in the social context of other actors engage ongoing circumstances from which they extract cues and make plausible sense retrospectively, while enacting more or less order into those ongoing circumstances" (409).

Because TAs are positioned at a moment in time when their identities as professional teachers and scholars are in flux and when they are trying to figure out these identities in the midst of interactions with many others (WPAs, other TAs and instructors, students, and so on), they are very much involved in the sensemaking process whether or not they or others explicitly recognize it as such. Part of this sensemaking is TAs' active participation in underlife as their identities as teachers, students, and even individuals are being formed, and the boundaries between these identities are often quite fluid. Weick, Sutcliffe, and Obstfeld's (2005) more descriptive explanations of sensemaking offer insight into how TAs are involved in sensemaking processes. I briefly work through these here to illustrate how TAs participate in sensemaking and how making this process explicit, especially in thinking about sensemaking as connected with underlife, can be useful to TAs and their mentors, including WPAs who supervise them.

The first description of sensemaking offered by Weick, Sutcliffe, and Obstfeld (2005) is that "sensemaking organizes flux" and that "sensemaking starts with chaos" (411). It may be quite easy to imagine the flux and chaos that first-year writing TAs can feel as they teach, often for the first time. Making syllabi and lesson plans, creating teaching materials, managing students, creating assignments, grading, and so on create a constant stream of small (and large) things that TAs must juggle. This leads to Weick, Sutcliffe, and Obstfeld's second description, which is that "sensemaking starts with noticing and bracketing" (2005, 411). While having many balls in the air, TAs have to notice when something is different and pull it out so that it can be understood. For example, a TA might identify a high number of students who are missing many classes early in the semester and pull this out of the chaos to begin to understand what might be causing such absences. This can lead to what Weick, Sutcliffe, and Obstfeld call "labeling," or figuring out how to categorize something so that it makes sense and something can be done about it (2005, 411). A TA might thus think that a student has an attendance issue if they have missed three classes in the first two weeks of a course; this is the TA's way of labeling what is happening (as an "attendance issue").

In the course of this labeling, a TA has to go through the retrospective process of thinking back and identifying this pattern of absences. The process of retrospection, or thinking through what has happened after it occurs, is another element Weick, Sutcliffe, and Obstfeld (2005, 412) claim is necessary to sensemaking that relies upon presumption, connecting "the abstract with the concrete." During this retrospection, TAs often rely on presumptions about this type of behavior—that they have either experienced or heard about from others—to help them understand actual classroom behavior. For example, they might assume that a particular student is struggling to adapt to life in college. As Weick, Sutcliffe, and Obstfeld point out, however, this part of the process is "social and systemic" (2005, 412), relying in part on what others have said about student absences and in part on how the field of writing has constructed attendance in writing courses. Weick, Sutcliffe, and Obstfeld argue that this process then leads to action and communication. A TA must determine what to do about a particular student with attendance issues, whether that is a private conference, reporting the student to an alert system, or nothing. They often will then share their stories with others as part of an organizational sensemaking process that builds up in particular writing programs and across our field. TA sensemaking, because TAs so often teach first-year writing courses, is thus an important part of understanding how our writing program cultures are built and sustained, how instructors engage in underlife as they navigate institutional and programmatic structures, and how, as WPAs, we might cultivate a positive sensemaking process for TAs and our writing programs.

Because communication built on sensemaking is so important, as rhetoricians, we can bring to this examination of the sensemaking process a deeper understanding of how people (in this case, TAs) make arguments to themselves and each other built on their sensemaking and how these contribute to organizational and disciplinary cultures. Particularly, attention to narrative rhetorics reveals how sensemaking narratives "permit actors to manoeuvre between contradictions, to ignore and to gloss ambiguities, to both mask and disclose emotional responses and intellectual positions, to simultaneously make and to unravel sense in organizational settings" (Brown, Colville, and Pye 2015, 269). Unlike the organizational storytelling that Yiannis Gabriel discusses, in which people generate stories "with plots and characters, generating emotion in narrator and audience" (2000, 239) within their organizations, the narratives TAs construct are often half-formed and involve questioning or exploring what something means. However, their interactions with others often rely on organizational stories that more experienced instructors have formed that inform their teaching and how they talk with others about their teaching. Even though TAs do not typically have as clearly formed stories to inform their teaching, their form of narration does have, as Walter Fisher (1984) explains about narration, "sequence and meaning for those who live, create, or interpret them" (2). Narration applies to both real as well as fictional situations, and it allows those going through a sensemaking process to construct meanings from events that they make understandable. As TAs reflect on their experiences to make narratives out of them, they are creating sensemaking narratives that they think about on their own and share with others; in the process, they often engage in underlife.

TA underlife forms an integral part of a writing program's personality and community. Similar to Brooke's (1987) explanation of how students interject themselves into the educational system, TAs can use sensemaking narratives both to understand and to push against the educational structures in which they are teaching, some of which writing programs embrace and others that they also resist. By identifying common ways that TAs undertake this sensemaking process and construct such narratives, WPAs can better understand how TAs engage in underlife and what they can do to help TAs negotiate their identities at the nexus of institutional expectations and resistance to these.

TAS' RHETORICAL SENSEMAKING

In order to examine the sensemaking rhetorical practices of TAs, I collected reflective writing produced by six TAs in the spring 2017 and spring 2018 semesters.[1] These TAs were all part of the first-year writing program I directed at a midsize, regional, MA-granting public institution in Texas. They produced weekly reflections about their teaching as part of a one-credit-hour, two-semester-long practicum that met once per week as they taught for their first two semesters at this university. Three TAs—Anna, Lily, and Diane—participated in spring 2017, and three TAs—Penny, Alex, and Jennifer[2]—participated in spring 2018. Anna and Alex were in their first semester of teaching, while Lily, Diane, Penny, and Jennifer were in their second semester of teaching, and all were teaching one of two courses in the first-year writing sequence. All but two—Lily and Jennifer—were completing creative thesis projects in the MA program; Lily and Jennifer wrote literature theses. In total, I collected 222 pages of written material to analyze.

Following methods outlined in Johnny Saldaña's (2016) *The Coding Manual for Qualitative Researchers*, I coded the material by reviewing the reflections and developing broad codes based on rhetorical strategies TAs used in their written work to make sense of what was happening in their classes, with their teaching, and so on. Originally, I identified thirty-two individual sensemaking moves that I collapsed into ten codes; I then combined these codes into the five broader codes represented here (seeking advice, narrating what happens in the classroom and why, praising and blaming self and students, solidifying a teaching approach, and focusing on the self and personal needs). Although these codes certainly are not exhaustive, they reveal common ways TAs reason through what is happening as they teach. They also can show WPAs and others who mentor and work with TAs what types of narratives are part of a writing program underlife and how to support TAs and others in the writing program who are figuring out who they are as teachers, how to work with students, how to grade ethically, and all of the other issues that arise as they teach, often for the first time.

Seeking Advice

A common sensemaking move TAs made in these reflections was seeking advice from me as the WPA, other faculty mentors, each other, and other instructors in the program. Given the ways in which sensemaking is attached to identity construction through social interactions, it is natural that TAs would look to those they assume have already figured out their teacherly identities to help them navigate their own experiences. TAs use this rhetorical move to explicitly ask others to help with the bracketing, labeling, retrospection, and actions their sensemaking process requires.

Jennifer perhaps most frequently asked for my specific advice during spring 2018 when she faced a semester with higher numbers of students with absentee issues and when she struggled to make her absence policy clear to one student athlete. In one reflection, she explains her thinking about this issue and asks me to help her think through what is happening:

> For the future, I think that I will continue to hold everyone to the same standard without deviation . . . but I do wonder how other instructors can get away with having little to no attendance policy? . . . I still find myself thinking that even if I had more absence allowances to give, some students would still ask for more so where is the line drawn in the sand? P.S. I know that I keep writing and asking you about this issue, but I find that I am still unclear on it. There are so many interpretations on this policy [the university's policy that students should be given up to three weeks of

absences for university-related participation in sports, organizations, etc.] that I am left wondering whether I am correct or not, or if there is even a right or wrong on this?[3]

Some of the difficulties TAs face in the sensemaking process is that there are not always right and wrong answers; in this case, Jennifer struggles because she is trying to determine the appropriate actions to take after she has labeled attendance problems in her class. However, because teaching is largely interpersonal work, there are frequently loopholes or different perspectives on these issues (such as some instructors choosing not to have an attendance policy at all) that make it difficult for TAs such as Jennifer to determine how they should or want to act as teachers.

Since WPAs can only represent one perspective on sensemaking, TAs also turn to other faculty mentors, each other, and other instructors to help them understand different perspectives on teaching writing and how they want to navigate this work. This is when sensemaking engages with underlife since the multitude of stories being told in a writing program can show how different instructors align with, deal with, and differ from writing program or university policies. The instructors Jennifer has heard about who simply do not have attendance policies are exercising their beliefs about student participation and attendance by circumventing the institutional issue of attendance altogether. These types of negotiations can extend outside of our programs and departments too, into other places on campus. Diane mentions her and Lily attending a workshop on active learning in the teacher center on campus, finding "comfort" in the fact that "other professionals" need "reminders" about how to approach student learning.[4] Such interactions with others can be especially helpful to new TAs who need help bracketing and labeling issues and then determining appropriate—in their own eyes and/or in the eyes of the writing program and institution—actions to take. Anna discusses how another of her faculty mentors "gave me the advice (since we are both theatrically inclined) to *act* like I'm playing the role of a teacher if I wasn't sure how to be a teacher. . . . And it seems to work because they [students] don't know that I don't know what I'm doing" (emphasis in original).[5] These types of advice help TAs deal with the conflict they feel as graduate students who are in charge of their own classrooms, especially those who may feel as if they do not belong in such positions. They also represent the social aspect of sensemaking, helping TAs notice some things they may not have on their own, then working through the labeling, retrospection, and action process with them. Such advice is complicated, however, by the negotiations every teacher makes about how to engage in underlife and the individual negotiations TAs are constantly making about their identities as teachers, students, and individuals. In other words, TAs can struggle to make sense of the advice offered when it conflicts with their sense of their own identities and their roles in a program and/or institution.

Narrating What Happens in the Classroom and Why

As part of their sensemaking, TAs often think about what is happening in their classrooms and seek to explain this to themselves and others. Sometimes this is framed as a justification for things they are doing to WPAs and others in a writing program, while other times it is presented as their working through these issues. These explanations tap most fully into Fisher's (1984) narrative theory through the noticing, labeling, retrospection, and action parts of the sensemaking process TAs use to make sense of their work. Such explanations also most closely resemble stories being passed to others as part of writing program underlife, even as TA stories are still often more open-ended than more experienced instructors' stories because they are seeking validation from others about their interpretation of events.

A common trope in this rhetorical move is TAs' attempts to identify external factors that affect what happens in the classroom as part of their labeling and retrospection process. While this could be viewed as a deflection onto things they cannot control (thus letting them off the hook for their own responsibility in the classroom), it could also be viewed as their struggle to understand an activity—teaching—that seems mysterious at times and to negotiate underlife and its conflicting identities. Alex, for example, frequently wonders about his students' previous preparation for college and how this impacts what they do in his classroom. Early in the semester, he notices their knowledge of rhetoric and labels it as a sign that they received a sound education that "made them prepared for a college level institution."[6] In this instance, students' previous educational experiences are labeled as a positive since they seem adequately prepared for this first-year writing class. However, about twelve weeks into the semester, Alex claims, "I do believe a lot of the in class frustrations of not coming to class or being mildly disruptive stems from their high school education system which could have potentially failed them in preparing them for college. I too was a victim of such a thing when I was a freshman in college."[7] Speaking to students' behavior, Alex's retrospection in this case labels previous educational experiences as a possible negative factor in their transition into the first-year writing classroom. Such narratives illustrate his attempts to understand what is happening in class by hypothesizing previous experiences that have affected his students and their work. His identification of their presumed background with his own illustrates how this sensemaking process is clearly tied to underlife and his negotiation of his own identity as an underprepared student and, now, his role as a TA.

TAs also noticed and reflected on factors on campus that influenced their students' behavior and ability to learn as they sought to label what was happening in their classrooms and what actions to take in response. In thinking about the university's scheduling of spring break and a two-day Easter break that were only a week apart—meaning that students only returned for three days in between—Alex grumbles, "I don't understand why the breaks have to be fashioned the way they are. Not only does it put the students in a lazy state of mind but it happens in the middle of the semester where productivity and classroom input needs [*sic*] to be the highest."[8] Similarly, Diane spends some time thinking about external factors influencing her teaching: "Comparing the four classrooms of my limited teaching experience, I am trying to understand whether the classroom facility itself is as large an influence as I thought at the beginning of my teaching journey last semester. Even this early in the semester, I suspect it is not . . . time of day is beginning to appear to me to be more important a factor."[9] While these aspects of teaching are out of the TAs' control, they are not out of the university's control. Bracketing and labeling them helps the TAs consider their and their students' positioning within a university that does not always seem to act in ways that will best help students learn and what actions, if any, they and their students can perform to counter these circumstances. Doing so engages TAs in underlife because they recognize that the institution may not always consider what is best for students, setting the stage for their thinking through the institution as something that can be negotiated with instead of simply obeyed.

Praising and Blaming Self and Students
A natural evolution of TAs explaining what is happening in their classrooms is praising and blaming themselves and/or their students for any problems, responses that are often emotionally inflected (see Williams's chapter in this collection for more attention to the emotional aspect of attending to sensemaking in writing programs). Typically, this occurred in this study when TAs noticed something positive or negative and sought to label what had happened in personal terms as they also

considered what (if anything) they could or should do in response. In these reflections, TAs equally identified praise and blame with themselves and their students, although each experienced their own progression in thinking about where praise and blame lay. These shifts indicate an active engagement in underlife as TAs considered what their roles as teachers are, regardless of what institutional or programmatic expectations might be.

One TA, Penny, had a very busy semester between working at the university in another role, teaching two classes, and finishing her creative thesis project. Such busyness, sometimes verging on chaos, contributed to her feelings of inadequacy in teaching even as she simultaneously identified where students were not taking responsibility for their own learning. Throughout the semester, Penny identified a few times when she felt as if she had not adequately taught her students, including their struggle with writing a literary analysis, discerning scholarly sources, and giving presentations. Near the end of the semester, she reflects back on the disruptions she experienced throughout the semester and how these may have affected her students: "I feel bad for my students because they've kind of gotten shortchanged this semester; I had to cancel the week of AWP, then there was spring break, then Easter break, then I had to cancel another week for the writing seminar, not to mention that I've been swamped with my own work so I can graduate."[10] While these were unavoidable absences, Penny labels missing so much class—even for university holidays—as a problem for students that she created, even though they overall performed quite well. Other absences that engaged her in her work as a creative writer are similarly viewed as her own problem, despite her role as a student in the university with her own career goals outside of teaching writing. In other words, Penny struggled to negotiate clashing identities in the underlife, perhaps especially because both seemed institutionally sanctioned (in her role as a teacher and in her role as a student). Although this retrospective process did not alter these absences, it did lead Penny to shift around some of her due dates to give students more time to work on major projects as she tried to make both identities work together.

However, despite recognizing some of these problems, Penny does not fully place blame for student failure on herself. She also identifies how some students do not do those things they should in order to succeed in her first-year writing class. For example, she recounts the story of a student who asked for a class extension on an assignment that the class had had for four weeks, a few students who stopped attending class, and students' resistance to finding scholarly sources. This tension about whose responsibility teaching and learning are reflects the multiple identities she was trying to navigate simultaneously in an institutional structure that was not always helpful. Her back-and-forth between labeling some things as her own distractions and some as student issues is a common thread in the reflections of other TAs, including Diane, who early in her second semester works through her feelings about teacher and student responsibility and ends, "Seriously, IT IS NOT ME. Please tell me it's not me."[11] Lily also bounces back and forth between thinking issues are her problem and thinking they are her students' problem, ultimately trying to find a middle ground in which "I am going to simply try my best to help them succeed and learn. . . . The rest is up to the students themselves."[12] The intensity with which TAs focused on who was to praise or blame for successes and failures shows how deeply these affected them and their perceptions of themselves and their students as well as how difficult the underlife—with its identity negotiations—can be.

Solidifying a Teaching Approach

Because TAs have yet to fully define who they are as teachers, part of their sensemaking process is solidifying their own teaching approach in relation to the writing program they are a part of and to other instructors around them. Much of the back-and-forth that the previous rhetorical moves identify occurs as TAs try to label who they want to be as teachers and how they can take actions and engage in communication with students that express this teaching philosophy. Their sensemaking processes lead to more concrete narratives about who they are or want to be as teachers that can become part of the writing program underlife more generally and that express their own involvement in underlife specifically.

One example of this is Lily's journey to figuring out what teacherly ethos she wants to have, a clear facet of the underlife she experienced. As I discussed in the previous section, she spent a lot of time going back and forth figuring out where to assign praise and blame in her classroom. In part, this happened naturally, as her semester began very well and then became more stressful as her own studies—and trying to complete her thesis—piled up (which eventually led to her decision to postpone her graduation from May to August). About a month into the semester, as she worked through the chaos and flux she felt, she provides an analogy about who she wants to be as a teacher:

> After careful consideration, I have decided that I want to be a marshmallow teacher; however, just a little on the toasty side. I have picked this analogy for a few reasons: (1) I am a little bit of a softie, which, while some may

say is a negative trait, I have to disagree, (2) A toasty exterior gets my policies across to students, but they do not resent me, and (3) Nobody likes a burnt "unedible" marshmallow. . . . I like this analogy because it shows that I can stand by my rules when I need, but I can also be understanding and flexible with the needs of my students. And as a student myself, I have always admired professors who are able to understand things from a perspective other than their own.[13]

Such an extended analogy shows Lily's deep thinking about her teaching approach and how she, in her second semester of teaching, is trying to negotiate her teacherly identity as she receives different institutional messages about who teachers are and how they should act. As Lily works out this identity, she feels the need to counter how some other instructors may think being a softie is "negative" to stake out her own way of being. Such sensemaking occurs as she tries to bracket her feelings out of the chaos to label who she is as a teacher and how this can be communicated to her students.

Other TAs in their first semester of teaching, such as Alex, explored their teaching approach without coming to as firm of an understanding of it as Lily did, perhaps indicating the time needed to find a way into and through underlife. Alex frequently remarks on his experimentation in class and how his students reacted to it as he worked through his teaching approach. Building much of his classroom around activities, about a month into the semester he comments, "It is an exercise to come up with a series of new creative assignments every week which incorporate group work and classroom participation. But seeing how an extreme positive response it [*sic*] taken from it then it makes it all worth it."[14] His approach to teaching took a lot of time and energy, but in his reflection, he felt as if it were worth this investment because his students responded so well to this type of teaching. However, he has yet to think clearly about whether this is an approach that works well with his own beliefs about teaching and his identity as a teacher. Anna, also in her first semester of teaching, used acting as a way into identifying her teaching approach with two difficult classes, even as this is partially a façade that she uses to navigate her teacherly identity. At the end of the semester, she reflects, "My motto for the semester is to appreciate the small miracles."[15] Having spent much of the semester trying to handle an unusually high number of student problems while navigating her identity as a young, petite woman, Anna labels her teaching approach as recognizing the positive things her students are doing while trying to mitigate the negative. As part of the sensemaking process, solidifying a teaching approach was very much a focus for these TAs as they tried to construct their identities in relation to those in the writing program in which they taught, sometimes engaging in underlife and other times avoiding such identity construction by allowing others to guide who they are as teachers.

Focusing on the Self and Personal Needs

In constructing their teacherly identities, TAs faced the additional complication of acting as graduate students and teachers while also having personal identities outside of the university, circumstances that create a unique kind of chaos. As part of their sensemaking process, TAs sometimes bracketed out the interactions between the personal and the professional, seeking to build a coherent sense of self that acknowledged the complications of their personal lives and how these impacted their work as teachers. The ways that TAs and instructors figure out a work-life balance is a large part of a writing program underlife that illustrates how they are trying to approach the various identities they have and consider the fluidity between these.

As a nontraditional student with a family and health complications, Diane's reflections are perhaps most illustrative of the ways that TAs had to focus on themselves and their needs during times of flux, times that they often viewed as disruptive to their roles as teachers. Throughout the semester Diane often reflects on how her health and personal needs impact her teaching and the ways she is trying to work around or with these complications. At one point, she remarks on how she is spending upwards of sixty hours per week studying and working, which is not sustainable, and what habits she needs to cultivate to be healthy: "If I want to have longevity in this career, I must begin now to develop positive habits beyond simple reflection, including the habit of tracking time spent in study and work."[16] Her line of thinking allows her to notice a habit, label it as unhealthy, and determine actions to take to avoid this habit continuing. Speaking to her ongoing struggle with the interactions between the personal and professional, near the end of the semester she asks, "It's that conundrum of work-life balance again. How do I best care for myself physically, spiritually, emotionally?"[17] The question of TA work-life balance is one that this particular writing program—and the field of writing program administration—is only beginning to adequately reflect upon and address,[18] and it is especially complicated for TAs who are trying to figure out how all of their identities work together.

Lily similarly questioned how to balance the personal and the professional when her father was hospitalized near the middle of the semester, which put her behind in her work. She rationalizes the way she balances these many needs by explaining how she prioritizes them: "The biggest goal I have right now is to try to put myself and my family first. I am trying to keep my health in order, both mentally and physically. I know it's what I need to do. It's tough, but it's what I need to do. And I know that if I do this for myself, my students will also benefit."[19] Both Diane and Lily recognize that they must take care of themselves if they are going to be available for students, understanding this as a concrete action they must take. Lily, however, recognizes the more direct ties between her personal life and work life in her claim that taking care of herself will ultimately benefit her students. Although writing programs do not always directly address issues of work-life balance, it is certainly a part of the underlife in writing programs, as evidenced in the ways that TAs figure out how to handle the workload they have been given and how they try to negotiate the many identities that inform their lives as individuals and teachers.

Although many teachers experience problems with work-life balance, these problems are especially complicated for TAs who have to balance their own graduate study workload with teaching, which takes additional time if they have not taught before, and their personal relationships. This can lead to their noticing healthy or unhealthy habits, labeling them, and trying to determine what actions they can take to achieve work-life balance. Cumulatively, part of their sensemaking process must involve figuring out how to preserve their selves and their connections with family and friends while also teaching. Doing so forms a large part of the underlife in writing programs, in which TAs and other instructors figure out how to meet writing program or university goals while also preserving their selves.[20]

TA SENSEMAKING IN WRITING PROGRAM UNDERLIFE

Because TAs can make up large parts of writing programs, their sensemaking processes can have a large effect on writing programs and how these programs engage with underlife. Although underlife can be difficult for WPAs to navigate, in part because it opens up room for the questioning of a program and its goals, purpose, methods, etc., TAs necessarily work through sensemaking processes that overlap with underlife. It is not productive, then, for WPAs to try to ignore or constrain these processes; instead, we should work to understand what types of sensemaking TAs are going through as they explore underlife and how we can help them make such processes productive for themselves and others in the program.

Perhaps one of the most important ways WPAs can help TAs with this process is by providing explicit opportunities for reflection and dialogue about their roles as teachers, students, and individuals (see also Smith et al.'s chapter in this collection about how reflection and dialogue can make space for sensemaking in writing centers). Especially in programs with large TA populations, regular opportunities to reflect on what is happening in and out of the classroom and how to negotiate these is vital to their pausing to make sense of what is going on and to talk with others meaningfully as they navigate their identities. Without our weekly meetings and reflections, I am not confident that I would have had the opportunity to work so closely with these TAs as they figured out how to respond to particular situations and as they thought about who they were as teachers. They also would not have had the opportunity to so deliberately dialogue with each other, as well as with me, as they worked through their experiences. As scholars in our field have pointed out,[21] reflection is an important component of working with TAs and one that should not be taken lightly. It is a primary means of engaging them in sensemaking and the negotiation of their identities.

As part of this sensemaking process, TAs also need to be given room to negotiate programmatic and institutional expectations so that they can consider whether they will or will not meet these and in what way. Reflections allowed me to see how TAs worked through sensemaking in part by talking with different faculty and thinking through how those faculty approached similar situations (such as Jennifer with the absence policy). As they did so, the TAs figured out how other instructors resist institutional or programmatic policies that they do not agree with and were provided examples of ways to push back as instructors instead of simply becoming cogs in the machine. While there are programmatic policies WPAs expect instructors to follow, we must acknowledge that productive questioning—productive in that it pinpoints specific issues or problems, draws attention to inconsistencies, points out tensions at work on them or others, and/or centers around what is best for themselves and students—is a necessary part of TAs learning who they are as teachers and who they want to become. An attitude of openness and listening as WPAs can help foster this type of questioning while offering space for us to provide guidance as TAs engage in underlife.

Finally, if WPAs are going to guide TAs, then we have to be open about our own sensemaking processes that engage us in underlife. In my own work, there have been times when I have engaged in sensemaking when confronted with seemingly puzzling policies or institutional constraints, such as how to work around institutional policies that did not seem to account for material realities. Instead of acting as if our teacherly identities are completely formed and perfectly negotiated, it helps our TAs to see our own teacherly identities as works in progress that we show by rethinking our teaching decisions with them. Similarly, we must model behaviors that we hope TAs will take up, such as setting boundaries for themselves on the amount of time they spend on work so that they can be more fulfilled in their everyday lives. Showing how we constantly engage in underlife, too, can help TAs view this as a meaningful process that will necessarily continue throughout their academic careers rather than something that they alone are going through.

Sensemaking, then, necessarily engages TAs—and everyone else in a writing program—with underlife as we all think about how to best teach our students within educational contexts that do not always work with us. All of us would do well to regularly engage in reflection and dialogue about our work and the identities we are asked to assume. The tension between institutional and programmatic expectations and the complex identities we have outside of these structures continues to push our field forward as it grapples with the realities of an increasingly globalized world in an often racist, sexist, homophobic, xenophobic American context. The sensemaking processes TAs go through as they cultivate underlife can help us all consider ways to engage in similar processes as we think about who we are as a field in this context as well as how we, as WPAs, want to respond to it both individually and programmatically.

NOTES

1. This research received IRB approval from Stephen F. Austin State University in November 2016 and January 2018.
2. All names are pseudonyms to protect the identities of the TAs involved in the study.
3. Jennifer. March 10, 2018. Reflection. Practicum in Teaching First-Year Composition.
4. Diane. February 6, 2017. Reflection. Practicum in Teaching First-Year Composition.
5. Anna. January 24, 2017. Reflection. Practicum in Teaching First-Year Composition.
6. Alex. February 7, 2018. Reflection. Practicum in Teaching First-Year Composition.
7. Alex. April 18, 2018. Reflection. Practicum in Teaching First-Year Composition.
8. Alex. N.d. Reflection. Practicum in Teaching First-Year Composition.
9. Diane. January 23, 2017. Reflection. Practicum in Teaching First-Year Composition.
10. Penny. April 18, 2018. Reflection. Practicum in Teaching First-Year Composition.
11. Diane. January 31, 2017. Reflection. Practicum in Teaching First-Year Composition.
12. Lily. February 17, 2017. Reflection. Practicum in Teaching First-Year Composition.
13. Lily. February 26, 2017. Reflection. Practicum in Teaching First-Year Composition.
14. Alex. February 28, 2018. Reflection. Practicum in Teaching First-Year Composition.
15. Anna. April 11, 2017. Reflection. Practicum in Teaching First-Year Composition.
16. Diane. February 28, 2017. Reflection. Practicum in Teaching First-Year Composition.
17. Diane. May 2, 2017. Reflection. Practicum in Teaching First-Year Composition.

18. While WPA work-life balance has been discussed in scholarship such as Diana George's (1999) *Kitchen Cooks, Plate Twirlers, and Troubadours* and Courtney Adams Wooten et al.'s (2020) *The Things We Carry: Strategies for Recognizing and Negotiating Emotional Labor in Writing Program Administration*, the field does not often consider the work-life balance of TAs, perhaps because their busyness is seen as temporary. (Although I would argue that three to six years is not very "temporary.") However, the long-term effects of such stresses include the growing numbers of graduate students who struggle to see how they can balance the demands of faculty positions with the personal lives they want to lead (June 2009), a trend writing programs need to consider as we demand that TAs be responsible for teaching their own classes as they complete advanced degrees.
19. Lily. March 31, 2017. Reflection. Practicum in Teaching First-Year Composition.
20. This also appears in discussions about the labor conditions in which many first-year writing instructors work that circle around the question of what amount of work it is ethical to ask those who are underpaid and unsupported to do (see Kahn, Lalicker, and Lynch-Biniek 2017).
21. See Hesse 1993; Estrem and Reid 2012a; Grutsch McKinney and Chiseri-Strater 2003; Reid 2009; Welch 1993.

REFERENCES

Adams Wooten, Courtney, Jacob Babb, Kristi Murray Costello, and Kate Navickas, eds. 2020. *The Things We Carry: Strategies for Recognizing and Negotiating Emotional Labor in Writing Program Administration*. Logan: Utah State University Press.

Brooke, Robert. 1987. "Underlife and Writing Instruction." *College Composition and Communication* 38 (2): 141–153.

Brown, Andrew D., Ian Colville, and Annie Pye. 2015. "Making Sense of Sensemaking in Organization Studies." *Organization Studies* 36 (2): 265–277.

Dobrin, Sidney I., ed. 2005. *Don't Call It That: The Composition Practicum*. Urbana, IL: NCTE.

Estrem, Heidi, and E. Shelley Reid. 2012a. "What New Writing Teachers Talk About When They Talk About Teaching." *Pedagogy* 12 (3): 449–480.

Estrem, Heidi, and E. Shelley Reid. 2012b. "Writing Pedagogy Education: Instructor Development in Composition Studies." In *Exploring Composition Studies*, edited by Kelly Ritter and Paul Kei Matsuda, 223–240. Logan: Utah State University Press.

Fisher, Walter R. 1984. "Narration as a Human Communication Paradigm: The Case of Public Moral Argument." *Communication Monographs* 51 (1): 1–22.

Gabriel, Yiannis. 2000. *Storytelling in Organizations: Facts, Fictions, and Fantasies*. Oxford: Oxford University Press.

George, Diana, ed. 1999. *Kitchen Cooks, Plate Twirlers, and Troubadours: Writing Program Administrators Tell Their Stories*. Portsmouth, NH: Heinemann.

Grutsch McKinney, Jackie, and Elizabeth Chiseri-Strater. 2003. "Inventing a Teacherly Self: Positioning Journals in the TA Seminar." *WPA: Writing Program Administration* 27 (1–2): 59–74.

Hesse, Douglas. 1993. "Teachers as Students, Reflecting Resistance." *CCC* 44 (2): 224–231.

June, Audrey Williams. 2009. "Grad Students Think Twice About Jobs in Academe." *The Chronicle of Higher Education* 55 (20). https://www.chronicle.com/article/grad-students-think-twice-about-jobs-in-academe-1453/.

Kahn, Seth, William B. Lalicker, Amy Lynch-Biniek, eds. 2017. *Contingency, Exploitation, and Solidarity: Labor and Action in English Composition*. Fort Collins: The WAC Clearinghouse and University Press of Colorado. https://wac.colostate.edu/books/perspectives/contingency/.

McCauley, William J. Jr., ed. 2021. *Standing at the Threshold: Working Through Liminality in the Composition and Rhetoric TAship*. Logan: Utah State University Press.

Pytlik, Betty P., and Sarah Liggett. 2002. *Preparing College Teachers of Writing*. New York: Oxford University Press.

Reid, E. Shelley. 2009. "Teaching Writing Teachers Writing: Difficulty, Explorations, and Critical Reflection." *CCC* 61 (2): W197–W221.

Reid, E. Shelley. 2017. "On Learning to Teach: Letter to a New TA." *WPA: Writing Program Administration* 40 (2): 129–145.

Restaino, Jessica. 2012. *First Semester: Graduate Students, Teaching Writing, and the Challenge of Middle Ground*. Carbondale: Southern Illinois University Press.

Saldaña, Johnny. 2016. *The Coding Manual for Qualitative Researchers*. Los Angeles: Sage.

Saur, Elizabeth, and Jason Palmeri. 2017. "Letter to a New TA: Affect Addendum." *WPA: Writing Program Administration* 40 (2): 146–153.

Weick, Karl E., Kathleen M. Sutcliffe, and David Obstfeld. 2005. "Organizing and the Process of Sensemaking." *Organization Science* 16 (4): 409–421.

Welch, Nancy. 1993. "Resisting the Faith: Conversion, Resistance, and the Training of Teachers." *CCC* 55 (4): 387–401.

3
CELEBRATING SENSEMAKING CULTURES IN THE WRITING CENTER
Scaffolding Transparent Communication between Tutors and Directors

Jeanne R. Smith, Shannon McKeehen, Barbara George, and Yvonne R. Lee

Because ongoing, frank conversation among staff and writing center directors about everyday operations is essential to running a successful writing center, in this chapter we employ a narrative case study that outlines the relationship between the microinteractions inherent in tutor communication and problem solving and a tutor-training program grounded in reflection.[1] In particular, we focus on a problem-solving sequence that resulted in establishing online writing lab (OWL) protocols, informed by tutor discussions. To flesh out this case study, we ground ourselves in ecological rhetorical theory and an emerging understanding of sensemaking to note the many interconnected ecological, or networked, rhetorical relationships that inform multiple literacies. Our case study offers practical application for writing centers seeking ways to better align theory and practice. By listening to tutors and centering their sensemaking in the development of our pedagogy, we not only enact a comprehensive and balanced understanding of the sensemaking cultures within our programs, but we also effectively address our community's needs for agency in methods of professional development. These goals adhere to the writing center's overarching aim to be a site for educational harmony (Boquet 2002; Van Waes, Van Weijen, and Leijten 2014). These theoretical considerations help us to answer the following: *What sensemaking cultures exist within our programs and centers, and how might knowledge of those cultures influence, inform, or complicate our work as administrators?*

A writing center's culture and knowledge are mutable (because of the swift turnover that happens in them over the course of a few semesters)

https://doi.org/10.7330/9781646424368.c003

and vulnerable (because of who the practitioners are). Other authors in this collection have seen how sensemaking is central to a writing center. Andrea Rosso Efthymiou, in this volume, recognizes that tutors make sense of theory differently than do administrators and that their sensemaking is a form of theorizing that directors not only can make room for but should center in their practice. In our own practice as directors, because one tutor cohort's shared sensemaking can seem like rigid rules imposed on the next generation of tutors (whose sensemaking context is different and whose voices could not have been included before they arrived), we've learned to renew guided sensemaking with every new cohort of tutors. As Alba Newmann Holmes observes in her chapter in this volume, "Sensemaking is happening in our writing centers, whether we guide the process or not." Like Newmann Holmes, after guiding our tutors in theory building, we want our shared sensemaking to encourage "reflection and self-critique," not to create a "culture of policing." We discovered that the breakthroughs of one tutor cohort's theorizing and sensemaking must be captured and taken up for revision by new cohorts of tutors, and that makes the documents we create, circulate, and revise key to sensemaking. In their chapter, Genie Nicole Giaimo and Joseph Cheatle advocate for documentation and deliberate knowledge management within the writing center to capture and retain both explicit and tacit knowledge of successive generations of tutors. As Giaimo and Cheatle note, much of what happens to a writing center is outside its control and is in the hands of outside stakeholders. We have chosen to center tutor sensemaking and to document it because it is an activity that we ourselves can support and protect among our internal stakeholders, the tutors.

INSTITUTIONAL CONTEXT

We work at a large midwestern doctoral-granting university whose writing center usage and funding for tutoring much more than doubled between 2005 and 2013 but whose institutional support for training, professional development, and the management of the center remained at the 2005 levels. The thirty-plus tutors in 2013 (up from twelve to fifteen in 2005) were still each trained in a one-credit-hour independent study course conducted by the director in addition to her teaching load. This course introduces new tutors to procedures in the tutor program, including theories and processes used at the writing center. But it was the way in which *online* tutoring was taught that led to our inquiry. In subsequent semesters, tutors learned online response in a series of one-on-one meetings with the director, Jeanne, or with graduate assistant directors Barbara or Shannon, using documents we had created in-house. The online training also included readings from Beth Hewett's 2015 *The Online Writing Conference: A Guide for Teachers and Tutors*, analysis of sample completed asynchronous sessions, and practice sessions. Training culminated in assigning the tutors authentic submissions to our online writing lab. The tutors received feedback on their responses from the director or an assistant director before those responses were released to the writer. Under the on-the-job training model, tutors were offered professional development in asynchronous response each semester, and those who earned online certification received a raise and a new rank. In 2013, with a usage rate of 100 percent and a strong demand for drop-in sessions, "downtime" for this on-the-job training in online response had become scarce. We realized later that the online training, which was initially held in isolation out of necessity, in the independent study course would lead to deeper reflections of our tutor-training practice.

In their initial training in the independent study one-credit-hour course, we helped tutors learn ways of providing cognitive and motivational scaffolding to writers by listening, asking questions, and responding as a reader. These ways of collaborating with writers were sometimes difficult for our tutors to translate to an asynchronous online environment because there is no writer physically present. To cope with this absence of a writer, some of our tutors at first reverted to editing papers as an early misstep in online response training. Others became attached to a limited range of decontextualized responses that could become formulaic. In our intense on-the-job training, we believed our tutors eventually attained abilities to work with writers asynchronously that were *comparable* to abilities to work in person. Our beliefs were about to be challenged.

The challenge came at the same time that institutional pressures pushed us to provide much more online writing support, exposing our assumptions about online tutor training. We will tell the story of how we moved through this challenge and developed a model of whole-staff reflection and collaborative sensemaking to improve all aspects of our online tutoring. Jeanne and current graduate assistant director Yvonne are currently refining our system to make it as sustainable as it has been effective.

Our ideas about sensemaking, reflection, and tutor development, however, did not come to us whole. We ourselves went through a process of sensemaking during the successive and overlapping terms of

Shannon, Barbara, and Yvonne. We struggled to make sense of what was happening with our tutors, and the tutors struggled to make sense of their own theories of online tutoring and those of each other. We believe attending to these sensemaking struggles itself is a form of reflection on action that can help address the complex issues of practice that many centers face.

Our case study is guided by the exigence many in writing centers must address: the dissonance that often occurs when a center educates tutors to work with writers in an online asynchronous environment (Van Waes, Van Wijen, and Leijten 2014). The shifting ecologies and variables that are outside the center's control—changing writing center staff, changing technological tools, changing faculty, changing university policies, changing understanding of online expectations from users—lead us to focus on what we *can* control: our own pedagogical practices. Interactions between director and tutors, and among tutors, are key. We will show how listening to tutors' sensemaking, even—and especially—when that sensemaking differs from the director's, can result in tutor ownership of theory and tutor agency in applying theory to practice. By showing examples of tutors' felt difficulties, we are able to advocate for transparent communication and give tutors an opportunity to join in inquiry that establishes writing center practice (Williams 2016). This communication can drive practice and improve the center's pedagogical ecologies. The entire tutoring staff now helps develop, apply, use, critique, and revise standards of online asynchronous response in a program where power and responsibility are shared. The decentralization of managerial power and the attention to employee sensemaking go together in program development. Directors can more attentively listen to what tutors know by inviting dissonance and listening for the gaps in the "official" narrative. By bringing tutors' narrative sensemaking into the official conversation of the writing center, we are now able to recursively reflect upon and reenvision our practice, while maintaining a healthy community.

METHODOLOGY AND RATIONALE

For this project, we arrive at the intersection of narrative case-study methodology as informed by sensemaking theory and methodology. Narrative methodology mirrors the sensemaking activities engaged in by writing center staff. Storytelling is a significant method for meaning-making among all people, as interacting with others by telling stories is how we create structure and meaning in our world and how we invite others to collaborate in our meaning-making processes (Brown 2000; Clandinin 2006; Patriotta 2003). Thus, we provide the narrative of a moment in the history of our writing center when the concerns of the tutors created a pathway for significant and beneficial growth of our center's practices. We use the case study as a means of presenting a singular exemplar (Flyvberg 2006; Petty, Thomson, and Stew 2012) of sensemaking in action to demonstrate the often overlooked effectiveness of tutors' sensemaking practices.

Rhetorical Ecology

Inherent in our understanding of sensemaking practices is an understanding of various nested and networked relationships within rhetorical ecologies that tutors were navigating in developing online tutoring protocols. Dobrin and Weisser (2002) discuss the socially situated manner of meaning-making by noting "the relationships between discourse and any site where discourse exists" (573). Amy Patrick (2010) discusses the need for writing pedagogy to understand the writer within as an agent in an ecosystem, encouraging an understanding of "the ways in which a writer successfully adapts, functions, and innovates in a dynamic society by engaging critical thinking, judgement and communication" (4). Ecological rhetorical theory allows for understandings of how composition might happen within and outside of academic classrooms by accounting for multiple variables that writing tutors might encounter as students from many disciplines and genres within disciplines seek a tutor. Bawarshi (2001) refers to genres as "rhetorical ecosystems" that enable a system of communication within a given social context (71). Further, Marilyn Cooper (1986) proposes an understanding that writing ecologies interact in varied ways within social systems (in and out of the classroom) as dynamic "webs" where meaning might be made through moves by individuals to write within or, at times, to challenge a genre (367). Tutors had a deep understanding of these complex writing situations as they worked with students from across varied disciplines within a writing center system that engaged in its own particular practices. As such, we observed and encouraged tutor sensemaking in writing across disciplines at our writing center. We had trained our tutors to discern different writing approaches for different rhetorical situations. At times, tutors were learning to challenge or dialogue about assumptions pertaining to writing from many genres that might move through our center. Our rhetorical ecology training, however, did not transfer to asynchronous online sessions as well as we thought it had.

Additionally, tutors often had differing understandings of online platforms by which tutoring might occur that could inform the so-called official writing center asynchronous online protocol. Here, tutors were often unofficially at the forefront of emerging patterns of how they and their peers might use emerging and shifting online platforms. For example, tutors might struggle with sensemaking to know about and discuss functions of chat rooms that they used personally but that were not being used at our writing center. Tutors discussed, among themselves, different constraints and affordances of emerging systems of online tutoring that might not be part of formal online protocol at the writing center. Amy Patrick (2010) discusses the ways by which innovations (in our case, online tutoring) emerge by referring to Everett Rogers's notions of diffusion of innovation:

> Writers often seek to communicate and diffuse innovations in their writing. According to Rogers, "Diffusion is the process by which an innovation is communicated through certain channels over time . . . communication is a process in which participants create and share information with one another in order to reach a mutual understanding." (4)

In understanding the online platforms as an additional ecological element that might impact meaning-making, we can more clearly see the tutors' varied sensemaking approaches to these online platforms and attend to various genres of writing that they might encounter; thus, they can then be mindful of the ways they might "make sense of" their extensive personal online practice experience into the ecology of tutor practice. At this point, the writing center might be intentional about the need for dialogue about tutor sensemaking of online tutoring practices.

Sensemaking and Educational Harmony

Sensemaking is a theory and methodology articulated and outlined by Karl Weick (1995) in his influential text *Sensemaking in Organizations*. Weick and many others have taken up the sensemaking mantle and expanded it by using it as a lens through which to understand practical, real-world situations (Brown 2000; Gioia and Chittipeddi 1991; Patriotta 2003; Weick, Sutcliffe, and Obstfeld 2005). Sensemaking is the art of asking two questions: "What is happening?" and "What do I do next?" (Weick, Sutcliffe, and Obstfeld 2005). Thus, it is about reflecting on what the current situation is and acting on that situation. Weick, Sutcliffe, and Obstfeld (2005) argue that explicit sensemaking occurs when our expectations of the world are different than our perceptions of how the world is (409). In our narrative case study, the tutors each had specific and different expectations of what online writing lab interactions should look like. However, several perceived that their expectations were not being met by the current practices of others. This disconnect between expectation and perception answers the "What is happening?" aspect of sensemaking theory. The act of visiting the writing center director and voicing their concerns enacts the response to the "What do I do next?" question and seeks to ensure harmony in the writing center space. In the process of dealing with this specific challenge, we responded with reflective practice models. We were striving for educational harmony, so we theorized learning practices that encouraged sensemaking. For example, a valuable principle of John Dewey's (1931) that is commonly employed in the writing center is the idea of discovery learning, which plays a significant role in tutors' sense- and meaning-making processes, especially as they work with writers. The value peer tutors place on their relationships to others and to their learning often contributes to eventful collaboration (Mullin 2001; Macauley 2004; Bohney 2016). Students learn best when discovering for themselves the complexities of various lessons, and training peer tutors to successfully communicate with their writers online is no exception. This concept has been adapted into constructivist theories of learning, giving many writing centers the chance to operate more harmoniously through cooperation and transparency. Effective discovery learning is a celebrated feature of our communities of learners, where our students are taught to uncover and share expertise. Thus, it makes sense for writing center tutors to want such harmony to exist with their directors. Regularly consulting with tutors about their felt difficulties on the job helps directors refine our training protocols. What's more, regular check-ins and professional development in the form of additional training throughout a tutor's tenure allows for educational harmony to flourish, as our sensemaking becomes more concrete and synchronous. Such discovery learning is a powerful means to these ends in many writing centers, including our own.

NARRATIVE CASE STUDY

Any writing center director who has helped undergraduate tutors learn asynchronous online response has probably experienced a familiar disconnect: Otherwise masterful tutors revert to surface editing or pat, formulaic responses as they tackle the sophisticated challenges of working with writers online asynchronously (Breuch and Racine 2000; Rilling 2005; Wolfe and Griffin 2012). In our center, we had worked hard for years to develop a training protocol for online tutoring that had served us well in helping tutors learn to be as responsive, adaptable, and improvisational in asynchronous online sessions as they had been in face-to-face sessions, and we were proud of the quality of their online tutoring.

During the semester that we focus on in this chapter, however, four challenging trends came together to intensify the difficulty of online tutoring. First, our writing center had more than doubled in size and was growing each semester, rendering our training protocol for online asynchronous tutoring too labor-intensive to be sustainable. Second, our institution expanded its online course offerings, including writing-intensive courses. Third, our administration was investigating third-party online options to meet expected increased demand for online writing support. Fourth, and most important, was a long-held traditional belief among our tutors that online tutoring was both difficult and unsatisfactory compared to in-person on-site tutoring. The resulting sensemaking behaviors of our own tutors within this challenging period inspired us to act, and it is only in retrospect that we have come to understand the significance of our experience and how our own sensemaking in response to the challenges above can form a heuristic for other writing centers and writing programs facing similar pressures.

A Puzzling Trend among Tutors

Just before the middle of the semester, a tutor approached Jeanne, concerned that a peer was incorrectly tutoring online because she did not insert bubble comments within the paper. Shortly after, another tutor discussed her discomfort that one of her fellow tutors had become too directive by addressing lower order concerns (LOCs) in an online submission. A week later, another tutor shared concern that a colleague had commented too much, and another asserted that this peer was not commenting enough. In each case, Jeanne reviewed the online responses, seeing that each tutor had addressed the specific context well in the online submissions, and she worked with the concerned tutors to help them expand their notions of good practice. This resolution should have been reassuring to Jeanne. After all, writers were being served well, writing center response principles were being upheld, and tutors were learning. But it was not reassuring. The experience left Jeanne with a felt difficulty: *Why this sudden "tattling" behavior? Did tutors feel a need to validate their own response style with the director? Why? Were tutors afraid to raise issues with each other? Why? What had happened to the collaborative group of tutors she had trained? Was the staff getting so large that now there were social factions? How do we address this?* All of these issues worried us, but the behavior also made us doubt our online tutor training. We needed to know why experienced tutors were not seeing what the director could see: the variety of appropriate responses in each rhetorical context. And, more to the point, we wondered what tutors were demonstrating to us that we had been oblivious to. The troubling trend seemed to be social, theoretical, structural, and substantive.

At first, we reasoned that our online training had simply started to miss the mark, and that the tutors were resorting to formulas instead of learning from each other (De Smet, Van Keer, and Valcke 2008). This reasoning was logical, but not sufficient, to explain what we saw. For example, we had seen tutors develop so-called false rules by finding a technique that works in one context and generalizing it to most asynchronous online sessions. Examples of false and even contradictory rules were easy to recall: *Always insert comments. Never insert comments. Always ask questions. Never make directive statements. Never correct an error. Always comment on errors. Never provide suggestions. Always give examples. Discuss no more than three issues. Address everything the writer asks about. Prioritize and prune your comments.* False rules could be on the rise, we thought, because they are easier to build than a flexible theory of response. We hoped that what we saw happening was that when tutors trained for online response in isolation by the director in the independent study course, and in subsequent semesters, in individual online modules, they had simply generalized what they had learned to do themselves and had privileged that technique as good practice for everyone. We hoped that getting all the tutors into an environment where they could discuss online tutoring would help them see diversity in practices that could all be theoretically sound. The complaints about each other's tutoring, we reasoned, represented a failure of our training to develop the sophistication and flexibility we had been known for when we were a smaller center (a center with downtime and ample opportunity for tutors to discuss their work between sessions). We believed we had to recreate the downtime theory discussions of the small center for our now large and busy center. We reasoned that scaffolding a discussion among the tutors would solve both problems. We now see that, like us, the tutors were responding to external pressures that made the need for change urgent.

A Perfect Storm: Internal and External Forces

As directors, our own reflection on action revealed problems in our online training program as well as mounting institutional pressures on that program. We could see that our online training was slow, labor-intensive, and top-down, concentrating authority for "what counts" as good tutoring in the directors' offices and inhibiting tutors from looking to each other for continued learning and expertise. Our intensive, individual training methods were no longer sustainable in a larger center at a university that was increasing online courses for all students, leading students to seek more online writing support. At the same time, our institution also began exploring the possibility of outsourcing online feedback in our distance education programs. Grammarly, the Ohio eTutoring consortium, paid tutor-matching services, and textbook publishing companies' on-demand online writing help were all posed by administrators as alternatives or supplements to the campus writing center. The administrators proposing such outsourcing did not consult with the writing center regarding the soundness of pedagogical practices nor how the writing center might modify its practices to better suit student needs. It was an environment ripe for outsourcing, which we believed would marginalize our center and create, in effect, two writing centers: one for in-person students and another for distance learners.

These mounting internal and external pressures spurred us to take action, and we devoted a mid-semester, in-service tutor development meeting to the subject of asynchronous online response. Feeling pressured to keep up with demand, the tutors were all eager to have their say about online tutoring, so participation in the meeting was robust. Our intention was simply to help tutors see one another's practices as valid, which the directors could see, but the tutors could not. The exercise accomplished much more than this later.

Applying Sensemaking Strategies, Part 1: Listen to Everyone in a Scaffolded Discussion

Our approach was to divide our usual mid-semester idea-exchange meeting (a meeting that every tutor attends as part of their employment each semester) into three sessions: a scaffolded discussion about tutoring values, some candid talk about the affordances and constraints of online tutoring, and a brainstorming session on how tutors translated their in-person practices to an online environment. Imagining that our tutors had more values in common than they realized, we hoped to encourage them to see multiple methods for accomplishing their intentions in online sessions. We were surprised at the end of this meeting how readily the tutors listened to the variations in their practice when those practices were connected to their shared values and intentions.

Session 1: What do you value most in your in-person tutoring?
During the first session, the director asked the tutors to articulate their highest goals for their in-person sessions and what they valued most about working with writers in the in-person environment. Nothing was too aspirational. Listening, writer agency, writer comfort and well-being, and writer independence were mentioned, as they might be in any writing center. Tutors talked about giving voice and empowerment to people who had previously been silenced. As the tutors spoke, we listed their ideas on a whiteboard and consolidated the items into a list that everyone agreed on. As a writing center, we clearly saw ourselves as a sounding board for students, as agents for social change, as mentors, and as coaches. It was a unifying moment. With everyone feeling pretty good about themselves as a team, we were ready to move on to a more contentious discussion question.

Session 2: What are the affordances and constraints of asynchronous online response?
Next, an experienced and respected tutor lead a brainstorming session on the affordances and constraints of asynchronous online tutoring. He pushed for complaints about asynchronous tutoring. Discussion was spirited. Some tutors disliked online sessions, but others saw them as advantageous. Not having the full array of communicative modalities topped the constraints list, while thinking before responding, revising responses, and embedding to resources emerged as commonly recognized affordances. Again, the list was pruned to only what everyone recognized as significant. Tutors easily connected the affordances of online tutoring to their overall tutoring values, and they all recognized the constraints as genuine challenges requiring creativity and admitted that they posed challenges they needed help to overcome. For example, the affordance of easily embedding resources in an online session matched the shared value of writer independence. The constraint of the absent writer challenged the shared value of demonstrating to the writer that they were listening. Unified, they were ready—perhaps—to learn from each other. We moved on to the final, and likely contentious, portion of our discussion.

Session 3: How do you accomplish the tutoring values that are most important to you in the asynchronous online environment, or even in spite of the asynchronous environment? How do you enact your tutoring values online?
Finally, the assistant directors led the most important part of the discussion, asking how tutors tried to accomplish their goals and to enact their values in asynchronous online sessions, given the affordances and

constraints we had listed. At first, tutors shared simple techniques to personalize their sessions, such as using the writer's name, referencing the concerns in the writer's submission form, and complimenting specific elements of the paper that helped them as readers understand a writer. Then, amazingly, a tutor who had been recently accused of being overly directive explained how he models an editing technique in his sessions, highlighting other sentences with similar editing issues, and embeds a resource. Far from being "directive," this tutor was trying to help the writer develop independence by using the affordances of the highlighter to get over the constraint of being unable to point and ask questions about sentences.

Tutors who previously had complained about each other's practices proudly articulated the connections between our common goals (such as writer independence) to their specific online tactics (how to point). For example, some tutors write in bubble comments, others do not type anything in the paper itself, and both camps call attention to specific sections of the paper (they "point") in different ways. (All camps were enacting the value of being specific to make the feedback actionable for the writer.) Tutors questioned their own tactics publicly in this meeting and invited others to make suggestions to help them retheorize their online practices. One tutor in particular, whom everyone respected, admitted that she often wondered if she was accidently overwhelming the writer by commenting too much. Another tutor wondered if he commented enough for writers to notice a pattern (both tutors were very much concerned that the feedback be understandable and usable). These admissions of vulnerability, and references to specific practices in relation to common goals, were powerful. Tutors trusted each other enough to question their own practices because they recognized each other's commitment to the shared goals of the group. When they disagreed, they did so based on a perceived connection between the specific feedback practice and a shared goal or value. For example, a tutor who does not comment inside the paper was asked how she was able make the feedback specific. In other words, how does she "point"? And that tutor responded that she used paragraph numbers, explaining how important it was to her to preserve writer autonomy by not touching the paper itself. When discussion was framed in this way, the tutors saw that their common goals and values could be enacted in numerous ways, depending on the context. Better still, they learned from each other. People who previously accused each of other of using wrongheaded tactics instead listened to each other's rationale or theory and saw each other's techniques as options for achieving a mutually cherished goal.

We summarized the discussion by listing our common values for online responses in rough draft form as the outcome of the meeting.

Applying Sensemaking Strategies, Part 2: Write It Up, Invite Feedback, and Use the Resulting Document

After the meeting, we distributed the list of common tutoring values and solicited comments from all tutors. Consensus in this document was easy to achieve because it was nothing more than the list from the meeting turned into parallel grammatical units and labeled as "common standards" to give the list the imprimatur of officiality, and it arose from the good will that had developed in the meeting. While tutors differed in their tactics from session to session, they all agreed that the twelve standards below represented quality online tutoring, and they could explain their individual tutoring moves based on what they were trying to do with regard to the criteria. By calling them standards, we now had a training and professional development document based on the tutors' sensemaking instead of the directors' sensemaking. We had distributed responsibility for articulating online asynchronous standards of tutoring, and we were very surprised that this could happen.

1. The tutor **demonstrated respect** for the writer.
2. The tutor **established rapport** with the writer.
3. The tutor **demonstrated** that they were **listening** to the writer's concerns.
4. The tutor used **previewing/forecasting language** prior to providing feedback.
5. The tutor **pointed to specific sections** of the writing when providing feedback.
6. The tutor explained the feedback **clearly and at the writer's level**.
7. The tutor focused on helping the writer **develop writing strategies**.
8. The tutor directed the writer to **resources**.
9. The tutor **limited feedback** so as not to overwhelm the writer.
10. The tutor provided **sufficient feedback** to address the writer's concerns.
11. The tutor **invited the writer to contact the Writing Commons** with questions.
12. The tutor **thanked the writer** for using the OWL service and **invited the writer to return**.

None of the tutors could have come to this theoretical moment alone. It required being in conversation with each other and making sense of each other's tactics and their own. We understand that we have not listed every desirable trait in asynchronous online tutoring, that many of these ideas are common, and that some of the items are in dynamic tension (standards 9 and 10, for example). As directors, we understand that there may be additional items to include; however, the *process* we uncovered here is more important that the twelve standards themselves. The tutors abstracted the values/theories from each other's narratives of practice by connecting those stories to what they all viewed as essential to tutoring writing in *any* session. For example, instead of accusing each other of writing too many comments (or worse, "tattling" to the director), the tutors could now discuss whether or not they felt the comments might overwhelm the writer, something they all recognized as something to be avoided. In retrospect, we believe that in the initial collaborative reflection meeting we had scaffolded a conversation in which tutors could hear each other make sense of practice and theory, where they could mobilize what they knew about in-person tutoring practice, discuss their feelings about asynchronous tutoring, and build knowledge together about the challenging aspects of online tutoring.

The document above is now used in initial tutor training, in quality control and mentoring work, and in ongoing professional development. Most important, it is used to productively discuss differences in practice, encouraging tutors to learn from each other as they do in their in-person sessions. The document is our anchor. However, because tutors graduate, we need to learn how to engage in such sensemaking all the time; otherwise, the standards become just another set of rules imposed on the tutors rather than a set of values articulated and used by them. This need to use the document well is a lesson we still had to learn and are relearning even today, as Jeanne and current graduate assistant director, Yvonne, work to keep the document fresh.

Applying Sensemaking Strategies, Part 3: Crowdsource the Center and Distribute Leadership

The common standards allow us to distribute responsibility for asynchronous tutor training and professional development among the whole staff, so it helps with our sustainability issue mentioned above. We have even used use the standards to help other writing centers grow their online tutoring. In our current tutor-training program (now a three-credit course that includes online response theory), trainees use the criteria to observe and reflect on the sessions of experienced online tutors prior to being assigned practice sessions of their own. Using the criteria, experienced tutors provide feedback to trainees as they practice asynchronous responding. Using the criteria, student managers sample the asynchronous sessions to look for trends in our feedback practices as a whole. Using the criteria, team leaders help established online tutors reflect on their practice. Experienced tutors have contributed examples of asynchronous sessions they have found challenging and invited other tutors to use the criteria to provide feedback. Tutors have used the criteria to observe and critique each other's asynchronous sessions for professional development. Tutors reflect on their online sessions using the standards as points of departure.

Before these standards, only about half of the tutoring staff at any given time was online-certified. As of this writing in 2018, the center employs fifty-five tutors, and all but one is online-certified. Tutor ownership of the standards drawn from sensemaking together is the value for us. The collaborative effort successfully exemplifies Weick's (1995) "cognitive apprenticeship" as tutors each lend their voices, their revisions, and their expertise to the standards and are ever-growing professionally as a result.

The misunderstandings among the tutors we saw in 2013 represented a failure of the directors to appreciate the sensemaking process of tutors and to integrate that process fully into professional development and ongoing reflection—especially during what was a challenging period of growth. We have learned from our experiences that false rules about online tutoring and the zeal to which tutors espouse them can reveal a pattern of sensemaking in which we can intervene. We have learned that interventions such as offering communication tools to promote sensemaking dialogue can provide tutors a platform for collaborative sensemaking to scaffold their theories of response with one another. However, no matter the breakthroughs we make in such scaffolded sessions, they are temporary. Sensemaking must be continuously renewed and must be woven into the official practices of the center, as seasoned tutors graduate and new tutors enter. Otherwise, the response theories of one cohort of tutors can be reduced by the next cohort to a list of rules. Without continuous, scaffolded reflection on action and ongoing opportunities for collaborative sensemaking within the official writing center culture, our interventions fall flat.

Applying Sensemaking Strategies, Part 4: Build Recursive, Valuable Collaborations

When we reflect on the semester of the perfect storm, we realize we have built something valuable out of what looked like a baffling problem. It *was* baffling, but it was not a problem we needed to fix. Instead, it was a signal of the need to intentionally bring tutor and director sensemaking together into our everyday practice as writing center professionals and to engage in reflection together. Below are the stages of that process presented as a heuristic built over several semesters and that continues to be refined. The centerpiece is attending to practitioner sensemaking, regardless of the area of practice under discussion: online sessions, group sessions, whole class sessions, unfamiliar genres, etc.

- Model genuine listening to reveal how practitioners' stories about their practice make sense of the complexity of the issue at hand.
- Facilitate practitioners' genuine listening to each other's stories as they build theories from stories of their practice.
  - Ask everyone to articulate what they value, building strong consensus.
  - Talk about the challenging practice honestly and openly.
- Assist practitioners in moving from stories/narrative to theory-building and empower them to word the theories that account for what they value in tier work.
  - Discuss individual ways of meeting the common values, despite the challenges and differences.
  - Make sure judgments are expressed, not about individual practices themselves, but about the connections of those practices to the consensus values.
  - Record the insights from these discussions as an official document.
- Formalize methods of continuous mutual listening to build practitioner sensemaking into the program's initial training and professional development culture.
  - Use the group-negotiated document; do not shelve it.
  - Encourage and reward continuous discussion of diverse methods for achieving common goals.
  - Revisit the goals themselves periodically to see how they resonate with practitioners.
- Develop processes in which all practitioners—including newcomers—collaborate in continuous assessment of the theories they develop together, negotiating adjustments as new cohorts of practitioners make sense of previous practitioners' theories.
  - Develop a system for repeating this process at least once a year, if not every semester.
  - Adjust the criteria as needed with each community of practitioners to ensure continuous, strong buy-in.

While we use the word *practitioners* above to expand our thinking to other writing programs, we see the last item, in which practitioners collaborate in continuous assessment, as critical in writing centers because of the normal turnover rate of student tutors. Without that step, the theories of previous generations of tutors seem helpful only until the last of that cohort graduates.

DISCUSSION

As directors, our first indication that we may have been lax in attending to tutor sensemaking (or encouraging negotiation and adjustment) can be a sudden uptick in misunderstandings, such as those we saw at the beginning of our narrative. The misunderstandings can mean that tutors are doing their sensemaking in isolation instead of in community. To overcome isolation with practices that are genuinely challenging and complex—as most writing program and writing center work is—practitioners need to hear the wisdom of their colleagues rather than a ruling from a leader. As leaders, directors can scaffold negotiations of complex theory, and we can build continuous sensemaking conversations into our tutor development programs. We can think of these conversations not only as brainstorming sessions but also as feedback sessions. A few years into our center's current online tutoring practices and after a number of management- and director-level assessments of online tutoring practices, we came to the realization that we need to follow our own advice to consistently involve tutors in the continued reflection on our practices. We had been using the collaboratively developed protocols for those assessments and were sharing our findings with the tutors to encourage reflective practices. However, we realize we must always guard against a modified version of the "tattling" and promote a view of the online tutoring standards as a living document, one that needs to be continually renegotiated by those responsible for upholding those standards—namely, the tutors. We must always be ready to take challenges back to the tutors and work through developing a new set of best practices that cohorts of tutors moving through the writing center can feel ownership of.

We realize now that writing center practices should not be condensed to a set of how-tos, as each writing center serves its institution and community in varying ways. Rather, the ongoing sensemaking practices among everyone in the writing center community amplify the principles that dictate tutoring practices, as supplied by expert and developing knowledge. Prioritizing relationships among veteran and beginner writing tutors involves regular reflection that supports the development of a writing center community of interrogation and method. After all, "a pragmatic perspective toward writing center knowledge accepts contradiction between theory and practice" (Hobson 1994, 22). Adaptability should be among the only constants in a writing center space; this is especially true in online environments, which can be unpredictable. Having tutors research innovations in online tutoring and communication is a wise approach with regard to professional development. In doing so, sensemaking can begin and continue among multiple sensemakers, without a need for strenuous hierarchy. All tutors can therefore ground their identities as sensemakers, without the need to reinforce gatekeeping among them (Weick 1995, 18). Ongoing professional development can also reinforce the variety of response that happens in online tutoring environments by centering accountability among all writing center staff. If writing centers are indeed what Boquet (2002, 16) calls "academic cleaning services," then writing center directors should be asking themselves how they can make online and offline tutoring practices as helpful and individualized as humanly possible, to avoid making their efforts "factory-like." Asynchronous tutoring practices can sometimes involve sterile, cookie-cutter experiences if we are not careful and do not welcome a variety of legitimate response (Van Waes, Van Weijen, and Leijten 2014). Online tutoring can have its perks when it comes to thorough feedback, which some tutors struggle with during face-to-face interactions, despite the flow of conversation during in-person sessions:

> Though practitioners may intuit the back-and-forth real-time affordances of face-to-face sessions as lending themselves more naturally to global concerns, asynchronous sessions are not necessarily limited to directive comments or surface issues—nor are these sessions defined by these concerns or approaches. (Weirick, Davis, and Lawson 2017, 29)

Thus, discovery learning has the potential to make asynchronous situations more manageable through patient trial and error. What we also had to remember was that our own practices as directors needed to add to the promotion of discovery learning as a form of sensemaking in those moments when things seemed to be running smoothly with little to no friction, and our sensemaking practices could come full circle when we came to terms with the continuous and ongoing nature of learning.

Attending to tutor talk (even when it's not what directors want to hear) and facilitating tutor crosstalk (even if it starts in uncomfortable misunderstanding) is how we can use sensemaking for deep learning and professional development. Under the strain of institutional pressures, misunderstandings among practitioners can seem negative. However, the misunderstandings are valuable. If we can bring ourselves to listen, tangible, useful, abundant evidence exists everywhere for how tutors and directors make sense of complexity. The stakes of failing to listen can be high. In the case of asynchronous online writing center tutoring, increases in online-only courses at colleges and universities can tempt institutions to outsource online writing support and can pressure writing centers to cede this work to others (because it is difficult, labor-intensive, and perhaps unpopular among tutors). Possibly even worse, the increases in online submissions can allow tutors to fall into formulaic responses in order to reduce complexity and keep up with increasing demand. The result of failing to attend to tutor sensemaking and to feature it in the center's culture could have been that online students would have less sophisticated feedback responses than our in-person students receive. Furthermore, the implications of having two versions of tutoring—one for brick-and-mortar students and one for online students—should concern us all because it replicates privilege for students whose life circumstances afford them the opportunity for in-person sessions. By contrast, we attempt to attend to the richness of tutor insights on the complex practice of online tutoring by building recursive reflections that encourage critical discussions of sensemaking that stem from what tutors are experiencing. In this way, we can continue to investigate, then reinvestigate, our online practices that might serve all students.

NOTE

1. This research was determined to be exempt from IRB review.

REFERENCES

Bawarshi, Anis A. 2001. "The Ecology of Genre." In *Ecocomposition: Theoretical and Pedagogical Approaches*, edited by Christian Weisser and Sidney Dobrin, 69–80. New York: State University of New York Press.
Bohney, Brandie L. 2016. "'Discovering' Writing with Struggling Students: Using Discovery Learning Pedagogy to Improve Writing Skills in Reluctant and Remedial Learners." Master's Thesis, Indiana University-Purdue University, Indianapolis.
Boquet, Elizabeth H. 2002. *Noise from the Writing Center*. Logan: Utah State University Press.
Breuch, Lee-Ann M. Kastman, and Sam J. Racine. 2000. "Developing Sound Tutor Training for Online Writing Centers: Creating Productive Peer Reviewers." *Computers and Composition* 17 (3): 245–263.
Brown, Andrew D. January 2000. "Making Sense of Inquiry Sensemaking." *Journal of Management Studies* 37 (1): 45–75. https://doi.org/10.1111/1467-6486.00172.
Clandinin, D. Jean. 2006. "Narrative Inquiry: A Methodology for Studying Lived Experience." *Research Studies in Music Education* 27 (1): 44–54. https://doi.org/10.1177/1321103X060270010301.
Cooper, Marilyn M. April 1986. "The Ecology of Writing." *College English* 48 (4): 364–375. https://doi.org/10.2307/377264.

De Smet, Marijke, Hilde Van Keer, and Martin Valcke. 2008. "Blending Asynchronous Discussion Groups and Peer Tutoring in Higher Education: An Exploratory Study of Online Peer Tutoring Behaviour." *Computers and Education* 50 (1): 207–223.

Dewey, John. 1931. *The Way Out of Educational Confusion*. Cambridge, MA: Harvard University Press.

Dobrin, Sidney I., and Christian R. Weisser. May 2002. "Breaking Ground in Ecocomposition: Exploring Relationships between Discourse and Environment." *College English* 64 (5): 566–589. https://doi.org/10.2307/3250754.

Flyvbjerg, Bent. 2006. "Five Misunderstandings About Case-Study Research." *Qualitative Inquiry* 12 (2): 219–245. https://doi.org/10.1177/1077800405284363.

Gioia, Dennis A., and Kumar Chittipeddi. September 1991. "Sensemaking and Sensegiving in Strategic Change Initiation." *Strategic Management Journal* 12 (6): 433–448. https://doi.org/10.1002/smj.4250120604.

Hewett, B. 2015. *The Online Writing Conference: A Guide for Teachers and Tutors*. New York: Bedford/St. Martin's.

Hobson, Eric H. 1994. "Writing Center Practice Often Counters Its Theory. So What?" In *Intersections: Theory-Practice in the Writing Center*, edited by Joan A. Mullin and Ray Wallace, 16–24. Ann Arbor: The University of Michigan.

Macauley, William J., Jr. 2004. "Paying Attention to Learning Styles in Writing Center Epistemology, Tutor Training, and Writing Tutorials." *The Writing Lab Newsletter* 28 (9): 1–5. https://wlnjournal.org/archives/v28/28.9.pdf.

Mullin, Joan A. 2001. "Writing Centers and WAC." In *WAC for the New Millennium: Strategies for Continuing Writing-Across-the-Curriculum Programs*, edited by Susan H. McLeod, Eric Miraglia, Margot Soven, and Christopher Thaiss, 172–199. Urbana, IL: National Council of Teachers of English.

Patrick, Amy. 2010. "Sustaining Writing Theory." *Composition Forum*, 21 (Spring). http://compositionforum.com/issue/21/sustaining-writing-theory.php.

Patriotta, Gerardo. March 2003. "Sensemaking on the Shop Floor: Narratives of Knowledge in Organizations." *Journal of Management Studies* 40 (2): 349–375. https://doi.org/10.1111/1467-6486.00343.

Petty, Nicola J., Oliver P. Thomson, and Graham Stew. 2012. "Ready for a Paradigm Shift? Part 2: Introducing Qualitative Research Methodologies and Methods." *Manual Therapy* 17 (1): 378–384. https://doi.org/10.1016/j.math.2012.03.004.

Rilling, Sarah. 2005. "The Development of an ESL OWL, or Learning How to Tutor Writing Online." *Computers and Composition* 22 (3): 357–374.

Van Waes, Luuk, Daphne Van Weijen, and Mariëlle Leijten. 2014. "Learning to Write in an Online Writing Center: The Effect of Learning Styles on the Writing Process." *Computers and Education* 73 (April): 60–71. https://doi.org/10.1016/j.compedu.2013.12.009.

Weick, Karl. E. 1995. *Sensemaking in Organizations*. Thousand Oaks, CA: Sage.

Weick, Karl. E., Kathleen M. Sutcliffe, and David Obstfeld. 2005. "Organizing and the Process of Sensemaking." *Organization Science* 16 (4): 409–421. https://doi.org/10.1287/orsc.1050.0133.

Weirick, Joshua, Tracy Davis, and Daniel Lawson. 2017. "Writer L1/L2 Status and Asynchronous Online Writing Center Feedback: Consultant Response Patterns." *Learning Assistance Review (TLAR)* 22 (2): 9–38.

Williams, Jessica. 2016. "Writing Center Interaction: Institutional Discourse and the Role of Peer." In *Interlanguage Pragmatics: Exploring Institutional Talk*, edited by Kathleen Bardovi-Harlig, Beverly S. Hartford, 37–66. New York: Routledge.

Wolfe, Joanna, and Jo Griffin. 2012. "Comparing Technologies for Online Writing Conferences: Effects of Medium on Conversation." *The Writing Center Journal* 32 (2): 60–92.

4

TUTOR-TO-TUTOR
Attending to the Operations of Race and Privilege among Writing Center Staff Members

Alba Newmann Holmes

INTRODUCTION

For more than twenty years, writing center scholars have recognized the need to diversify writing center staff to better reflect and engage with the campus communities they serve (Barron and Grimm 2002; Grimm 1999; Okawa et al. 2010; Greenfield and Rowan 2011a; Green 2018). As directors respond to this need, the composition of their centers shift; but deeply seated white assumptions and privilege often remain in place.[1] Writing center staffing reflects larger institutional patterns in which efforts to recruit a more diverse student body may occur "without simultaneous attempts to decenter whiteness" (Smith and Tuck 2016, 13).

Scholarship on race and the writing center has tended to focus on tutor-to-writer interactions (Bawarshi and Pelkowski 1999; Barron and Grimm 2002; Mendez Newman 2003; Innes 2006; Zhao 2017; Haltiwanger Morrison 2018; Lockett 2018). Attending to the operations of race within writing consultations makes sense: the tutor/writer dyad is clearly a space in which power is evoked and negotiated, and the operations of race often exacerbate these dynamics. Tutors may meet with hundreds of writers over the course of their time in a center; these meetings tend to define the job. That said, working in a writing center also often involves face-to-face interactions with others employed by the center—fellow tutors, assistant directors, coordinators, directors, and receptionists. Although less has been written about these interactions, they too are informed by the operations of race (Geller et al. 2007; Suhr-Sytsma and Brown 2011).

In this chapter, I focus on tutor-to-tutor interactions, particularly in the context of staff meetings. I attend to the specific experiences and voices of tutors, drawing upon their contributions to meetings, their

https://doi.org/10.7330/9781646424368.c004

reflective writings, and my own experiences directing two undergraduate writing centers at liberal arts colleges. While awareness of white privilege may be growing on college campuses, my experiences with undergraduate writing tutors suggest that there is often a distance between what students understand in theory and what they understand about themselves, their peers, or their behaviors toward one another. In other words, not all peer tutors belong to the same sensemaking cultures or access the same sensemaking frameworks when it comes to questions of race and racism. The same can certainly be said of writing center administrators. In primarily white institutions, open communication about race and privilege is often circumscribed by assertions of positive intent, a skewed emphasis on the individual's responsibility to recognize and address so-called microaggressions[2] in real time, and uncertainty about how to move forward individually, or as a group, in the face of the profound problem of white privilege.

This chapter documents my own sensemaking process regarding the operations of race in the writing center: from an initial "trigger"[3] through the steps I took to make meaning of events—reaching out to colleagues, reading, discussing with students in small groups and individually—then, calling the peer tutors into my sensemaking process in hopes of affecting theirs, so that we could collectively, intersubjectively, map a path forward (Balogun and Johnson 2004, 524). Before sharing that work, however, I would like to take a moment to reflect on the relationship between my own identity and the information included in this chapter.

I am white. Like many (if not all) of the students I discuss below, my personal sense of identity is more complicated than the way in which I am read by others. I was born and raised in New Mexico. My father's first language is Spanish; most of his family members were killed in Auschwitz—he and his parents and sister escaped Europe in 1939, landing eventually in Colombia. My mother's people were farmers; she was the first in her family to go to college. Both of my parents are artists. Each of these realties influences my sense of who I am. That said, I have been educated, formally and informally, as a white person, and I have benefited from that whiteness.

I have worked on this chapter over a long period of time—the experiences at its core took place more than six years ago. After the document had been through several iterations, I came to the not-wholly-welcome realization that what I had written was a white lady discovery story. In a book about sensemaking, a discovery story is appropriate. Sensemaking scholarship attends to the ways in which individuals and organizations move from not knowing and not understanding to understanding and taking action—integral to that is the process of discovery. As Rita Malenczyk points out in the introduction to this collection, storytelling is an integral part of sensemaking, as well. And storytelling belongs in/as antiracist work (Green and Condon 2020). Still, I had some questions about what I had written. As Neisha-Anne Green, Vershawn Ashanti Young, and others have amply documented, for people of color, sensemaking about the operations of race—inside and outside the contexts of writing centers—happens early, often, and in destructive ways. My "discovery" of the operations of white privilege—when and how it happened for me—highlighted the very privilege I was seeking to challenge. And in a field with a superabundance of white women's voices, I wondered what it meant to add another piece that might be relevant only to white readers.

I trust that my readers, like the BIPOC peer tutors with whom I have worked, will come to their own conclusions about what is relevant. In my own appraisal, the most important parts of this text are those in which I lift up the voices of students, amplifying their voices with the authority granted to me by position, age, and (with an irony lost on few) my race. But sensemaking is not just a process of listening or interpreting. It is also a process of taking action. When I began this work, Neisha-Anne Green had not yet given her 2017 keynote address at the International Writing Centers Association (IWCA) conference highlighting the differences between allies and accomplices, but I was aware that positive intention alone would not suffice. I took steps, and missteps, in my efforts to become an accomplice, and those are documented here too—for any writing center administrators who may find them useful in taking steps themselves. As Green cautions, it's not the label but the WERK that matters (2018, 32). Antiracist work and sensemaking work can be powerfully allied when we recognize in them a shared purpose: to arrive at "consensually constructed, coordinated system[s] of action" with which we can make change in our institutions (Taylor and Van Every 2000, 275).

STRUCTURAL DIVERSITY IS NOT A PANACEA

I admit my own naivete when, in the spring of 2013 while I was directing a writing center for the first time, I had the opportunity to hire a diverse group of peer tutors into a center that had been historically white. My arrival as director of that program served as one of the "ecological changes" described by Weick (1969)—a space and time in which organizational sensemaking is likely to occur (Maitlis and Christianson

2014, 60). In that center, all the peer tutors, or consultants, were undergraduates. Their large number (thirty-five for a total student population of just over two thousand) was driven by a program that paired each consultant with a first-year seminar. These same tutors staffed the writing center.

Our hiring process began with a call for faculty nominations. In order to hire a more diverse staff, I would need faculty collaboration. I asked my colleagues to please diversify who they nominated—in terms of race, gender, and major—and they did. And I hired every student of color who was nominated. Had you asked me at the time, I would not have recognized this as tokenism. All the students I hired were qualified. They interviewed well. I thought I was addressing a problem from the ground up. I still think it was an important move; but, as I said, also a naive one.

First off, my claim that I hired every student of color who was nominated is probably wrong. I hired every student who presented as a student of color based on what I knew about them from their nomination and application (which did not ask about their racial or ethnic self-identification) and those utterly unreliable methods: how they looked and their surnames. And, as I learned in my work with them, I hired a number of students who I identified as students of color but who did not define themselves or identify with others on the basis of skin color, race, or culture. As Valentine and Torres (2011) caution, students' physical features, names, or geographic backgrounds cannot be read as "unproblematic confirmations of their identities" (194). They offer this observation in the context of profiling writers who visit the center, but the same can, of course, be said of hiring peer tutors.

At the time, however, I felt happy that I was able to offer positions to eleven people of color—just under one third of the total staff for the year. I imagined that the writing center culture would change just by having these people present in the center. I wasn't completely off base, but as Okawa et al. (2010) and Smith and Tuck (2016) caution, meaningful, productive working relationships don't emerge simply based on proximity. Structural diversity does not guarantee "genuine interaction": "Genuine interaction among diverse populations invokes a much messier, more complicated notion of diversity. It goes beyond the sheer presence of diverse students to include diverse human beings in relationship to and with each other" (Valentine and Torres 2011, 199). Hiring, in and of itself, does not build these relationships.

While I was aware that some writers felt uncomfortable coming into a predominantly white center, my exposure to antiracist pedagogy and literature was still limited, and as a white person, I had not considered the ways in which white privilege was deeply and invisibly entrenched in our center, in our staff members' behaviors and experiences—what Brian Hendrickson describes in his chapter in this collection in terms of "institutional disposition" or what Asao Inoue (2016) terms a "white racial habitus"—and in how that wasn't changed by making these new hires. I am deeply indebted to the student of color who finally made this clear to me—by inconsistently attending our weekly staff meeting. This was the first impetus for the sensemaking journey I document here, as her absence "violated expectations," which triggered sensemaking (Maitlis and Christianson, 2014, 66). Cornelissen (2012) describes sensemaking as the processes of making meaning through which "people interpret events . . . that are somehow surprising, complex, or confusing" (118); and I was perplexed, perhaps even frustrated, by her apparent lack of engagement.

When I followed up with her by email, she said, "I do not feel like my presence contributes to the discussions we have in staff meetings and, in all honesty, I did not think my absence would be noted. This, I think, represents a larger invisibility and lack of entitlement I feel within the work I do at the writing center." Of course, I *had* noticed her absence. I had hired her, along with the other students of color, because I wanted them in the room.

What I had not noticed, and what staff members of color eventually began to articulate for me, was that our large staff meetings were rife with microaggressions: the students of color were being interrupted by fellow tutors in small discussion groups. When I asked for staff members to share their experiences, white voices were dominating the conversations, and in some cases, consultants of color felt their work with writers was being disrespected. One told me, "In the large group I am safer because you are watching, but when we break into small groups, people act differently—without you monitoring, they behave disrespectfully, and I don't feel safe." The actions I had taken thus far had exacerbated tensions between race, privilege, and the work of the writing center. I needed to plot a course forward, acknowledging the complexity, the messiness, my own missteps, but also the importance of our ongoing work together.

STAFF MEETINGS AND TUTOR INTERACTIONS

Centers that offer a quarter- or semester-long tutor education course have some significant advantages when it comes to working intensively with tutors to recognize the operations of race and white privilege and to practice antiracist pedagogies. This is especially true when those teaching the class avoid the "week twelve approach," which puts racism on the syllabus, but without giving it the sustained attention that its complex ethical, historical, and social ramifications require (Greenfield and Rowan 2011b). In robust tutor-education courses, there is time to read, discuss, come to know one another as a community, and develop trust—that is, create relationships—all of which are instrumental in raising awareness and accountability within the staff. A course can also offer a space in which the authority of the professor gradually shifts toward the authority of the group (Warnock and Warnock 1984, Okawa et al. 2010). There is a lot to be said for this model.

As the National Census of Writing documents, however, not all campuses have tutor-education courses (Gladstein and Fralix 2013).[4] According to the 504 programs that responded to the 2013 census, workshops held before the semester are the most common method of preparing undergraduate peer tutors for their work with writers (273 responses). These workshops may be offered alone or in conjunction with other forms of tutor education, including full-credit courses (184 responses), weekly meetings (174), monthly meetings (143), or half-credit courses (55). In other words, more than half of responding centers did not offer a tutor-education course. The center I was directing at that time was one of these; we paired a beginning-of-the-year workshop with weekly staff meetings.

In the absence of a tutor-education course, where can antiracism work occur? Writing center orientations at the beginning of the year or semester offer community-building opportunities of the meet-and-greet variety. They are often charged with the energy and enthusiasm of the beginning of the term. They may strike a tone for future work together, highlight foundations and expectations. They are, however, removed from the everyday interactions of the center, frequently taking place before the proverbial rubber meets the road.

Staff meetings, on the other hand, typically recur throughout the term and are informed by the rhythms and stresses of its progress. They meld necessary housekeeping with the intellectual and ethical work of the center, offering space (at least in principle) for writing tutors to engage in sensemaking—to reflect on their own experiences and put these into broader contexts. Beyond learning from faculty or staff leaders, the peer tutors with whom I have worked have emphasized the importance of meetings as a space for learning from one another.

The opportunity to mentor and learn from one another is one of the acknowledged boons of writing center work, whether it takes place in a meeting, on shift, or in a class. The makeup of writing center staff—drawn from a variety of disciplinary backgrounds—also allows students who are already familiar with critical pedagogies and the language of antiracism; for instance, from sociology coursework, to engage in dialogue with those from fields in which explicit discussions of race and privilege are not the norm. Taking students' disciplinary preparation for antiracist pedagogy into account is important too, because we should not expect the work to be done solely by those who are themselves people of color (Carroll 2008, 46–47).

A number of factors can affect how this learning takes place during staff meetings, specifically. One of them is size. Like a traditional class, if you have six people in the room, or twenty-six, you have a different set of possibilities. Staff size affects engagement (who contributes and in what ways). It can also affect the tutors' sense of purpose, that is, *why* they are present in those meetings. In general, I have found peer tutors in staff meetings less attuned to their audience (that is, their fellow tutors) and their responsibilities to that audience than they would be to the writers with whom they work. So, although they may appreciate learning from one another, they do not always engage with one another in ways that foster this learning.

At the time when the peer tutor wrote to me of her experience of invisibility, I was holding one weekly staff meeting for thirty-five people. It is easy to imagine how size alone could limit participation based on who felt comfortable speaking up in front of a large audience. I had thought of small breakout groups within the meeting as a means of encouraging more voices to join the conversation. With seven or eight groups and only one of me, however, the small groups without my supervision had become unchecked spaces of white privilege. I myself had contributed to the problem by emphasizing that the newer consultants should learn from the more experienced staff members; those given the authority to share their experiences were, then, almost all white.

EXAMINING WHITE PRIVILEGE

A microaggression is an interaction in which one person casually, sometimes unknowingly, asserts their dominance or assumes their priority over another. We can predict likely aggressors based on markers of status: race, gender, class. As such, microaggressions are subtle reenactments of long-standing inequalities, and they are damaging because they happen over and over again. As the *American Handbook of Psychiatry* acknowledged in 1974, the insidious danger of microaggressions is that they are "incessant and cumulative" (Pierce 1974, 515). Viewing microaggressions through a sensemaking lens highlights how an event may hardly register for some (typically those not on the receiving end), therefore remaining unexamined or "senseless," while the same event may be profoundly meaningful for others—intimately connected to the sense the individual has of an organization and their role within it.

In her initial email to me explaining why she had not been attending staff meetings, the tutor said, "I did not approach you about these feelings because, firstly, I did not want to be viewed as the typical person of color who always makes things about race, and secondly, because I've engaged in enough dialogue surrounding these issues to be emotionally exhausted." She agreed to start coming to the meetings again but asked that she not be required to confront these issues.

In my response to her, I thanked her for explaining to me the experiences she and others were having, and I said: "While you do not have to address the issues that you identify, I do." Then I knew I needed help, because I did not know how to address them, which is where my process of sensemaking began in earnest. I was very fortunate. I had a marvelous colleague, a sociologist, who specializes in the sociology of race, identity, and racism. I went to her and said, "I have a hot mess in the writing center, and I need help." And she helped me.

I told her what I knew: I had staff members who were feeling systemically marginalized, and I had been complicit in this marginalization. The large group meeting wasn't working. Many of our new consultants were feeling disrespected, invisible, excluded, and exhausted. I wanted to broach these issues with the staff, without putting undue pressure on students of color to represent these concerns. I wanted to intervene as soon as possible, with the long-term goal of building a more authentically inclusive community[5] in the writing center.

My colleague gave me several important pieces of advice. First, if you really want the peer tutors to reflect on the operations of race, you have to let that be *the* focus; don't try to tackle other aspects of diversity at the same time. If you put other things on the table—like gender or sexual orientation—students will rush to them, because they feel easier to tackle. I have since heard this advice expressed elsewhere, as well. In the introduction to *Transforming the Academy*, for instance, Sarah Willie-LeBreton shares feedback she received from colleagues who cautioned against engaging the multiple dimensions of diversity in her edited collection, because "institutions use other forms of diversity to avoid working on racial diversity" (Willie-LeBreton 2016, 3). In the introduction to

Writing Centers and the New Racism, Greenfield and Rowan (2011b) also observe that bringing other identity markers into the discussion serves as a distraction (3).

Second, don't treat this as an "inoculation"—the "race day" intervention. You have to take a sustained, multi-pronged approach, and you have to tell students we will be taking a sustained, multi-pronged approach. This is the same advice Greenfield and Rowan (2011b) and Diab et al. (2012) offer.

Third, do not let intentions be on the table. In my subsequent antiracist work with white students, I have returned again and again to this point. Not allowing our intentions to be on the table may offer white people the first intimations of what it feels like to be without privilege. It is frustrating, frightening, even infuriating to be misunderstood, to feel your actions are misrepresented by others, to sense the disconnect between how you understand yourself and how others understand you. That is an important sensation for white people to have. I like very much Nancy Grimm's (1999) articulation: "My goal is to make well-intentioned people uncomfortable. . . . My hope is that uncomfortable people will search for more complicated understndings" (x). Cultivating in white students the ability to remain present, open, and engaged while experiencing these sensations may be one step toward addressing white fragility.

Finally, my colleague told me, as a white person, be prepared to be the bad guy—no matter how good you may be. In part, she explained, this has to do with the age group of the consultants I was working with and their processes of identity formation through disidentification or othering.[6] At least some of the time, I was going to be that other because I cannot step outside of my whiteness, just as I cannot step outside of my authority and privilege as a professor and writing center director. Jona Olsson elaborates, in "Detour Spotting for White Antiracists": There are no "exceptional white people"; no matter how committed to antiracism we may be, "we still experience privilege based on our white skin color. We benefit from this system of oppression and advantage, no matter what our intentions are," and those who do not have the same privilege know it (1997, 4).

I shared with my colleague my plan to hold a series of required breakout meetings, in lieu of the large group meeting, during which I would ask the staff members to reflect on a number of sample scenarios drawn from recent writing-center meetings—situations in which microaggressions or other problematic interactions had occurred. She and I talked about the range of responses I might get and how to facilitate the conversation productively. I viewed staff meetings as both the problem and the solution—the same spaces in which students were experiencing the effects of race and racism were also the spaces in which I would work with them to address and acknowledge their behaviors and experiences. Of course, the meetings themselves were neither problem nor solution, merely the vehicle—first for unexamined assumptions and behaviors, and then for explicit attention to these.

The next week, I asked each of the staff members to sign up for a group of no more than eight. I let people see who was in the groups so they could sign up with others with whom they felt affinity. Because peer tutors of color remained in the minority, and because a number of them had expressed not feeling safe or not feeling respected in the larger group, I felt it important that they be given the opportunity to enter those meetings among friends. The meetings were to be one hour long. In the end, I held five of these breakout meetings.

When each group was assembled, I began by saying that I was holding these meetings because a number of our colleagues in the writing center had had experiences that made them feel unwelcome and, as the director of the writing center, it was my responsibility to help all of us recognize and address these experiences. I had hired every consultant for what they could contribute to the center, and if they were not able to make those contributions, as an employer, ethically and pragmatically, I must try to make changes so that we *could* benefit from everyone's contributions. I described how our meeting would proceed: first, I would read aloud some excerpts from *Writing Centers and the New Racism*. Then, I would ask them to read over several sample scenarios that were based on things that had happened in our center, and I would ask them to reflect on how each of the scenarios impacts a culture of inclusivity in the writing center.

I also laid out the ground rules: no talking about what had been intended or meant by any of these interactions, only a focus on the outcome, the impact. No one was to interrupt anyone else. No one, except for me, was obliged to speak, but I hoped that we would be able to have some discussion. I also told them that I recognized how uncomfortable the conversation could become. I, too, would be uncomfortable. They would very likely see my face getting red as we proceeded, but that I was okay with it because I was serious about wanting to talk about this.

I have since thought about how the ground rules I provided echoed and differed from the Four Agreements laid out in the *Facilitators Guide to Courageous Conversations About Race*, described by Smith and Tuck (2016): (1) "Stay engaged" in the conversation, (2) recognize that there will be moments in which [we] will "experience discomfort," (3) "speak [your] truth" and honor others' truths, and (4) expect and accept that such conversations may not end in "closure" (34, quoting Singleton and Linton 2006, 58). Acknowledging discomfort and emphasizing that these conversations were part of a process, not the conclusion, were both part of my framing for our meetings. I was not as explicit in requiring that students stay engaged or speak. Given that the meetings I had called were both out of the ordinary and short, I was not particularly concerned about people tuning out or lacking engagement. I would have done well to place more emphasis on what it means to honor others' truths, I believe.

The excerpts I read aloud from *Writing Centers and the New Racism* served two purposes: they showed that the conversations we were about to engage in were part of a much broader, national dialogue that others were taking seriously, and they helped to calm me, as I was momentarily able to rely on other voices to explain my thinking. To frame my decision to hold these smaller breakout meetings and discuss real scenarios, I drew on Jane Cogie's (2011) use of Tagg (2003), who encourages us to "embrace the 'hot cognitive economy of the Learning Paradigm college'" (97), in which teachers actively engage students in the making of knowledge (Cogie 2011, 231). I hoped to serve, I told the tutors, as the kind of leader who "opens space" rather than fills it, recognizing the kind of "heat" this could produce for all involved. One potential source of heat was the very tension between opening space for students and yet not obligating them to do all the work of filling that space: I wanted to honor the students of color who felt they had already said their piece, repeatedly. Silence could be a form of participation, as far as I was concerned.

I also drew from Cogie's (2011) use of Levinas (1998) to emphasize that "we are responsible [for our actions] beyond our intentions" (Levinas 1998, 3, qtd. in Cogie 2011, 229). I shared part of Michelle Johnson's "Racial Literacy and the Writing Center" (2011), which calls upon the work of Victor Villanueva Jr. (2006), pointing out that my own use of terms such as *inclusive* and *diverse* may have allowed me initially to focus on structural diversity, without attending to interactions occurring within the writing center community. I was now deliberately moving away from those tropes (Johnson 2011, 215) to ground our conversation in the "messier, more complicated" experience of "genuine interactions" (Valentine and Torres 2011, 199). I then had the students read over the scenarios, silently at first. One-by-one we began to discuss them. Here are three of the five scenarios I included:

A white writing center director hires eleven students of color as new writing consultants. They join a staff of twenty returning consultants who are white. In staff meetings, the director emphasizes the importance of learning from the more experienced consultants.

In a staff meeting, during a small-group conversation, a white consultant interrupts a consultant of color, taking the conversation in a different direction. The consultant of color is not given an opportunity to complete their thought.

A consultant of color is meeting with a student in the writing center. A white consultant is listening nearby and interjects to offer a suggestion.

In perhaps all but one of the five group meetings, a white student wanted to address the fact that the scenarios were not intentionally hurtful actions. In each case I said succinctly, "Yes, but as I explained at the outset, we aren't concerning ourselves with why this happened, rather with what the consequences were." In this regard, it was helpful to have one of my own mistakes as the first in the list. By and large, students were able to see and articulate the negative impact of these interactions on our community. A white, male sophomore shared, "I never thought that my actions could be understood as having anything to do with race, but as I read these, I see how they could." A white, female junior reflected, "I would feel unwelcome, too, if this was happening to me." A white, female senior commented, "I get really excited about things. I think I am an interrupter. I need to be more tuned in to how that can impact others, not just in terms of what they are saying but in the bigger picture."

Valentine and Torres (2011) emphasize "that interaction is reciprocal" and that tutor education "must help tutors come to a deeper understanding of their own identities" (207). Smith and Tuck (2016), similarly, observe that through antiracist pedagogies, students who have "never directly experienced the more oppressive consequences of racism" can be invited to reflect on why that is, what that means (25). While these initial meetings were only a very early step in this direction, I did note that a number of the tutors continued to reflect along these lines in subsequent semesters, as well.

Of course, not all was self-reflection and acceptance. Some group members tried to see the scenarios in terms of common courtesy, civility, or professionalism regardless of racial dynamics. In one case, a tutor said, "Yeah, but these kinds of interactions could happen to anyone, they aren't necessarily about race." These were not explicit "post-racial" or "color-blind" arguments; indeed, I am struck that none of the peer tutors with whom I worked at the time claimed that we were operating in a post-racial world. Still, recourse to "it could happen to anyone" or "that's not the operation of race, that's rudeness" comes close. I agreed that not being rude was a best practice; I even acknowledged that anyone in the room might at some point in their life be interrupted or overlooked, but that did not allow us to imagine that race was not operating within these specific interactions. Instead, I said, "If the person on the receiving end of this kind of behavior is a person of color, they can't step outside of their experience; and if it is part of a larger pattern of interactions they have witnessed frequently, they know from experience that race has something to do with it."

I was grateful when a female student of color, a junior, shared this: "I haven't been thinking about these things in my work in the writing center, but now that we are reading these, I have an example of something that has happened to me in the classroom and in our meetings. I'll make a contribution to class conversation or to a small group discussion. And the person who talks after me, who is not a person of color, will begin their comment with, 'Actually. . . .' When they start that way, they are de-actualizing what I just said." In addition to helping her peers recognize the often-subtle manifestations of microaggressions, she was modeling an attunement to the effects of language that is fundamental to peer tutoring in writing. Starbuck and Milliken (1988) argue that "putting stimuli into frameworks (or schemata) that make sense of the stimuli" is central to sensemaking (51). In this instance, the student was reflecting aloud her own process of placing these interactions, or stimuli, into the framework of her prior experience, at the same time helping others in the class to recognize the stimuli, and perhaps, to begin constructing frameworks of their own that would integrate her testimony.

In at least four of the group meetings I held, I believe we "attend[ed] to and bracket[ed] cues in the environment" for the purposes of "creating intersubjective meaning," as Maitlis and Christianson (2014, 67) suggest. In other words, I felt as though highlighting the scenarios and responding to and discussing them as a group began the necessary work of understanding the experiences of others and the significance of those experiences to our work together as a whole.

The last meeting, however, was more challenging. In that group there were four staff members of color—including the woman who had sent me the initial email and two other women who had spoken with me privately about negative experiences they had had or witnessed as members of the writing center staff. The one male student of color in the room began his response to the scenarios with: "I probably shouldn't say this, but I don't really think these are issues." He went on to explain that if individuals were having these experiences, he did not understand why they didn't just address them directly with the person who'd been rude. He felt that directly addressing the person in question was the best way to handle it, and then closed with, "if this is really going on as often as you seem to be suggesting."

Here, an agreement to honor one another's truths would have been beneficial. Lacking one, I pushed back and stated bluntly that it wasn't a question of what *seemed* to be going on; these things were going on, and it was our collective responsibility to recognize and respond to them. I asked, too, how it would be possible to make it safe for students to intervene in the moment of a microaggression and whether it was appropriate to assume that if someone "has a problem" they should "deal with it," when the problem wasn't theirs but instead was systemic.

To have one student of color undermine the legitimacy of the experiences of others was not something I had expected or experienced in the previous meetings. What further speaks to my novice status in dealing with issues of race and privilege was my lack of attunement to the impact of intersectional identities on staff members' experiences. Another male student of color later told me in a one-on-one conversation that he had never been interrupted by other consultants and was not aware of being on the receiving end of any microaggressions, while almost all of the female consultants of color shared with me that they had. I have since thought about how I might have better designed and facilitated the meetings—so they would not have been seen as a "proving ground" in which differences in student perceptions could have detrimental effects on one another but rather as a space in which we could "consensually construct" a shared understanding and plan of action (Taylor and Van Every 2000, 275).

Valentine and Torres's (2011) point that we cannot know "how the various aspects of students' identities will shape their interactions" was further brought home for me in the tutors' responses to Geller, Condon, and Carroll's (2011) article on *punctum*, which they read as a follow-up to our scenario meetings. In it, the authors identify "significant and often shame-inducing moments . . . that catch us unaware and force us to acknowledge racism" (120), and they share their "urgent sense that we needed individually and collectively to move past paralysis around moments that cause us shame," to move forward with important antiracist work (108).

The consultants' responses showed a high level of engagement. One commented: "I appreciated the emphasis the reading put on embracing discomfort. I think that individuals in positions of privilege often become incredibly uncomfortable in situations where they are forced to confront that privilege because that means also realizing that such a privilege is an unfair, social construction." The same student continued,

> I did have a few concerns with the chapter, however. Most saliently, I was bothered by the focus, I felt, the authors put on people of color educating whites. For instance, referring to an interaction between a white consultant and a writer of color, the authors explain that the writer's paper . . . "served as a punctum for Sandy—and then for the whole staff and the director" (Carrol 2011, 114). Although I understand the benefits of this situation, I don't feel that the authors adequately addressed how one-sided this dynamic was. . . . The writer of color is offering up her very personal experiences, and the authors frame it as a moment of education for the white consultant.

Another tutor, who identified as BIPOC, suggested similarly that the article was written by white authors for a white audience, and that she didn't find it particularly relevant to her experience. In part, this had to do with a flaw in the way I set up the activity. I asked students to reflect on whether they'd had an experience of punctum. Based on the article's framing, this was a question more pertinent to white students than students of color. Cheryl Jones-Walker (2016) invites teachers to recognize that "what is valuable for majority students may come at the price of not adding value or meeting the needs of students of color" (63). This is clearly as relevant in tutor training activities as it is in the context of the traditional classroom.

A number of the peer tutors pushed back on the emphasis on shame in the Geller, Condon, and Carroll (2011) article. They had difficulty granting shame any redemptive potential, or they equated shaming with silencing and opposed the silencing of anyone, even as a means of dismantling privilege: "The intentional fostering of shame, be it for reflection or equalizing . . . cannot work to create spaces of empowerment or inclusivity. Being mindful, well-versed, and aware of privilege is great, and I am glad so many people are passionate about it. But choosing one approach—forcing shame—reifies privilege that may be assumed more than actual." This student went on to say that as a first-generation college student from a low-income, white family, "I don't know how to create a more inclusive space, but the last few weeks have left me feeling disinherited from the conversation." For some, the article and the activities we had participated in were not sufficient to move past a sense of paralysis in the face of punctum or privilege.

Here, again, intersectional identities complicate matters. When I have experienced resistance to antiracist conversations among thoughtful, engaged white members of the writing center community, what seems to stand in the way is a profound awareness of their own vulnerability. Vulnerability—whether it be a result of class, gender, religion, sexual orientation, or institutional position—sometimes serves as a catalyst, drawing individuals and groups together, even when their specific experiences of privilege and oppression differ. Other times, vulnerability produces a counter-magnetic force that resists recognizing one's own privilege or another's oppression. As a teacher, I continue to think about how to honor these students' truths and ways of sensemaking, while not allowing it to "detour" us from the antiracist work we need to do.

CONFLICT, INDIVIDUALISM, AND COMMON UNDERSTANDING

Conflict is a well-recognized aspect of productive teamwork (Tekleab, Quigley, and Tesluk 2009). Organizational behaviorists make a distinction between "task conflict"—when team members define a task or understand how best to accomplish that task differently—and "interpersonal conflict,"[7] which is based upon differences in identities, beliefs, and how we read or understand one another. Collaboration often entails both these types of conflict; and if students in the writing center are reporting no conflicts, it may mean they are not actually collaborating in meaningful ways (Valentine and Torres 2011, 204).

Peer tutors become well-acquainted with task conflict in writing conferences and learn how to negotiate those moments in which the writer's and tutor's agenda differ, for instance. Sometimes interpersonal conflict occurs in conferences as well—when people feel profiled, misunderstood, out of sync, or disrespected. Ideally, when interpersonal conflict occurs between writers and tutors, writing center mentors and directors can help—Suhr-Sytsma and Brown's (2011) heuristics for recognizing and addressing the "language of everyday oppression" offer examples of how to identify and begin to respond to some of these scenarios. In less ideal circumstances, tutors may wait out an uncomfortable conference, and conflict may be avoided. Ultimately, when tutors and writers cannot establish rapport or respect, they may arrange (informally or formally) not to work together again.

Task conflict may crop up between peer tutors as well, especially if they collaborate on projects, but interpersonal conflict can have more profound negative impacts on tutors and the centers in which they work. The same time constraints and "escape hatches" are not available to staff members who will have ongoing contact with one another over semesters or years; sometimes a tutor will leave a center altogether if interpersonal conflict goes unacknowledged. In all four of the centers with which I have worked, I have been struck by the goodwill and positive energy of the tutors (let this serve as my acknowledgment of their positive intent). The issue is that interpersonal conflict produced by the operations of race and privilege often is not recognized as conflict—it manifests in the kinds of microaggressions I have described above, which are visible to some but not all. This invisibility can give the appearance of the well-tempered writing center, when in fact staff members are experiencing friction based not on the nature of their work but on who they are—the bodies they occupy and their racialized experiences.

In their longitudinal study of fifty-three student teams, Tekleab, Quigley, and Tesluk (2009) found that with effective conflict management, which included the direct and open acknowledgment of interpersonal conflicts and a willingness to address them, teams ultimately experienced "higher levels of cohesion, team member satisfaction, and internal team trust" (175). The question is, how do writing center directors help undergraduate writing tutors both acknowledge and address these conflicts? How do we get that particular sensemaking process started?

To help tutors engage with one another productively and manage conflict productively, we may first need to make it more obvious to them that they are a team. Just as many outside of writing centers assume that peer tutors are hired for their individual skills (as writers or peer editors, etc.), peer tutors may assume that their work is individual rather than collective—based upon what they are good at and implicit in the structure of one-to-one conferences.[8] The individualism of writing tutors may be particularly accentuated in programs that feature a course-fellow or associate model, in which a great deal of each tutor's work happens in individual meetings with members of the class to which they are assigned and not in the context of a center.

Tutors understand well that they are supposed to collaborate with writers, and they express high levels of responsibility toward the writers with whom they work, but their sense of responsibility to function as a team with their fellow tutors is not as universal. Resources, writing center missions, and traditions dictate how closely and in what capacities tutors collaborate with one another on writing center initiatives. Some centers set up ad hoc teams or formal committees to take on projects, complete assessments, or conduct research. In others, tutor-to-tutor interactions occur only at very defined moments—on shifts or during meetings, for instance. Even if their writing center does not call on them to work together on initiatives beyond tutoring, as they develop their practice, mentor, and learn from one another, they are a team. This seems particularly important to reinforce at moments when new tutors join an existing staff, which in many centers occurs every year.

We can create guidelines for tutor-to-tutor interactions, making expectations more explicit. I did this with the consultants—in facilitated small groups—after our scenario meetings. Guidelines emphasize individual accountability for treating one another with respect. Like Suhr-Sytsma and Brown's (2011) heuristics, however, they also attempt to shift the weight off of individual decision-making and responses by coming up with a list of agreed-upon behaviors. These lists are helpful when they hone our attention—making visible to all what has previously been visible only to some. However, like structural diversity, guidelines are no cure-all. They are easily reified (divorced from the context or the social and intellectual communities that generated them), and they may create what one peer tutor described in a written reflection as a culture of "policing": "Most of the guidelines we established focused on how we could get consultants to police each other's behavior, as opposed to self-critique and reflection. This was especially frustrating because no one acknowledged the likelihood that were these 'policing' practices to take place, it would mean white consultants expecting consultants of color to educate them and help correct their behavior."

When tutors suggest that individuals should work out their own conflicts with one another (disregarding the operations of race) or when guidelines are put in place that rely on policing, it is worth highlighting with peer tutors the ways in which individualism and privilege may operate together to suggest strategies for addressing conflict that are not realistic or appropriate for those who are experiencing the negative impacts of the operations of race. Privilege tends to accentuate the sense that individual choice and accountability are what matters. This makes sense; if your privilege is unexamined, you can assume that the positive outcomes you experience are based on your choices, and that others, too, can have positive outcomes by making the kinds of choices you have or would make. Those who do not experience privilege, on the other hand, recognize that personal choices may have limited effect on the systems in which they find themselves.

Smith and Tuck (2016) encourage us in our antiracist work by emphasizing that "institutionally, we can talk about race if we establish and adhere to some common understandings." (34). Guidelines establish common expectations, but not necessarily common understandings. Common understandings are shared, intersubjective ways of making sense of interactions, behaviors, and experiences. Those come slowly. They come out of relationships. And relationships are more likely to emerge among writing center staff members when we take time to focus our attention on the interplay between individual and collective experiences, and individual and collective accountability, and when we accept the discomfort that often accompanies these messier, more genuine interactions.

Sensemaking is happening in the writing center, whether we guide the process or not. As Balogun and Johnson (2005) note, individuals are making meaning when they "engage in gossip and negotiations, exchange stories, rumours and past experiences, seek information, and take note of physical representations, or non-verbal signs and signals" (1576). If we wonder where writing center "lore" comes from, it comes from community members' (tutors', writers', and administrators') efforts to make sense of all of these experiences in the context of the center.

Sometimes that resulting lore is problematic, just as the experiences to which the lore responds may be better for directors in both cases, to take part in guiding the conversations about experiences and lore—to help ourselves and the peer tutors with whom we work develop "resourceful sensemaking" or "the ability to appreciate the perspectives of others and use this understanding to enact horizon-expanding discourse" (Wright et al. 2000, 807). We do this when we facilitate face-to-face conversations and when we make spaces for dialogue in textual spaces, such as the journal entries that Carroll (2008) describes. We do it in mindfully run staff meetings and any time we bring our tutors together to collaborate and then debrief on their collaborations.

Even when writing center directors do this work imperfectly, as much of it as we can do, our peer tutors pay it forward—to each other, to the writers with whom they work, and to us. Years have passed since I held those initial scenario meetings. Those students graduated; I moved on to another institution. But I know that the work we began of attending to the experiences of tutors of color was significant. I remain in contact with many of the consultants from that time, including ones who were skeptical. I see clear evidence that they are still learning from those conversations and carry them with them—into their work educating new tutors at new institutions, into their graduate studies, and into their lives. Even in the absence of a tutor-education course, my experiences suggest that we can do the necessary work of recognizing and challenging the operations of white privilege within the writing center and beyond.

Note: I would like to thank Noor Amr, Tiffany Chan, Marcela Harden, Astra Lincoln, Chanel Sulc, and the other writing associates with whom I worked in 2013–2014 for their insights and for allowing me to share their words. Also, my thanks go out to Mat Barreiro, Emily Drew, EDickey, Luis Rosa, Karen Woods, and the many other colleagues from whom I have learned along the way.

NOTES

1. See Asao Inoue's discussion of the "white racial habitus" in Inoue (2016).
2. I use the term "so-called" here, because I think the diminutive "micro" belies the significance of these instances and their impact.
3. I do not love this term because of its different connotations in discussions of content warnings or "trigger warnings"; however, "trigger" is the term frequently utilized in the scholarship on sensemaking to describe the initial event that requires interpretation or response—the impetus for sensemaking. See, for instance, Louis 1980; Hoffman and Ocasio 2001; Maitlis and Lawrence 2007; Nigam and Ocasio 2010; and Maitlis and Christianson 2014.
4. The reasons for this are many. At some institutions, it is difficult to add a tutor education course to the list of course offerings because of departmental politics or questions about where such a course fits into the curriculum. In some cases, it is difficult to convince or require students to take such a course. On some campuses, writing center directors who are staff members (and not faculty) are not given the opportunity to teach courses. Tutors may also work jobs outside of the writing center or program so that finding room in their collective schedules for an additional course, or even staff meetings, can also present a challenge.
5. See my later discussion of how this language may participate in what Victor Villanueva has termed "the new racism."
6. For a further exploration of this process, see Chris Weedon's *Identity and Culture: Narratives of Difference and Belonging*, especially chapter 1: "Subjectivity and Identity," and Margaret R. Somers's (1994) "The Narrative Constitution of Identity: A Relational and Network Approach," especially pages 608–611.
7. Using the term "interpersonal" to describe conflict gave me some pause as I was composing this chapter. I worried that it might suggest individual idiosyncrasies as a source of conflict within groups, when the type of conflicts I am interested in are not produced by individual actions or predilections but based on systemic programming that applies to persons.
8. The shift to describing conferences as "one-with-one" offers some resistance to this emphasis on the individual nature of the work.

REFERENCES

Balogun, Julia, and Gerry Johnson. 2004. "Organizational Restructuring and Middle Manager Sensemaking." *Academy of Management Journal* 47 (4): 523–549. https://doi.org/10.2307/20159600.

Balogun, Julia, and Gerry Johnson. 2005. "From Intended Strategies to Unintended Outcomes: The Impact of Change Recipient Sensemaking." *Organization Studies* 26 (11): 1573–1601.

Barron, Nancy, and Nancy Grimm. 2002. "Addressing Racial Diversity in a Writing Center: Stories and Lessons from Two Beginners." *The Writing Center Journal* 22 (2): 55–83.

Bawarshi, Anis, and Stephanie Pelkowski. 1999. "Postcolonialism and the Idea of a Writing Center." *The Writing Center Journal* 19 (2): 41–58. http://www.jstor.org/stable/43442836.

Carroll, Meg. 2008. "Identities in Dialogue: Patterns in the Chaos." *The Writing Center Journal* 28 (1): 43–62.

Cogie, Jane. 2011. "Breaking the Silence on Racism through Agency within a Conflicted Field." In *Writing Centers and the New Racism: A Call for Sustainable Dialogue and Change*, edited by Laura Greenfield and Karen Rowan, 228–252. Logan: Utah State University Press.

Cornelissen, Joep P. 2012. "Sensemaking Under Pressure: The Influence of Professional Roles and Social Accountability on the Creation of Sense." *Organization Science* 23 (1): 118–137.

Diab, Rasha, Beth Godbee, Thomas Ferrel, and Neil Simpkins. 2012. "A Multi-Dimensional Pedagogy for Racial Justice in Writing Centers." *Praxis: A Writing Center Journal* 10 (1). http://www.praxisuwc.com/diab-godbee-ferrell-simpkins-101.

Geller, Anne Ellen, Frankie Condon, and Meg Carroll. 2011. "BOLD: The Everyday Writing Center and the Production of New Knowledge in Antiracist Theory and Practice." In *Writing Centers and the New Racism: A Call for Sustainable Dialogue and Change*, edited by Laura Greenfield and Karen Rowan, 101–123. Logan: Utah State University Press.

Geller, Anne Ellen, Michele Eodice, Frankie Condon, Meg Carroll, and Elizabeth H. Boquet. 2007. *The Everyday Writing Center: A Community of Practice*. Logan: Utah State University Press.

Gladstein, Jill, and Brandon Fralix. 2013. "Four-Year Institution Survey." National Census on Writing. Swarthmore College. https://writingcensus.swarthmore.edu/.

Green, Neisha-Anne. 2018. "Moving Beyond Alright: And the Emotional Toll of This, My Life Matters Too, in the Writing Center Work." *The Writing Center Journal* 37 (1): 15–34.

Green, Neisha-Anne, and Frankie Condon. 2020. "Letters on Moving from Ally to Accomplice: Anti-racism and the Teaching of Writing." In *Diverse Approaches to Teaching, Learning, and Writing Across the Curriculum, IWAC at 25*, edited by Lesley Erin Bartlett, Sandra L. Tarabochia, Andrea R. Olinger, and Margaret J. Marshall, 277–292. Fort Collins, CO: WAC Clearinghouse. https://doi.org/10.37514/PER-B.2020.0360.2.15.

Greenfield, Laura, and Karen Rowan. 2011a. "Beyond the 'Week Twelve Approach': Toward a Critical Pedagogy for Antiracist Tutor Education." In *Writing Centers and the New Racism: A Call for Sustainable Dialogue and Change*, edited by Laura Greenfield and Karen Rowan, 124–149. Logan: Utah State University Press.

Greenfield, Laura, and Karen Rowan, eds. 2011b. *Writing Centers and the New Racism: A Call for Sustainable Dialogue and Change*. Logan: Utah State University Press.

Grimm, Nancy. 1999. *Good Intentions: Writing Center Work for Postmodern Times*. Portsmouth, NH: Boynton/Cook.

Haltiwanger Morrison, Talisha. 2018. "Being Seen and Not Seen: A Black Female Body in the Writing Center." In *Out in the Center: Public Controversies and Private Struggles*, edited by Harry Denny, Robert Mundy, Liliana M. Naydan, Richard Sévère, and Anna Sicari, 21–27. Logan: Utah State University Press. https://www.jstor.org/stable/j.ctvbq s9mw.5.

Hoffman, Andrew J., and William Ocasio. 2001. "Not All Events Are Attended Equally: Toward a Middle-Range Theory of Industry Attention to External Events." *Organization Science* 12 (4): 414–434.

Innes, Sarah. 2006. "Chapter 10: Literacy Myths, Literacy Identities: The Writing Center Regulates Institutional Constructions of Racial Identity." *Counterpoints* 298: 183–199.

Inoue, Asao. 2016. "Afterword: Narratives that Determine Writers and Social Justice Writing Center Work." *Praxis: A Writing Center Journal* 14 (1). http://www.praxisuwc.com/inoue-141.

Johnson, Michelle T. 2011. "Racial Literacy and the Writing Center." In *Writing Centers and the New Racism: A Call for Sustainable Dialogue and Change*, edited by Laura Greenfield and Karen Rowan, 211–227. Logan: Utah State University Press.

Jones-Walker, Cheryl. 2016. "Teaching Difference in Multiple Ways: Through Content and Presence." In *Transforming the Academy: Faculty Perspectives on Diversity and Pedagogy*, edited by Sarah Willie-LeBreton, 59–70. New Brunswick, NJ: Rutgers University Press.

Levinas, Emmanuel. 1998. *Entre nous: On Thinking-of-the-Other*. New York: Columbia University Press.

Lockett, Alexandria. 2018. "A Touching Place: Womanist Approaches to the Center." In *Out in the Center: Public Controversies and Private Struggles*, edited by Harry Denny, Robert Mundy, Liliana M. Naydan, Richard Sévère, and Anna Sicari, 28–42. Logan: Utah State University Press. http://www.jstor.com/stable/j.ctvbqs9mw.6.

Louis, Meryl Reis. 1980. "Surprise and Sensemaking: What Newcomers Experience in Entering Unfamiliar Settings." *Administrative Science Quarterly* 25 (2): 226–251.

Maitlis, Sally, and Marlys Christianson. 2014. "Sensemaking in Organizations: Taking Stock and Moving Forward." *The Academy of Management Annals* 8 (1): 57–125.

Maitlis, Sally, and Thomas B. Lawrence. 2007. "Triggers and Enablers of Sensegiving in Organizations." *Academy of Management Journal* 50 (1): 57–84.

Mendez Newman, Beatrice. 2003. "Centering in the Borderlands: Lessons from Hispanic Student Writers." *The Writing Center Journal* 23 (2): 43–62.

Nigam, Amit, and William Ocasio. 2010. "Event Attention, Environmental Sensemaking, and Change in Institutional Logics: An Inductive Analysis of the Effects of Public Attention to Clinton's Health Care Reform Initiative." *Organization Science* 21 (4): 823–841.

Okawa, Gail, Thomas Fox, Lucy J. Y. Chang, Shana R. Windsor, Frank Bella Chavez Jr., and LaGuan Hayes. 2010. "Multi-Cultural Voices: Peer Tutoring and Critical Reflection in the Writing Center." *The Writing Center Journal* 30 (1): 40–65.

Olsson, Jona. 1997. "Detour Spotting for White Anti-Racists." Cultural Bridges to Justice. http://www.culturalbridgestojustice.org/detour-spotting/.

Pierce, C. M. 1974. "Psychiatric Problems of the Black Minority." In *American Handbook of Psychiatry*, edited by Silvano Arieti, 512–523. New York: Basic Books.

Singleton, Glenn E., and Curtis Linton. 2006. *A Field Guide for Achieving Equity in Schools: Courageous Conversations about Race*. Thousand Oaks, CA: Corwin.

Smith, Michael D., and Eve Tuck. 2016. "Decentering Whiteness: Teaching Antiracism on a Predominantly White Campus." In *Transforming the Academy: Faculty Perspectives on Diversity and Pedagogy*, edited by Sarah Willie-LeBreton, 13–36. New Brunswick, NJ: Rutgers University Press.

Somers, Margaret R. 1994. "The Narrative Constitution of Identity: A Relational and Network Approach." *Theory and Society* 23: 605–649.

Starbuck, William H., and Frances J. Milliken. 1988. "Executives' Perceptual Filters: What They Notice and How They Make Sense." In *The Executive Effect: Concepts and Methods For Studying Top Managers*, edited by D. C. Hambrick, 35–65. Greenwich, CT: JAI Press.

Suhr-Sytsma, Mandy, and Shan-Estelle Brown. 2011. "Theory In/To Practice: Addressing the Everyday Language of Oppression in the Writing Center." *The Writing Center Journal* 31 (2): 13–49.

Tagg, John. 2003. *The Learning Paradigm College*. Bolton, MA: Anker Publishing.

Taylor, James R., and Elizabeth J. Van Every. 2000. *The Emergent Organization: Communication as Its Site and Surface*. Mahwah, NJ: Erlbaum.

Tekleab, Amanuel, Narda R. Quigley, and Paul E. Tesluk. 2009. "A Longitudinal Study of Team Conflict, Conflict Management, Cohesion, and Team Effectiveness." *Group and Organization Management* 34 (2): 170–205.

Valentine, Kathryn, and Mónica F. Torres. 2011. "Diversity As Topography: The Benefits And Challenges Of Cross Racial Interaction In The Writing Center." In *Writing Centers and the New Racism: A Call for Sustainable Dialogue and Change*, edited by Laura Greenfield and Karen Rowan, 192–210. Logan: Utah State University Press.

Villanueva, Victor Jr. 2006. "Blind: Talking About the New Racism." *The Writing Center Journal* 26 (1): 3–19.

Warnock, Tilly, and John Warnock. 1984. "Liberatory Writing Centers: Restoring Authority to Writers." In *Writing Centers: Theory and Administration*, edited by Gary Olson, 16–24. Urbana, IL: NCTE.

Weedon, Chris. 2004. *Identity and Culture: Narratives of Difference and Belonging*. Maidenhead, UK: Open University Press/McGraw Hill.

Weick, Karl. E. 1969. *The Social Psychology of Organizing*. Reading, MA: Addison-Wesley.

Willie-LeBreton, Sarah, ed. 2016. *Transforming the Academy: Faculty Perspectives on Diversity and Pedagogy*. New Brunswick, NJ: Rutgers University Press.

Wright, Charles R., Michael R. Manning, Bruce Farmer, and Brad Gilbreath. 2000. "Resourceful Sensemaking in Product Development Teams." *Organization Studies* 21 (4): 807–825.

Zhao, Yelin. 2017. "Student Interactions with a Native Speaker Tutor and a Nonnative Speaker Tutor at an American Writing Center." *The Writing Center Journal* 36 (2): 57–87.

5
MAKING SENSE OF HOW THINGS FEEL
Attending to Emotional Experiences in Writing Programs

Bronwyn T. Williams

If you read the websites and mission statements of writing programs and writing centers, it's not unusual to find emotion-inflected words and ideas sprinkled throughout. The range of words include *confident, respectful, supportive, inclusive, safe, responsible, nurturing, comfortable, engaging, creative, mindful,* and *enjoyable.* Turn to the Council of Writing Program Administrators' statement on the "Framework for Success in Postsecondary Writing" (2011) and, again, you find concepts such as curiosity, openness, engagement, creativity, persistence, responsibility, and flexibility, which all have connections—either implied or explicit—to emotions. Similarly, I can reach across my office, pluck off a copy of *WPA: Writing Program Administration,* and turn to almost any article and find descriptions of or references to emotions that include frustration, determination, satisfaction, puzzlement, anxiety, and, yes, even pleasure. In our work in writing programs, as in our daily lives, emotion is always there.

Yet, as we think about sensemaking in writing programs, emotion may not be the first framework we imagine. There are many factors that routinely come up in discussions of what constructs writing programs, ranging from institutional ideologies to material conditions to dominant cultural narratives about writing. Yet, in such discussions, emotion as an important element of meaning-making and program-building is not a common focus of scholarship, even though emotion is a central system for determining how we understand and respond to the world. Emotion is occasionally addressed in research on pedagogy and literacy practices (Kurtyka 2015; Madianou and Miller 2012; Micciche 2007; Newkirk 2017; Williams 2017, 2018); however, most of this research is focused on the impact of emotion on individual writers. Emotion is more typically one of what Rita Malenczyk in her introduction to this volume identifies as "often-unseen interactions" and is less likely to be regarded when we think about making sense of how our programs work or how we build them. As an explicit concern, we are largely quiet on the role of emotion in the goals, processes, and identities of writing programs.

Yet emotions gained by experience, shaped by social conventions and interactions, and performed rhetorically are central to sensemaking and a daily part of everything we do. Psychologist Margaret Wetherell (2012) describes affect as "embodied meaning-making" that is shaped and regulated by ongoing, recursive interactions between the individual and the social. Although emotions typically are not part of the formal structures or discussions of writing programs, they are crucial in shaping how everyone in a program—administrators, instructors and tutors, and students—make sense of their work to themselves and each other. The emotional experiences that are valued, acknowledged, tolerated, and taught construct both what Malenczyk calls organizational life and, just as important, an emotional identity of a program. The emotional identity of a program shapes both internal attitudes and orientations toward program and center work as well the identity of a program within the larger institution of the university.

In this chapter I draw on research in psychology to frame how emotion works as a crucial element of sensemaking in writing programs. I discuss how the emotional experiences of instructors, tutors, and students shape the emotional identity of the program and the work that takes place there. Every classroom or writing center experience is an emotional experience for students and instructors or tutors, and it structures their emotional responses to future classrooms or writing consultations. Every programmatic experience for teachers or tutors affects their emotional dispositions toward the program and colleagues in the same way. I discuss how attending to and articulating the emotional experiences of students and staff provides an important way for a writing program to make sense of and define itself. I reflect on examples from my work in two WPA positions to demonstrate how policies and practices can be understood as emotional experiences and to illustrate successes and failures in responding to these emotional contexts. Such approaches require more than simply saying a program is caring or nurturing. Instead, it is important to listen to the stories and experiences of the people in a program and to reflect explicitly on the range of emotions—including motivation, confidence, empathy, and even anxiety—that shape the sensemaking culture of a program. I will also draw on recent research in writing and literacy studies (Eodice, Geller, and Lerner 2017; Haswell and Haswell 2015; Newkirk 2017) as well as my own research (Williams 2018) to describe how attending to the construction of emotional dispositions as a programmatic focus shapes motivation and perceptions of agency for students and instructors or tutors.

Emotion is always there, and we are always working with the dispositions that grow from it. I argue that approaching WPA work with attention to emotional experience, both in policy and practice, is both a more humane and a more pedagogically effective model for teaching and administration.

EMOTION AS MEANING-MAKING

Emotion is often assumed to run counter to the larger goals and discourses of the university. If you asked, most faculty would agree that the focus of higher education should be disinterested analysis and dispassionate presentation. Rational inquiry is the ideal across disciplines, and there is a deeply rooted suspicion of emotion, which is regarded as manipulative and lacking rigor. Even more recent attention in rhetoric and composition and literacy studies to how writers experience emotion and the connections between embodiment and emotion, both in and out of the classroom, can be seen as exceptions to the more general perceptions about emotion in higher education. In terms of writing program administration, though there are some notable exceptions (Davies 2017; Micciche 2011), the focus of scholarship over the years would indicate that emotion, as a programmatic concern of administrators, would come far behind concerns such as assessment (Corbett 2017; Dryer and Peckham 2015; Lancaster et al. 2015; Moxley and Eubanks 2016), curriculum development (Burrows 2016; Davila 2017; Dean 2015; Sura 2015), and institutional politics (Estrem 2015; Fedukovich and Morse 2017; Phillips, Shovlin, and Titus 2016).

There are problems with this conception of emotion, however, and how it affects our work in writing programs.

First, and most familiar to our field, is the argument made by many feminist scholars and scholars of color that when we deny the knowledge created by emotion, we miss important ways of understanding the world (Delgado 1989; Kirsch 2005; Ronald and Roskelly 2001; Young 2004). Dominant cultural ideologies construct certain performances of emotion as acceptable, such as rationality and detachment, and use others as reasons to dismiss or criticize people. An expression of emotion interpreted as too exuberant or combative in the context of dominant cultural norms is often used to exclude an individual on the basis of race or class, while emotions perceived as overly sentimental may be coded as feminine and naive. Newmann Holmes, in this volume, vividly demonstrates the emotional experiences that are privileged or dismissed by dominant cultural norms, such as white supremacy, and their impact on members of a writing center staff.

In addition, it is important to keep in mind that we are *always* experiencing emotions. The popular conception of emotion is of those moments that draw explicit notice, such as when we feel noticeably joyful or angry or frightened. The truth, however, is that our minds are always experiencing and monitoring emotions, even when those emotions are rationality or calmness. Just as weather is always present, even when the conditions for a day are calm and unremarkable, emotions are always present, even when we feel calm and unremarkable.

Excluding emotion from our considerations, then, is problematic because, though we may think we can exclude emotion completely from teaching and administration, we then miss the ways it figures in the sensemaking that is present in our daily lives and work.

In order to understand the role of emotion in sensemaking, it is useful to understand what recent work in psychology reveals about how emotion works in our daily lives. Another common conception is that our emotions are both innate and individual. Given their immediacy and how inextricable they are from bodily responses, it is easy to imagine that we were simply born with certain emotions. Yet research indicates that emotions are instead the result of interplay between bodily responses and social interpretations and performance. We learn our emotions and will continue to learn them, feel them intimately, and perform them publicly. Margaret Wetherell (2012) defines human emotion as "embodied meaning-making" (4). I find it useful to extend this definition to include embodied meaning-making *and* performance.

Imagine, for example, there is suddenly a loud noise behind you. Though your body will respond with a range of automatic responses—narrowing blood vessels, jolts of adrenaline—just in case it might be danger, the initial embodied response is not an emotion. Your emotional response will depend as much on the social context and memory as it does on your body. First, in a series of rapid and recursive interactions, the sensory information is measured against memories of similar experiences. The brain "draws from a vast repository of stored representations in the blink of an eye, to associatively recombine what it has learned of the past" (Barrett 2009, 1292). If we've gone to many fireworks displays, and we immediately identify the sound as fireworks, we might feel excitement. We would respond differently—with concern—if it sounded like thunder and still differently—with wariness or puzzlement—if we were unsure. These recursive interactions of biological systems and memory quickly provide interpretations for sensory stimulus that create a meaning—an emotion—for the situation.

In addition to memory, the social and cultural context in which we live is a crucial factor in constructing and defining our emotions. While stimulus in our environment may provoke immediate biological responses, it is the social context that defines them as particular emotions. Take again the example of fireworks. The noise and explosion may cause our bodies to react, but if everyone around us is responding to the display with pleasure, we will learn to interpret that stimulus as pleasurable. What researchers call "affective inter-subjectivity" begins when we are infants (Meltzoff and Brooks 2007) and shapes how we learn to interpret, and then internalize, the emotions that we then consider central to our sense of who we are. At the same time, understanding, mimicking, and internalizing the emotional conventions around us are essential processes in fitting in to the groups in which we live (Hood 2014). If each time we have an experience, people around us respond to it by interpreting it as a particular emotion—fear, joy, or sorrow—such experiences create cognitive patterns that soon allow for almost instantaneous feelings of those particular emotions when we once again encounter such a situation. The emotions feel internal, spontaneous, and natural but have, in fact, been learned over time and with experience. As Wetherell (2012) notes about how we learn, our brains are "intensely responsive to the patterning of personal history, and designed to be social, intensely responsive, possibly from the very beginning, to the actions of others" (150). After a while, similar sets of emotional experiences create dispositions toward particular experiences or circumstances that mean we define ourselves as someone who hates arguments or loves big crowds or is always happy at Halloween. Such interpretations are ongoing and can be changed with a different kind of experience, or a different social context. We might have enjoyed celebrating a particular holiday with family, but if one year there is conflict and tears at the end of the day, the emotion and memory we draw from it may shift distinctly (Kahnemann 2011).

The fact that every experience is an emotional experience, immediately connected to emotional states that we felt the last time we had a similar experience, has implications for the writing classroom. When students walk into a writing classroom or receive an assignment or a response to a draft, they have emotional responses to that moment that have been patterned over years of experiences in school (Williams 2018). A history of rigid rules about writing and harsh, punitive comments on drafts can result in a student feeling frustrated or powerless about a writing assignment when it is first mentioned, even before it is distributed or discussed by the instructor. In the same way, a series of positive, encouraging experiences with writing helps shape a disposition of confidence. Whether it is confidence, frustration, anticipation, resentment, or any other emotion, the students in any class *feel* things about a writing situation before addressing them rationally. What's more, as teachers, we are teaching them in their context of these previous emotional experiences, even though more often than not we are unaware of what those experiences and emotions might be.

EMOTIONS AND DISPOSITIONS TOWARD STUDENTS

While I have addressed the implications of these emotional experiences in classroom and writing center tutorial contexts in other work (Williams 2017, 2018), I believe that understanding the importance of emotional experiences also has important implications for how we understand the emotional dispositions that develop in a writing program. Every experience, in a classroom or among instructors or tutors in a staff room, is interpreted through social conventions of emotion. Such conventions can reflect widely held cultural ideologies. Yet the conventions that influence interpretations of emotion can also be local and distinctive and reflect the collective dispositions of those in the program. For a writing program, recognizing what emotions are being promoted and acknowledged—or at least tolerated—can help reveal important values of the program and how it knows itself. Such conventions of emotion are not static and can be influenced by our work as administrators. The emotions we promote, that people then experience, accumulate to create social expectations and interpretations of emotions. If we encourage particular emotional approaches to sensemaking, as well as model these emotional responses ourselves, it can work to establish emotional identities for our program, both with students and in the university as a whole.

To illustrate my point, I want to first discuss the ways in which the emotional dispositions in a program can influence the pedagogical work that takes place with students.

Every teacher or tutor has moments of frustration. Working with students who appear to be disengaged, dismissive, or disrespectful can grind at the nerves of the best-intentioned teachers. At some point, when patience fails, it is common, and some would even say expected, for people to want to vent about their frustration. You can hang around any faculty hallway or writing center staff room and hear people expressing frustration now and again. In her chapter in this volume, Adams Wooten notes how these kinds of narratives about teaching among GTAs can exist in the underlife of writing programs, often disrupting the official goals or values of a program. Sometimes, however, instructors expressing frustration take the form of deriding or mocking students and their work. There is, unfortunately, a long tradition of this kind of venting, and there are teachers who defend it as necessary "blowing off steam." Yet, as Jessica Winck (2016) notes in her analysis of teachers posting student errors in order to mock them, this tradition is troubling in the way it reproduces a "deficit-oriented, remedial model that has for so long been used to interpret student writing" (36). In these kinds of exchanges, individuals learn to interpret their relationships with students through the dominant emotional conventions of the group around them. For example, I might come out of a class or tutoring session where students are not being particularly engaged and, feeling discouraged and confused, relate what took place to my colleagues. If their response is to shake their heads and try to commiserate by complaining about unmotivated students who will never be eager to learn, I may learn to interpret my unhappiness as resentment and disdain. If we understand the practice of teachers venting about or mocking students as a pattern of repeated and ongoing emotional experiences, we can see how such comments begin to create emotional dispositions about teacher-student relationships that can be adversarial, disrespectful, and, eventually, toxic. The way we feel about a moment in which a student tests our patience is shaped by the emotional conventions and dispositions of those around us. We gradually begin to develop and internalize a set of emotions about our students and our teaching that we feel every time we encounter a similar situation in our teaching, and we start to feel that is our normalized identity as a teacher.

I have been a teacher and then administrator for years and have heard many variations on the theme of venting about or mocking students and have seen the eventual toxic effects. My response is to have a long-standing practice at the university writing center of talking with our consultants about the ways we talk to each other about student writers. I explain why I have no tolerance for talk about students that is derisive or mocking. Not only does it create destructive emotional dispositions toward students, I tell them, but it is the kind of talk that students imagine—and fear—us doing about their work. Yet I also make clear that I know there will be moments in which they may feel frustrated or upset with students. I discuss other ways we can think about and talk about frustration. Rather than simply gripe and deride, I suggest they talk about the concerns and emotions and get support and feedback from colleagues that focuses on support, not just complaint. I also talk about how, even in moments of frustration, we can remain mindful of the humanity of the students involved, and what histories or reasons may be driving their emotional performances. I also model, in the practicum course and staff meetings or just in daily conversation, ways of talking about frustration that are focused more on support and empathy than on complaint and disregard. Such an approach doesn't ignore or dismiss frustration but rethinks and recreates the ways in which the emotions are interpreted. When emotions are reflected back as support, the pattern of interactions begins to shift the dispositions and narratives about the experiences, reducing the culture of complaint. As Winck (2016) notes, in talking about our students, "derision toward students and their writing is learned . . . [and] that it can also be unlearned" (36). In some ways, such an approach could be seen as a relatively simple intervention, and I wouldn't presume to say that it works miracles or eliminates a culture of complaint. That said, I do believe that discussing and modeling emotional responses in this way has a cumulative effect on how the consultants respond to students that results in more positive and productive emotional dispositions toward teaching. Indeed, I have had writing center consultants come back after moving on to other teaching positions to remark about their surprise and discomfort at programs with more negative emotional cultures of complaint.

A similar emotional context can take place in the ways we talk about so-called resistant students, both in classrooms and writing centers (Williams 2018). There are narratives that shape our conversations about students who don't do what we ask or do it begrudgingly. In these familiar narratives, the students are construed as bored, angry, or petulant. It is not uncommon for the narrative to frame the resistant student as a person motivated by trying to make the life of the instructor or tutor difficult. There is a frustration that the student won't engage, regardless of the best efforts or extra attention from the instructor. Yet research interviews with students can reveal other emotions and dispositions at work. A student who appears disengaged or resistant may be feeling anxiety, fear, or uncertainty about their position or competence in the classroom. Or the student may be responding to a pattern of harsh or unclear criticism of their writing by putting up emotional defenses to minimize the threat of future humiliation or feelings of failure (Williams 2018). Students often work hard to hide such experiences and narratives behind a façade of indifference or resistance.

Tutors and teachers may respond to such students with their own feelings of resentment or anger. Their comments often reveal a sense of hurt at feeling rejected in what they hope will be a positive teacher-student relationship. Again, such narratives can get repeated among colleagues and add to the emotional disposition in a program that is subtly—or even overtly—adversarial toward students. If we enter into our encounters with students ready to interpret the emotional experiences as adversarial, where humiliation and anger are likely, we are more likely to interpret the next set of student actions in that same emotional context.

Making explicit the role of emotion in how teachers make sense of the interactions with the students in their classes is one way I have tried to respond to these moments of mutual disappointment or antagonism. For example, urging tutors and teachers to ask students about their previous literacy experiences, whether in writing conferences or through assignments such as literacy narratives, can reveal the complexity of students' emotional experiences that they bring with them into our classrooms. Such a relatively simple intervention can result in a greater sense of empathy by the teachers and pause or redirect from a battle of wills. As a programmatic approach, discussing the role of emotion in sensemaking and encouraging teachers to reflect on the emotional experiences of students, as well as their emotional experiences and expectations in the classroom, can make a significant difference in the ways that tutors and teachers understand and respond to their students. One of the most pointed emotional experiences in teaching can take place when an instructor suspects the student of plagiarism. When teachers talk about cases of suspected plagiarism, there is often an intensity to their emotions and to the ways in which they describe students that indicate more is going on than just the successful completion of an assignment (Williams 2007). There can be hurt, anger, or even sadness, as the teacher deals with what feels to be a betrayal of trust by the student. The result can be that teacher responses can focus on punishment, even retribution, first, rather than instruction or finding out the reasons the student plagiarized. This can be driven in part by unacknowledged emotional responses. If it is necessary to sanction a student for plagiarizing, it should be a thoughtful, measured response. I'm not arguing that teachers and tutors should not feel upset by instances of student plagiarism. What I am advocating is that they should be encouraged to be aware of the nature, and source, of their emotions.

HOSPITALITY AND EMPATHY IN A WRITING PROGRAM

This is the moment when I can imagine some readers warily wondering if I am recommending tell-all, touchy-feely therapy sessions in writing programs. In fact, no. But I do think discussions of emotion, rather than emotional discussions, can be productive. Although it is moments of emotional intensity, such as instances of plagiarism, that make emotions most obvious because they are out of the norm; in fact the relationships between teachers and students are *always* mediated by a set of anticipated emotions and responses that are shaped by the context of the local community. If, for example, we frame the reading of student papers as boring and tedious in our conversations, then that is how we will interpret those experiences. When we get a stack of papers, we will begin to feel bored and unhappy even before we pick up the first paper. If, on the other hand, we interpret and talk about the experience of reading student papers as one that might lead to learning and surprise rather than disappointment and frustration, we will begin to include those different feelings when papers arrive and be more able to experience the different range of emotions when reading.

Toward this end, I find the work of Haswell and Haswell (2015) about an ethic and approach of hospitality in tutor and teacher relationships with students to be useful. They draw from traditional concepts of hospitality in which strangers and their hosts shared shelter and worked through customs of respect and reciprocity. Teaching and learning their conception of hospitality "welcomes and makes room for new ideas coming from any direction, including students, and undercuts the fatal expectation that knowledge transfer is a one-way street" (8). In a classroom or writing center that works through principles of hospitality, there is an ongoing exchange of ideas in which both sides make themselves open to learning and change. It doesn't mean that we don't have things to teach students or that we only provide positive comments. It does mean, however, that we respect the experiences and potential agency of students and respond more as collaborative colleagues than hierarchical judges. If we think about the most positive learning and emotional experiences we have had with collaborators or mentors, we can easily remember the give and take that Haswell and Haswell (2015) suggest are encouraging. As they point out, such relationships are more complex, and sometimes more risky or prickly, than just seeing ourselves as caring for students, in which the relationship between "carer" and "cared-for" is implicitly more hierarchical. When I work with tutors in our university writing center, I encourage empathy and listening, but also emotional dispositions of respect and openness that I hope will lead more toward concepts of hospitality and collaboration that can facilitate a mutual sense of agency and confidence.

Margaret Wetherell (2012) argues that emotion is constructed through "affective practice," (23) which moves constantly between embodied responses and social interpretations:

> This is a way of conceptualising social action as constantly in motion while yet recognising too that the past, and what has been done before, constrains the present and the future. Practice is both a noun and a verb. It is an activity and for the participants (and social analysts) it is also an established reference point and site of repetition—a practice—the way I, or we, do things, and sometimes cannot help but do so again. Practice is about improvisation, it is about training. (23)

Understood this way, we can see emotion as a set of social practices that can be shaped by our responses. The emotions we discuss, and the ways that we model and talk about emotions, can pervade a program and influence the dispositions teachers and tutors take toward their experiences with their students. As Malenczyk points out in her introduction, sensemaking in writing programs is an ongoing process that combines observation, experience, and reflection. It is important, then, that our discussions are not simply one-time considerations of the role of emotion in a program but instead ongoing conversations in practicum courses, in staff meetings, and in hallways and offices. While we sometimes talk about the culture of a program, it is less common to talk about the emotional dispositions, or emotional identity, of a writing program. Yet a number of the chapters in this volume (Newmann Holmes; Johnson and Dean; Smith, McKeehen, George, and Lee; Adams Wooten), though not focused on emotion as a central concern, also illustrate how emotions are present, constantly under construction and reconstruction, and part of the unofficial life of most writing programs. What's more, in addition to creating an emotional culture for teachers and students in the program, such a culture can begin to define a program within the larger university. There are programs and departments in universities that get reputations for being intractable or rigid and are talked about by students with exasperation or wariness. Yet if students have emotional experiences in a program that reflect hospitality and empathy, they will talk about those experiences with other students and the identity of the program will be framed by such emotions. If a program has a more constructive and positive emotional identity, that will influence students' emotional expectations when they enter a class or writing center, and that will benefit learning on all sides.

EMOTIONAL RELATIONSHIPS WITHIN A WRITING PROGRAM

In the life of a writing program, the relationships among staff, and staff and administrators, are as significant to the construction of a program's identity and culture as instructor-student relationships. Emotion, and the emotional dispositions created through the experiences outside the classroom, can be crucial to the sensemaking in a program. In their conceptions of a writing program, the tutors and teachers frequently include emotions in their interpretations of events, using descriptions of relief, frustration, anxiety, or gratitude or words such as *thoughtful, nightmare, rigid,* or *caring.* Although many of these emotional dispositions reflect the values of the culture at large, it is the case that such emotional contexts can be specific to different programs. Writing programs are no different than other social contexts in creating interpretive frameworks that shape these emotional experiences and, by extension, the sense of the emotional disposition of the writing program. And, as Alba Newmann Holmes demonstrates in her chapter in this volume, the social contexts in which we experience and interpret emotions are always constructed in systems of power, privilege, and oppression. The conversations that happen in a writing program can involve pain, silencing, or fear. Such experiences may not be immediately visible to those positioned in the dominant culture, and so require the kind of ongoing listening, reflection, and education she discusses. In addition, part of the discussion of emotion that happens in a writing program should include an explicit recognition of how cultural expectations, and systems of power, shape how we interpret and perform emotions in our lives and our programs.

Toward that end, though no single person can construct the emotional culture of a program, I do believe that the expectations the director defines in regard to emotions, and, just as important, the emotions the director performs on an ongoing basis, have significant effects on how people understand their emotional experiences in a program.

Given that we are all products of our emotional experiences, I think my emotional dispositions toward working in writing programs were constructed initially through spending a dozen years either as a graduate teaching assistant or an adjunct. The latter, in particular, established a clear set of emotional patterns for me. I remember feeling a sense of community and support from my colleagues and enjoying the emotional culture of the writing program that approached students with respect and the teaching of writing as something that should be pleasurable (Williams 2011). I also felt the respect of individual directors of the program. At the same time, to the rest of the faculty in the English

Department, we adjuncts were invisible at best, and disdained at worst. As many other contingent faculty have described (Fulwiler and Marlow 2014), such encounters often left me with a confounding mix of anxiety, resentment, and shame. When I became director of the first-year writing program, my first WPA position, I was determined not to forget how those emotions had been fostered and to do what I could to mitigate those feelings.

Yet, good intentions, particularly when we consider the way emotions mediate relationships, can be more complicated to understand and navigate than we expect. One example of this came in my first year as director of the first-year writing program. I was taking over from an administrator who was leaving for another job. I decided that the first thing I wanted to do was meet individually with each instructor in the program, from graduate students to tenured faculty, and find out from them what they regarded as the strengths and problems of the program. From a programmatic aspect, it was an illuminating process and shaped my priorities for changes and new initiatives. And, though I didn't articulate it this way at the time, I also hoped it would create an emotional experience for each person in which I would be perceived as someone who valued communication and transparency. I wanted people to feel trust and respect after they left my office. I finished the semester feeling pretty good about the process and what it had accomplished.

It came as a jolt, then, the following semester when a group of instructors, graduate students, and part-time lecturers, sent me an email with a list of complaints about the program. While none of the complaints were directed at me personally, the tone of email was negative and frustrated. My initial feeling in reading it was to feel annoyed and frustrated myself. I felt that my explicit actions in being participatory and responsive were being dismissed and that I was not being given any time to work toward making changes before I was being served with a list of angry demands. I felt defensive and, even worse, I knew that I couldn't do some of things people were asking, and didn't want to do others, and I worried that my inability or unwillingness to meet the demands would undermine my work from the start. I was hurt and frustrated.

When I voiced my hurt and frustration to a former fellow adjunct from my previous university, she reminded me that the people writing the email were writing about a program, not about me. I remembered then the emotional experiences from my days as an adjunct and how, and why, they seemed to either be ameliorated or exacerbated. I remembered the importance of transparency in understanding why things were happening and feeling I was trusted enough to understand that information.

Just as important, I remembered that being listened to, like a colleague, mattered immensely. I also realized that the context of the situation was the program and the university, not just me individually. Just as students don't always imagine the emotions of their instructors when they make what are institutionally motivated complaints, the instructors in the program were probably not focused on my feelings or how they might be hurt. The tone and content of the email made it clear that the complaints reflected issues that were both real and important in the program but also a pattern of previous emotional experiences as GTAs and contingent faculty, in our program and others, that preceded me becoming director. These experiences created emotions and expectations of what would happen in a writing program in dealing with the WPA.

Although I did not think of it in these terms at the time, I knew I had to offer a different emotional experience in my response. I set up a meeting with the people who wrote the email, conscious that not only was I a tenured faculty member with more institutional power than the instructors, but I was also a white male in a supervisory role meeting with a group of GTAs and contingent faculty who were all female. I understood at the time that I needed to be mindful of the cultural contexts of power and privilege in the situation. All of us entering the meeting were drawing on emotional experiences of similar meetings in the past and how they would have been shaped by gendered constructions of power. In the meeting I did my best to focus on listening carefully to what they said and understand the key issues at hand. I also had to be aware that, first, the emotions people had on arriving at the meeting were beyond my control. More important, I knew that the emotions they left with would not be determined solely by me but evolved through their interactions with me. Again, though I didn't conceive of it this way then, I believe I stumbled on to the idea that affective inter-subjectivity was constructing how people would feel about the meeting and me as the director. I did my best to be respectful, transparent, and honest and, in doing so, tried to continue creating a pattern of emotional experiences that I had started with the individual meetings.

It's impossible for me to say whether my response helped construct different emotional dispositions for the program, as I never followed up with any kind of formal research on such issues. What I will say is that, during my time as director, instructors often seemed willing to bring problems to me, which I counted as a success. What I also noticed is that the tone of the problems and complaints often shifted from one that was more confrontational and fatalistic to one that was, even when frustrated, more indicative that a solution might be reached.

The point of my example is not whether I was an enlightened director of first-year writing. The point is recognizing that every moment in a program is an emotional experience for the people involved that contributes to emotional social contexts in the program. If, for example, there is a shared culture in a program that interprets decisions by the director through emotional dispositions toward unfairness or envy, then decisions such as course scheduling, office assignments, or professional development funding will tend to be felt first as those emotions, regardless of what the director says. Such dispositions may predate the director but shape the emotional dispositions of those in the program and those new to the program. Research on emotion indicates that negative emotions can be particularly powerful and easily recalled (Fernyhough 2012), a finding not surprising if we understand that emotions and memories are often constructed to help us avoid similar negative, and even dangerous, experiences in the future. What may be good in terms of evolution, however, can be a problem in a writing program. The sharing of negative emotions in a social context creates cycles that influence how subsequent experiences are felt by people in that context. In such an emotional context, disagreement at a meeting, for example, may be felt immediately as unjust, hurtful, and another inevitable example of a rift between people or groups in a program. These unofficial emotional narratives are often more powerful than any mission statement on any writing program web page.

As a WPA I don't presume that I have the power to make every experience positive for instructors or tutors. At the same time, I am convinced by the research (Fernyhough 2012; Kahnemann 2011; Wetherell 2012) that the narratives we tell after an experience shape how we feel about it and how we will feel about similar experiences in the future. Creating different emotional experiences in a program takes many forms. For example, acknowledging emotions, even when negative, can help people feel they are being understood and respected. We may, indeed, get frustrated with students. But if the conversations that we have focus on taking into account students' emotional lives and never giving up on a student, that frustration may not become toxic. The systems involved in scheduling mean that someone will be disappointed. But if we make systems as transparent as possible and ask for and respond to feedback about the systems, people may not perceive the disappointment as unfair or conspiratorial. Framing a discussion in a meeting in terms of listening strategies toward each other and working toward negotiation, rather than simply winning argumentative points and a final vote, can shift perceptions of what takes place in the conversations.

Even seemingly small steps can matter. When I began starting casual conversations by asking not just "How is it going?" but also "What's been going well in class?," I found it began to change the ways in which people talked about their work and their students. If people had complaints, I was happy to hear them, but I also offered a chance to remember that there had been successes as well. Other small emotional experiences, such as celebrating teaching and tutoring achievements, thinking about the emotion-inflected words we use to discuss students in writing practicum courses, or simply knowing the names and backgrounds of people in the program and taking the time to go to their offices to talk with them about how they are doing, can accumulate into more positive dispositions in a program.

What I am advocating here is not a simple Pollyannaish prescription for positive thinking as the solution to all problems. That is not what the research indicates. What research on motivation does indicate is that the strongest, most powerful internal motivations come from situations in which we find meaning, have some aspect of control, and receive respectful and thoughtful responses (Deci and Ryan 2000; Sheldon and Schüler 2015). Indeed, even small changes in response that allow people to find their work more meaningful, and less futile, can result in significant changes in internal motivations (Ariely, Kamenica, and Prelec 2008). Research on student writing and perceptions of agency or meaning illustrate that students respond positively and with greater motivation to writing assignments and responses that emphasize these qualities (Eodice, Geller, and Lerner 2017; Sommers 2006). With that in mind, I find it persuasive to believe that the emotional experiences we attend to and try to create with instructors and tutors should also be mindful of emphasizing meaning, control and collaboration, and thoughtful and respectful response. We know that detailed, relevant, positive comments help students not just with their writing but also with their sense of agency and confidence. Literacy narratives of both students and professional writers are filled with moments in which encouragement—even a single, small comment—can shift the perspective of the writer (so, too, can a single moment of callous criticism). It is no different for teachers or tutors.

EXPERIENCES OUTSIDE OUR CONTROL

The reality of working in any institution is that emotional experiences are often constructed, or at least influenced, by systems and traditions that are not under the control of any single person. Every WPA knows how much is beyond their control, sometimes including key decisions such as budgets or personnel reviews or, most recently, how schools responded to the safety concerns of the COVID-19 pandemic. Yet every one of those moments involves a set of emotional experiences or expectations on the part of everyone involved. Take grading, for example. Grading is a central experience of most academic settings, yet one that more often than not evokes negative emotions for both students and instructors. Students often regard grading as arbitrary and opaque, if not manifestly unfair (Adams 2005; Alm and Colnerud 2015; Blum 2016) and talk about it with resentment and anxiety (Blum 2016; Chory, Horan, and Houser 2017; Vallade, Martin, and Weber 2014). Grading is influenced by dominant cultural conceptions of identity that can work against students not positioned as part of the dominant culture (Jacoby-Senghor, Sinclair, and Shelton 2016; Malouff and Thorsteinsson 2016). Teachers are not much happier with the stress and limitations of grading (Jiang, Tripp, and Hong 2017; Tannock 2017). These emotional responses to the moment of grading result from deep-rooted emotional conventions about grading that students develop from patterns of experience from primary school on. By the time they have reached the university level, they have equally powerfully rooted emotional dispositions toward how they will feel about the moment of grading. At best they may feel pleasure, or at least relief. But students often talk about feelings of dread, discouragement, and even anger when they discuss grading. Such emotional experiences of grading contribute to impact of grades on lower students' internal motivations in school (Klapp 2015).

What's more, the position of grading at the end of a writing project gives it an increased emotional impact in terms of how students feel about the writing process. Intense emotional experiences that take place at the end of an event or process have an exaggerated effect on how we remember or feel about the entire event (Kahnemann 2011). If a holiday trip ends with us coming down with an illness, or if an evening out ends with an argument, we are more likely to remember the trip or evening as spoiled than if the illness or disagreement had happened at the beginning of the trip or event. We don't average out our experiences to form emotional memories of them. Instead, the most intense experience, combined with the way the experience ends, has a much greater impact on how we feel about the experience in the future. From an emotional perspective, this puts grades at a problematic point in the academic writing process. Students focus on the judgment of the grade, often discounting what they felt they were learning during the writing process (Williams 2018). In a similar way, I have heard teachers talk, while grading, of their frustrations with students, seemingly dismissing good pedagogical work that had taken place during the class.

For teachers, course evaluations can sometimes be emotional experiences analogous to grades for students. The evaluations can seem arbitrary and opaque and shaped by dominant conceptions of identity (Joye and Wilson 2015; MacNell, Driscoll, and Hunt 2015) that can lead instructors to talk about the process with anxiety and resentment. What's more, like grades, the evaluations come at the end of the course and, as a result, can have an increased emotional impact on how instructors perceive the overall success of the course. Anyone who has taught knows that even a single particularly vituperative evaluation can sour an experience of a course.

Despite the widespread distaste for institutional systems such as grades and course evaluations, and the fact that there are many other possible approaches to assessment, such systems of assessment are ideological structures deeply embedded in our institutions and culture at large. Even as we may work to create programs that push against such systems (Williams, in press), the reality is that most of us are going to have to deal with systems such as grades and course evaluations for the foreseeable future. In the same way, other systems, such as pay levels for tutors or instructors or policies on who gets to participate in institutional governance, can seem intractable to a WPA, even as we know they can significantly shape the emotional experiences of teachers and tutors.

Though we cannot always control the ideologies and systems that affect the emotional experiences in a program, we can have an impact on the emotional dispositions that develop in the program. The ways in which we acknowledge emotions and the narratives that we construct around them can influence dispositions in productive ways. Take grading, again, as an example. For students, we may be institutionally obligated to assign grades. Yet, if in our conversations with students both before and after grading, we ask them to reflect explicitly on what they have learned, we can help them create an emotional counter-narrative of learning and growth that can mitigate the negative emotions they connect with receiving the grade. In the same way, if we encourage teachers and tutors to reflect on what they are learning and accomplishing in courses as the courses unfold, as well as at the end, we help them construct more balanced and useful emotional experiences about their work. Research in psychology demonstrates that ongoing, thoughtful—and honest—reflection can construct more productive and nuanced narratives and emotions about what has happened, as well as what can be accomplished in the future (Wilson 2011). Engaging in "story editing"

(Wilson 2011) of our autobiographical memories is not a matter of excising unpleasant memories but of putting them into context. Rather than letting a cognitive distortion shape our emotions about an experience, for example, that one unhappy student means you've failed as a teacher for the class or that one disagreement in a meeting means you are not respected in a program, putting things in context means paying explicit attention to the range of experiences and emotions taking place in a program. For a WPA, encouraging people to acknowledge and discuss the range of emotions in a program, as well as modeling emotional responses that value respect and empathy for teachers and students, can be helpful even in the face of larger institutional obstacles.

CONCLUSION

I often say to people with whom I work in writing programs that I regard the purpose of my job as director as making their work and lives easier. When I began my first position as a WPA, I understood that statement to mean that I would do things like support innovative ideas about pedagogy and to take on, and potentially clear away, administrative and institutional obstacles that could get in the way of their teaching. I still believe that those are important aspects of my job. Yet, in the years that have passed, I have also come to understand that statement to mean that I will do my best to facilitate and support a thoughtful and hospitable community in the program, to make sure that people are heard, even when I lack the power to make the changes they desire. In recent years I have understood that the building of community is also inextricable from attending to the emotional culture and identity of a program.

Talking about emotion in academic settings can feel risky. There are going to be people who set up dichotomies where compassion and empathy are pitted against rigor and intellect. Yet even those critics will tell stories about their teaching or tutoring in which emotion figures heavily. They hope their students will feel the same passion for intellectual exploration that they feel. They worry that students lack confidence in their writing or are seemingly bored in class. And they are grateful for moments in which the institutional response of a program may be caring toward them, such as when they may need time off to tend to a family emergency. Even those who express concern about talking about emotion in a writing program will, if asked, grant that our emotional states can be crucial to our ability to engage in an activity. We cannot do our best work if we feel insecure, intimidated, bored, or anxious. Yet, in the moments we feel confident, engaged, respected, and safe, we do well.

The role of emotion in how able and willing we are to engage in a task is not a matter of how we feel as an individual. The emotional context of a program will influence the ways in which teacher, tutors, and students interpret the experiences they have, and then how they feel about them the next time similar experiences occur. Too often, however, the emotional culture of a program is perceived as something that develops organically, beyond the influence of individuals in the program. Yet it is possible to address emotions in a program in a way that helps everyone involved understand more fully the role of emotions and the narratives through which we construct and perform them in how we make sense of our program and our work. Taking the time to acknowledge the role of emotions, and then talking about them explicitly, can help everyone understand how emotions are being constructed and reproduced in the program. The way we frame emotions in such conversations matters. The ways we respond to bad news or encounters, by admitting to problems and advocating transparency yet also responding with support and care, shapes how others will interpret those emotions. The emotions we talk about, and enact, as being at the core of our work—trust, empathy, confidence, reflection, respect, cooperation—communicate those values and emotions to others and contribute to the creation of an emotional culture and identity for the program that will benefit the working lives of teachers and tutors and the learning experiences of students.

REFERENCES

Adams, Jeffrey B. 2005. "What Makes the Grade? Faculty and Student Perceptions." *Teaching of Psychology* 32: 21–24.

Alm, F., and G. Colnerud. 2015. "Teachers' Experiences of Unfair Grading." *Educational Assessment* 20 (2):132–150.

Ariely, Dan, Emir Kamenica, and Dražen Prelec. 2008. "Man's Search for Meaning: The Case of Legos." *Journal of Economic Behavior and Organization* 67 (3–4): 671–677.

Barrett, Lisa Feldman. 2009. "Variety Is the Spice of Life: A Psychological Construction Approach to Understanding Emotion." *Cognition and Emotion* 23 (7): 1284–1306.

Blum, Susan D. 2016. *"I Love Learning; I Hate School": An Anthropology of College*. Ithaca, NY: Cornell University Press.

Burrows, Cedric. 2016. "The Yardstick of Whiteness in Composition Textbooks." *WPA: Writing Program Administration* 39 (2): 42–47.

Chory, Rebecca M., Sean M. Horan, and Marian L. Houser. 2017. "Justice in the Higher Education Classroom: Students' Perceptions of Unfairness and Responses to Instructors." *Innovative Higher Education* 42 (4): 321–336.

Corbett, Steven. 2017. "Toward Inclusive and Multi-Method Writing Assessment for College Students with Learning Disabilities: The (Universal) Story of Max." *WPA: Writing Program Administration* 40 (3): 23–38.

Council of Writing Program Administrators. 2011. *Framework for Success in Post-Secondary Writing*. Council of Writing Program Administrators, National Council of Teachers of English, and National Writing Project.

Davies, Laura J. 2017. "Grief and the new WPA." *WPA: Writing Program Administration* 40 (2): 40–51.
Davila, Bethany. 2017. "Standard English and Colorblindness in Composition Studies: Rhetorical Constructions of Racial and Linguistic Neutrality." *WPA: Writing Program Administration* 40 (2): 154–173.
Dean, Ann C. 2015. "Understanding Why Linked Courses Can Succeed with Students but Fail with Institutions." *WPA: Writing Program Administration* 38 (1): 65–87.
Deci, Edward L., and Richard M. Ryan. 2000. "The 'What' and 'Why' of Goal Pursuits: Human Needs and the Self-determination of Behavior." *Psychological Inquiry* 11 (4): 227–268.
Delgado, Richard. 1989. "Storytelling for Oppositionists and Others: A Plea for Narrative." *Michigan Law Review* 87 (8): 2411–2441.
Dryer, Dylan B., and Irvin Peckham. 2015. "Social Contexts of Writing Assessment: Toward and Ecological Construct of the Rater." *WPA: Writing Program Administration* 38 (1): 12–41.
Eodice, Michele, Anne Ellen Geller, and Neal Lerner. 2017. *The Meaningful Writing Project: Learning, Teaching and Writing in Higher Education*. Logan: Utah State University Press.
Estrem, Heidi, Dawn Shepherd, and Lloyd Duman. 2015. "Relentless Engagement with State Educational Policy Reform: Collaborating to Change the Writing Placement Conversation." *WPA: Writing Program Administration* 38 (1): 88–128.
Fedukovich, Casie J., and Tracy Ann Morse. 2017. "Failures to Accommodate: GTA Preparation as a Site for a Transformative Culture of Access." *WPA: Writing Program Administration* 40 (3): 39–60.
Fernyhough, Charles. 2012. *Pieces of Light: The New Science of Memory*. London: Profile Books.
Fulwiler, Megan, and Jennifer Marlow. 2014. *Con Job: Stories of Adjunct and Contingent Labor*. Logan: Utah State University Press.
Haswell, Richard, and Janis Haswell. 2015. *Hospitality and Authoring: An Essay for the English Profession*. Logan: Utah State University Press.
Hood, Bruce. 2014. *The Domesticated Brain: A Pelican Introduction*. London: Penguin UK.
Jacoby-Senghor, Drew S., Stacey Sinclair, and J. Nicole Shelton. 2016. "A Lesson in Bias: The Relationship between Implicit Racial Bias and Performance in Pedagogical Contexts." *Journal of Experimental Social Psychology* 63: 50–55.
Jiang, Lixin, Thomas M. Tripp, and Phan Y. Hong. 2017. "College Instruction Is Not So Stress Free After All: A Qualitative and Quantitative Study of Academic Entitlement, Uncivil Behaviors, and Instructor Strain and Burnout." *Stress and Health* 33 (5): 578–589.
Joye, Shauna, and Janie H. Wilson. 2015. "Professor Age and Gender Affect Student Perceptions and Grades." *Journal of the Scholarship of Teaching and Learning* 15 (4): 126–138.
Kahnemann, Daniel. 2011. *Thinking, Fast and Slow*. New York: Farrar, Straus, and Giroux.
Kirsch, Gesa. 2005. Friendship, Friendliness, and Feminist Fieldwork. *Signs* 30 (4), 2163–2172.
Klapp, Alli. 2015. "Does Grading Affect Educational Attainment? A Longitudinal Study." *Assessment in Education: Principles, Policy and Practice* 22 (3): 302–323.
Kurtyka, Faith. 2015. "Settling In to Genre: The Social Action of Emotion in Shaping Genres." *Composition Forum* 31 (spring). http://compositionforum.com/issue/31/settling-in.php.
Lancaster, Sonya, Heather Bastian, Justin Ross Sevenker, and E. A. Williams. 2015. "Making the Most of Networked Communication in Writing Program Assessment." *WPA: Writing Program Administration* 38 (2): 93–112.
MacNell, Lillian, Adam Driscoll, and Andrea N. Hunt. 2015. "What's in a Name: Exposing Gender Bias in Student Ratings of Teaching." *Innovative Higher Education* 40 (4): 291–303.

Madianou, Mirca, and Daniel Miller. 2012. *Migration and New Media: Transnational Families and Polymedia.* London: Routledge.

Malouff, John M., and Einar B. Thorsteinsson. 2016. "Bias in Grading: A Meta-Analysis of Experimental Research Findings." *Australian Journal of Education* 60 (3): 245–256.

Meltzoff, Andrew N., and Rachele Brooks. 2007. "Intersubjectivity Before Language: Three Windows on Preverbal Sharing." *Advances in Consciousness Research* 68:149.

Micciche, Laura R. 2007. *Doing Emotion: Rhetoric, Writing, Teaching.* Portsmouth, NH: Boynton Cook.

Micciche, Laura R. 2011. "For Slow Agency." *WPA: Writing Program Administration* 35 (1): 73–90.

Moxley, Joseph M., and David Eubanks. 2016. "On Keeping Score: Instructors' vs. Students' Rubric Ratings of 46,689 Essays." *WPA: Writing Program Administration* 39 (2): 53–80.

Newkirk, Thomas. 2017. *Embarrassment: And the Emotional Underlife of Learning.* Portsmouth, NH: Heinemann.

Phillips, Talinn, Paul Shovlin, and Megan L. Titus. (2016). "(Re)Identifying the gWPA Experience." *WPA: Writing Program Administration* 40 (1): 67–89.

Ronald, Kate, and Hephzibah Roskelly. 2001. "Learning to Take it Personally." In *Personal Effects: The Social Character of Scholarly Writing*, edited by D. Holdstein and D. Bleich, 253–266. Logan: Utah State University Press.

Sheldon, Kennon M., and Julia Schüler. 2015. "Agency and its Discontents: A Two-Process Perspective on Basic Psychological Needs and Motives." In *APA Handbook of Personality and Social Psychology*, edited by M. Mikulincer and P. R. Shaver, 167–187. Washington, DC: American Psychological Association.

Sommers, Nancy. 2006. "Across the Drafts." *College Composition and Communication* 58 (2): 248–257.

Sura, Thomas. 2015. "Making Space for Service Learning in First-Year Composition." *WPA: Writing Program Administration* 38 (2): 113–128.

Tannock, Stuart. 2017. "No Grades in Higher Education Now! Revisiting the Place of Graded Assessment in the Reimagination of the Public University." *Studies in Higher Education* 42 (8): 1345–1357.

Vallade, J. I., M. M. Martin, and K. Weber. 2014. "Academic Entitlement, Grade Orientation, and Classroom Justice as Predictors of Instructional Beliefs and Learning Outcomes." *Communication Quarterly* 62 (5): 497–517.

Wetherell, Margaret. 2012 *Affect and Emotion: A New Social Science Understanding.* Thousand Oaks, CA: Sage Publications.

Williams, Bronwyn T. 2007. "Trust, Betrayal, and Authorship: Plagiarism and How We Perceive Students." *Journal of Adolescent and Adult Literacy* 51 (4): 350–354.

Williams, Bronwyn T. 2011. "Dancing with Don: Or, Waltzing with 'Expressivism.'" *Enculturation* 13. https://www.enculturation.net/dancing-with-don.

Williams, Bronwyn T. 2017. "Having a Feel for What Works: Polymedia, Emotion, and Literacy Practices with Mobile Technologies." In *Social Writing/Social Media*, edited by S. Vie and D. Walls, 127–143. Fort Collins, CO: WAC Clearinghouse/Parlor Press.

Williams, Bronwyn T. 2018. *Literacy Practices and Perceptions of Agency: Composing Identities.* London: Routledge.

Williams, Bronwyn T. In Press. "Writing Centers, Enclaves, and Creating Spaces of Change within Universities." *Writing Center Journal.*

Wilson, Timothy. 2011. *Redirect: The Surprising New Science of Psychological Change.* London: Penguin UK.

Winck, Jessica. 2016. "Amused Teachers and Public Readers: Empathy and Derision in 'Student Bloopers.'" Dissertation, University of Louisville.

Young, Morris. 2004. *Minor Re/Visions: Asian American Literacy Narratives as a Rhetoric of Citizenship.* Carbondale: Southern Illinois University Press.

PART II

Sensemaking and Institutional Structures

6
NEW WRITING CENTER ECOLOGIES
Challenging Inherited Sensemaking in the Center

Genie Nicole Giaimo and Joseph Cheatle

INTRODUCTION

Writing centers have long viewed themselves as outsiders, rogues, and mavericks (see North 1984; Denny 2010; Sunstein 1998); meanwhile, institutions may have sometimes viewed them as remedial (Harris 1990). And while all of these figurations may have been more accurate early on in their history, writing centers are increasingly part of the fabric of institutions, which includes additional hiring lines that result in an expanded and more professionalized academic field (Wallace and Wallace 2010). Like other academic units, writing centers compete for resources, establish learning outcomes and goals, offer credit-bearing courses and embedded tutoring, and, often, further the mission of the institution. In short, like those who staff the writing programs, tutors in writing centers are "en-meshed in complex, circulative relationships" (Reiff et al. 2015, 3) that make up an ecology that works within—and sometimes against—the larger institution.

Because of these relationships, which sometimes extend far beyond the walls and virtual spaces of the writing center to include administrators, faculty, accreditation boards and other stakeholders, we rely on documentation to make sense of and justify our work (Hall 2017). As our field continues to professionalize, it is important that our documentation reflects the goals of our field and articulates what we do to both internal and external audiences. Documentation, both in the past and currently, includes client registration information, session notes/report forms, observations, focus groups, client surveys, institutional reports, and more. Most of the documents we use in our field have not radically changed over the years, and while there are studies that question the value of particular documents, such as session notes and client surveys, there is little research on how integration of novel documentation may enable us to sensemake about writing center work. It seems our field has failed to do continuous review of our documents and, thus, we are stuck with the same past practice, informed by similar lore.

Because we resist understanding writing centers in new ways, we risk restructuring and other hazards that accompany the practices put into place at many higher education institutions, such as austerity measures, formula-based budget models, and responsibility-centered budgeting. These measures are often out of our control. Nevertheless, universities and colleges run as businesses, with attendant organizational models and philosophies; therefore, writing centers could benefit from engaging with organizational research in order to make sense of the work that we do. As Malenczyk's introduction to this collection notes, at its core, sensemaking is the process of understanding. In his study on the history of the term, Weick (1995) argues that "sensemaking is about such things as placement of items into frameworks, comprehending, redressing surprise, constructing meaning, interacting in pursuit of mutual understanding, and patterning" (6). Weick's argument captures how sensemaking is about both the construction and reception of knowledge. Importantly for organizations, sensemaking is neither static nor stable, but is, instead, constantly in motion (Hernes and Maitlis 2010, 29–30); furthermore, it is a recurring and ongoing process of organizing knowledge and "meaning creation." While sensemaking is, as noted in other chapters in this collection and the introduction, often about storytelling, we take a somewhat different approach in our chapter to conceptualizing sensemaking that focuses on knowledge development, information dissemination, and frameworks. We believe it is critical to attend to how information is created and moves in ways that are predictable and patterned but also fluctuating and potentially novel. Analyzing our field's documents—and offering up for examination documents that are new to the field—can help expand our sensemaking about writing administration and enrich discussions (and defenses) about our work.

Although documentation is one of the primary ways that writing centers have defined and situated themselves within institutions, we do not always use the forms of documentation that best speak to institutional outcomes, strategic plans, or even ideals and values we support as a field, such as collaboration, mentorship, and professionalization. Therefore, we argue that as our field expands, in terms of staffing lines and links into broader college and university administration, our documentation must change to reflect new audiences and sensemaking ecologies. We are organizations within hierarchies that have policies, procedures, and goals that are often in flux and changing; therefore, rather than merely use forms of documentation that are holdovers from the origins of writing centers, we need to update current documents and develop new ones. In this chapter, we explore how we can make sense of the work of writing centers through the development and analysis of the documents that our work creates. In particular, we focus on three documents that we identify as the past, present, and future of writing center work: session notes, client surveys, and individual development plans (IDPs). Organizational theory, from which the idea of sensemaking emerged, allows us to examine current writing center documentation, like session notes and client surveys, and to frame how new documentation, like IDPs, can more effectively communicate the range of work and support we provide while updating our sensemaking ecologies for our current educational climate. And while at times our piece might sound like the onus is on WPAs to perform all of this sensemaking labor on their own, we also recognize that there are systemic issues related to our material (and psychosocial) conditions that need to be attended to. In short, we need a wide-ranging approach to sensemaking about our work. We need to attend to emotional experiences in WPA work and in our teaching (Williams, this volume). We need to resist austerity models of education and make visible (and challenge) documents that aim to remain obscure, such as Memorandums of Understanding (MOUs) and union contracts, as well as other "ruling relations" documents, which reveal so much about our working lives and the values of the institutions for which we work (Nicolas, this volume). Our colleagues and coauthors offer excellent complements to our chapter, and so we hope our contribution is read as one part of a constellation of new approaches to sensemaking in our professional field. In this chapter, we attempt to answer the questions, How do our everyday documents represent our work? and How can we better document this work?

Organizational Theory, Documents, and Writing Centers

At the center of organizational theory is a rational framework that can be applied to all aspects of an organization. Farazmand (2002) writes that organizational theory is necessary because "organizations were [initially] simple in structure and management, but as they grew larger they become sophisticated and complex in structure and function, requiring managerial skills and techniques beyond the comprehension of many people" (xv). Central components to organizational theory are understanding the organization and assessing effectiveness (Lund 2011). But achieving these is not easy; according to Henry (2002), organizations face a large number of issues: "Goals are vague, and public organizations are appropriately sprawling as structures meant to achieve the vagaries of large organizational missions; judging organizational effectiveness, as a result, is difficult" (8). As organizations grow larger, it becomes more difficult to judge effectiveness and make sense of them. One way to understand an organization and assess effectiveness is through documentation. For Buckland (2013), organizational knowledge is represented through documents, which are complex because they are both technical and social (Buckland 2013; Lund 2011). However, documents don't exist in a vacuum or outside of context; in fact, "the meaning of a document—what it is perceived as signifying—makes a document important, but what it signifies is influenced and extended by relationships with other documents and with people" (Buckland 2017). And while "documents are concerned with evidence and evidence implies fact. Meaning . . . is constructed in the mind of the observer, even where facts are concerned" (Buckland 2013, 3). Therefore, when considering documents, it is important to take into account both the technical aspects of the document as well as how it will be used and perceived.

So why, and how, is organizational theory important for writing centers? The history of writing centers generally tracks with the ways in which organizations develop and change over time from less structured to more structured, yet sprawling, workspaces. As Lerner (2003) points out in his study of writing centers from 1939 to 1970, "Punishment and Possibility," writing centers have traditionally been marginalized. Lerner is merely one among many who have pointed this out. Thompson (2006) echoes Lerner's viewpoint: "It is not difficult to find discussions of the low status and the lack of power writing centers have in their home institutions, in composition studies, and in the academy at large" (34). Many early writing centers were created as a response to the need facing higher education during the open-access movement (Boquet 1999). And many writing centers were often supported with minimal staffing and funding; some were created by graduate students, not by administrators or faculty. From these organic and perhaps less structured roots, programmatic shifts occurred, as writing centers increasingly began to occupy a solidified and more central position within institutions. Grassroots centers gave way to ones with tenure lines, which gave way to ones with staff administrators. Some of these changes in organizational structure were positive, such as securing a budget and hiring lines, which helped writing centers maintain their coherence and their scholarly legacy.

However, some of these changes were not necessarily positive. With more organizational structures and connections to central administration, writing centers have also become student support workhorses that are under intense scrutiny. Migration away from placement within English departments and toward student affairs or academic affairs has come with new challenges but also new opportunities for reimagining how we make sense of our work and our mission. Given this new positionality, we argue that writing centers should be viewed, and are often already viewed, as organizations: they have a budget, staff, mission, objectives, documentation, and more. Yet, at the same time that writing centers face organizational challenges regarding performance, overhead, staffing, and resource allocation, we lack such a model through which to frame our work. By applying an organizational theory framework, we can begin to identify how our centers map onto our mission and our goals; however, we can also gauge how central administration and the "powers that be" support this work. Because we are already documenting what we do in writing centers, we argue that this is a relatively low-stakes way to engage stakeholders outside of the writing center about the meaningful and vital service that writing centers provide—not only for writers but also for the tutors that staff our centers. In this way, we can be better advocates for our staff and be better prepared to identify their needs, which include not only professional development but also labor incentives and support. By naming what we already know intuitively—that writing centers require far more administrative support than they are ever provided with—we can make sense of our work and the work of our tutors and staff. However, we can also identify what is within our power to develop, organizationally, and what is outside of our power to correct. Figure 6.1, from *Organizational Assessment: A Framework for Improving Performance* (Lusthaus et al. 2002, 10), provides a helpful diagram for understanding the facets of an organization and how they overlap with organizational performance.

In figure 6.1, *organizational performance* is defined in terms of three driving contextual forces: *organizational capacity, organizational motivation,* and *environment. Organizational capacity* "is the ability of an organization to use its resources to perform" (Lusthaus et al. 2002, 11); *organizational motivation* "represents the underlying personality of the organization . . . what drives the members of the organization to perform" (11); and *environment,* which "is the key factor in determining the level of available resources and the ease with which an organization can carry out its activities" (12). In the center, and representing the overlap of the three larger circles, is *organizational performance.* Organizational performance

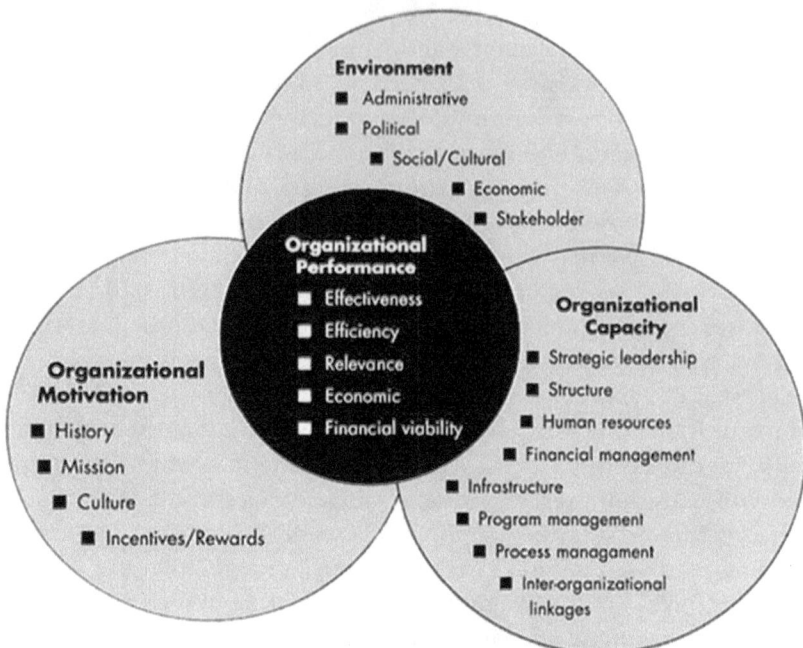

Figure 6.1. Diagram of organizational performance. Reproduced with permission from Lusthaus, et al., Organizational Assessment: A Framework for Improving Performance *(Ottawa, Canada: International Development Research Centre, 2002), 10.*

takes into account all three driving contextual forces; through this framework, writing centers can begin to think about how to make sense of our organizations through our documentation.

Document: Improving Session Notes/Client Report Forms (CRFs)

The *organizational capacity* of a writing center can be measured through many kinds of documents—strategic plans, annual reports, budget reports, personnel and policy documents, exit interviews, observations, and so on—and all of these documents (and so many more) are evidence of the writing center's ability to perform its day-to-day and long-term duties. However, one document often overlooked for assessing the daily functioning of writing centers is the session note. Session notes are an almost universally implemented practice in writing centers in which tutors (either in concert with a client or independently) fill out a record of a session's events (Larrance and Brady 1995). Past research on session notes has focused frequently on the use-value of the document and how it is perceived by stakeholders, which often takes the shape of exploring ethical and philosophical issues surrounding sharing these documents with external populations, such as faculty (Crump 1993; Pemberton 1995; Jackson 1996; Conway 1998). A recent study by Bugdal, Reardon, and Deans (2016) explores some of the technical aspects of session notes—coding the notes into five types—but ultimately focuses on the use-value of the notes for stakeholders rather than how writing centers rely upon, expand, and utilize these documents for organizational purposes. Other authors, like Cardaro (2014), identify the ways in which session notes "can act as a vital link between writing centers and classrooms" (1). Indeed, as Weaver (2001) notes, a lot of research on session notes is focused on "the benefits and drawbacks of conference summaries" for stakeholders (35).

With the notable exceptions of Cogie's 1998 study "In Defense of Conference Summaries: Widening the Reach of Writing Center Work" and Malenczyk's 2013 " 'I Thought I'd Put That in to Amuse You': Tutor Reports as Organizational Narrative," not many studies explicitly discuss or identify the organizational purposes that session notes perform within the writing center. While Cogie (1998) identifies—through surveys of tutors, writers, and faculty—the role that session notes play in writer motivation and confidence, Malenczyk (2013) argues that referring back to session notes written about an individual writer might help tutors to further develop their tutoring practice and better support writers.

Ultimately, the early studies on session notes, such as Pemberton's 1995 work "Writing Center Ethics: Sharers and Seclusionists," seem to heavily influence even most current research on session notes. It seems, then, that session note research is split between studying the use and the perception of the document, on one end of the spectrum, and the technical aspects of the document, on the other end. However, from an organizational perspective, the technical aspects of session notes matter just as much as the purpose of the document and how it is perceived by stakeholders. Hall's 2017 book *Around the Texts of Writing Center Work: An Inquiry-Based Approach to Tutor Education* is perhaps one of the first studies to not only identify the important role that documents created in a writing center play in its organizational development but also to analyze the form and content of these documents. In it, Hall uses a variety of analytical tools to examine common documents that writing centers produce, including session notes, and how these documents help to sustain knowledge production in the writing center and foster a "community of learners" (3). Building on the work of Hall and others, the authors of this study conducted a large-scale discourse analysis of session notes from writing centers across four large public universities, producing a two-million-word corpus that, in the future, others can contribute to, explore, and analyze (Giaimo et al. 2018). While Hall's work studied how tutors engage with these documents, we were interested in how administrators can utilize session notes, potentially cross-institutionally, to understand the scope and purpose of this document.

From our inter-institutional project, we discovered that session notes are an ideal way to understand the ecology of a writing center and whether its organizational structure is productive and healthy. Session notes help to identify whether or not the mission of the writing center is being carried forward by staff members. They can also reveal whether or not concepts from training are making their way into staff members' tutoring practices, as they do at the Michigan State University Writing Center. Additionally, session notes can reveal, as they did in The Ohio State University Writing Center, the unique kinds of challenges that tutors experience in their daily work, such as performing emotional labor with clients, with colleagues, and for themselves. Furthermore, analyzing session notes from multiple institutions allows administrators to learn about local cultures within writing centers and what carries over, organizationally, from center to center. In short, session notes can be used to assess and update process management and program management; they can also reveal whether or not to foster interorganizational linkages, such as advisory councils, partners meetings, research collaborations, and joint trainings, among others.

Document 2: Why Satisfaction Isn't Enough: Improving Client Surveys

The client survey is one document that can help to assess the *environment* of an organization (see figure 1 above). Client surveys ask stakeholders (writers) to identify whether or not they are satisfied with the writing center's services, staff, philosophy, and so on. These documents also help to assess the culture of the writing center—what clients identify as valuable as well as their perception of the center's ethos and mission. Finally, they also serve an administrative function, as they are one of the largest and most consistent sets of input about organizational structure and performance. Often, data from client surveys are used in annual reports to justify budgets, though there are some recent studies that identify issues with only surveying people who attend the writing center and not those who don't (Salem 2016; Giaimo 2017). Often, client surveys gauge client satisfaction rather than measure other factors that contribute to engagement (or lack of engagement) with writing centers.

Depending on the center, client surveys can be administered in a number of ways: after each session, for a set time during the academic year or randomly, or weeks or months after the session. In whatever ways it is disseminated, however, this document is frequently used to demonstrate that writing centers are considered successful. Usually, a question to the effect of "was your session successful?" gives respondents the option to check yes or no or to respond on a Likert scale. According to Schendel and Macauley (2012), satisfaction surveys "can help you to gauge whether the people with whom you come into contact find the writing center open, helpful, and professional; whether the services you offer suit their needs; and, whether consultations result in a self-perceived change in one's writing or one's writing development" (127). While, ideally, client surveys ought to track a host of factors connected to the tutorial process and the writing center's mission and structure, responses to surveys are often overwhelmingly positive (or negative) and rarely nuanced enough to hinge programmatic development and change upon.

Furthermore, though satisfaction surveys are widely used in writing centers, they have been generally discredited and viewed with suspicion as documents in organizational theory. There are many issues with satisfaction surveys, particularly surrounding bias: "Although surveys are typically offered to a random sample of customers, the recipient's decision whether or not to respond to the survey is not random" and can result in low numbers of completions and a situation where "the group of people who choose to answer a survey is not necessarily representative of the customer population as a whole" (Brogle 2013). In addition to not being objective—despite the guise of objectiveness—surveys tend to capture extreme responses at the expense of a representative sample.

Even though client surveys are frequently used in writing centers, they are not often used beyond satisfaction surveys and present some problems. While satisfaction surveys can be useful, Gofine (2012), Kalikoff (2001), Thompson (2006), Salem (2016), and Giaimo (2017), among others, have all pointed out problems with client surveys because they predominantly measure client satisfaction. For Gofine (2012), client surveys are problematic because "those who did complete the forms were so appreciative that the surveys were more like thank-you notes" (42); this is often the case with client surveys, especially those completed immediately after a consultation. Gofine found that, "although the center's staff appreciated the gratitude that they received, the feedback from the surveys was not conducive to the greater goal of improving services or detecting variation in client experiences of the writing center" (42). Survey data did not provide any actionable measures or provide the breadth of clients' experience. Meanwhile, Kalikoff (2001) found a number of issues with client surveys: students believe they don't have time to fill out surveys and "gave perfunctory answers or left the center without completing a form," surveys were not given to all clients, and surveys were overly positive (5). These issues with writing center surveys echo the broader bias issues with satisfaction surveys. And as Thompson (2006) points out, while satisfaction surveys were particularly effective for young writing centers to demonstrate their viability, as centers become more complex, they need to develop more sophisticated uses for surveys (35). Client surveys, as Gofine (2012), Kalikoff (2001), and Thompson (2006) note, are often overly positive and provide little in the way of accurate and constructive feedback for organizational development. Furthermore, as Giaimo (2017) notes, "widely surveying a student population ought to be the 'gold standard' of the field's methodological approach to studying habits and perceptions within writing center contexts. Those that refuse to attend a writing center can act as a control group for researchers to compare with students who do attend the writing center" (56). Survey design, then, must be considered alongside survey dissemination approaches, in assessment work.

Client surveys don't have to be discarded, however, but can be improved upon to better suit our organizational needs. For this reason, we offer six areas of improvement for centers that currently use them:

1. Expand surveys out from assessing mere satisfaction. As Thompson (2006) notes, although necessary, surveys "do not provide much direct information about student learning" (45). For example, surveys might ask how clients perceive themselves as writers and measure if perception is correlated with use (Giaimo 2017).

2. Structure survey questions carefully. Creating a good survey is difficult and, often, setting up dichotomous questions can lead to false limitations in responses (MacNealy 1999, 161). For example, utilize the Likert scale and make the tone of questions neutral.

3. Determine what drives happiness or unhappiness and track that. For example, assess the emotional state of clients before they have their sessions and after they have their sessions and analyze change in affect over time.

4. Approach the creation of client surveys with thoughtfulness. For MacNealy (1999), it is important that surveys determine a clear purpose before implementation (148). Client surveys can't be all things to all people; rather, they should have specific and clear goals that can change over time. For example, test survey language before implementation to identify what questions yield detailed or variable responses and share the survey with tutors, as they often have good insight into the emotions and needs of clients.

5. Have broader audiences in mind. For example, consider what external stakeholders would be interested in knowing about the writing center and its role in student learning.

6. Survey outside of the writing center to identify general attitudes regarding the importance of writing across majors, writing habits and motivations, and knowledge of the writing center and its practices. These findings can be compared against writing center attendees or used as a control for assessing development of writing center clients over time (Giaimo 2017).

Drawing on these recommendations can help lead to an improved client survey, one that moves beyond satisfaction and that can be used to improve not only student learning outcomes but also reportage outcomes.

Document 3: Introducing Individual Development Plans (IDPs)

Individual development plans (IDPs) can affect *organizational motivation* and help to set the standards for how staff members perform and are supported in doing their jobs. This document can affect an organization's mission and culture, as well as help to set incentives/rewards (figure 6.1). A common professionalization tool, IDPs are utilized in a broad array of academic and professional spaces, including biology (Marcus 2016; Mayer 2011; Gitlin 2008), early childhood education (Sugarman 2011), medicine (Ko and Kimple 2018), chemistry (Krone and Wenzel 2016), MBA programs (Rubens et al. 2018), governmental organizations, and beyond (Marcus 2016; Kaye 2010). IDPs have been found to increase performance and career success in a wide range of populations, including graduate students (Marcus 2016), postdocs (Gitlin 2008; Mayer 2011), new and seasoned teachers (Sugarman 2011), and corporate employees (Goffnett 2014; Kaye 2010). Those who participate in the IDP process have demonstrated "higher performance, increased career satisfaction and rapid advancement" (Goffnett 2014, 2), increased professional outcomes in academic disciplines (Gitlin 2008; Mayer 2011), strengthened skills in professional and academic settings (Goffnett 2014; Krone and Wenzel 2016), and increased career performance and higher career satisfaction (Gitlin 2008; Goffnett 2014).

A number of funding agencies, such as the National Science Foundation (Mayer 2011), National Institutes of Health (Ko and Kimple 2018), as well as accreditation and granting agencies in education (Sugarman 2011), require IDPs as part of their professionalization and mentorship processes. Yet, despite their successful integration into many different professional spaces, IDPs are not common practice in the humanities, particularly in writing centers or the broader field of rhetoric/composition. Therefore, as one part of our "new" sensemaking ecology that forms "complex circulative relationships" (Reiff et al. 2015, 3) for writing centers, we propose the implementation of individual development plans for graduate and/or postdoctoral researchers who work in our writing centers.

An IDP is a form of two to three pages and contains particular subheadings such as, but not limited to, professional goals, mentors, training skills assessment, annual objectives plan, and long-term goal setting, as well as a section for establishing specific, measurable, achievable, relevant, and time-bound (SMART) goals. The three major components in an IDP, as Goffnett (2014) identifies, include:

1. Development goals
2. Timelines to accomplish each development goal
3. Activities necessary for development (1)

Many institutions of higher education offer templates for IDPs, and models can be found on the NIH website.

The Ohio State University (OSU) Writing Center selected one of a number of IDP templates offered university-wide, which was then adapted and applied to its professional development program for graduate administrators. The implementation of IDPs has yielded generative conversations regarding professional aims as well as helped to establish professional development goals (such as specific skills development) in order to achieve those professional aims. Although the evidence so far is only anecdotal—now, IDPs have only been a part of the OSU WC professionalization program for three years—IDPs have helped to shape the leadership team of graduate students in the OSU WC as well to facilitate engagement in career reflection and identification of transferable skills. Also, anecdotally, of the three graduate students who engaged in the IDP process in year one, all three have graduated and accepted writing center positions—two of the three graduate students were in fields adjacent to writing center studies, such as English and education. Therefore, particularly among graduate students who want to make a career pivot into writing center studies, IDPs can help to set appreciable goals and identify the skills necessary to achieve those goals.

Within writing center work itself, IDPs can provide a low-stakes but still engaging way to think about how writing center work transfers into other academic and professional contexts. As Rubens et al. (2018) have found, "most graduate students, and perhaps many working professionals, often do not allocate time for needed self-reflection and introspection on their strengths and weaknesses as managers and leaders in organizations; nor do they devote full consideration of where and how they will achieve their personal and career goals" (10). Therefore, even if writing center employees are not interested in pursuing writing center administration work, IDPs can prove to be a necessary tool in that they promote intentional career planning and goal setting. In short, IDPs can act as a professionalizing tool for staff members, undergraduate and graduate alike.

IDPs should be part of an ongoing professionalization conversation (Kaye 2010) and embedded into everyday organizational practices. They should not stand in as "a job description, a performance evaluation, or a program evaluation" (Sugarman 2011, 27). Rather, they should be part of an ongoing conversation on professional development and career objectives. In the second year that IDPs were offered at OSU as a professional development program (this time optional, rather than required), none of the five graduate administrators participated in the professional development process. This is a troubling if not unsurprising result of making the IDP process optional; if graduate students and others do not often take time to reflect on their professional goals organically, then offering them an optional professionalization program might not be the most effective way to facilitate buy-in. Writing center administrators might need to take additional steps to engage students. Therefore, we provide suggestions for integrating IDPs into current and ongoing mentorship and professionalization programs:

1. Because graduate students often do not engage in skills or career goal planning on their own, make the IDP part of required professional development rather than optional (Rubens et al. 2018).
2. Managers/directors should engage in the IDP creation process with their employees (Goffnett 2014).
3. Managers/directors need to provide resources to help employees meet their goals (Goffnett 2014).
4. Managers/directors should build the IDP into ongoing professional development, returning to it, post write-up, to assess the success of the plan.
5. IDPs should have specific goals, while allowing those IDP goals to be amended (Sugarman 2011), with specific timelines and plans for completion.
6. The IDP should not be used in lieu of a performance review, a job description, or a program evaluation, although such documents can inform the IDP plan (Sugarman 2011).

In short, IDPs are a useful way to prepare tutors for their careers after the writing center; however, they are also a useful document for cultivating leadership in the writing center and encouraging retention among staff members (Goffnett 2014). Other potential benefits include increased investment in the organization (be it a company, a laboratory, or a writing center), career preparation, and better work performance. Also, IDPs respond to the workers' needs and identify future opportunities for the worker within the organization, all of which lays "paths toward success for the organization and its employees" (Goffnett 2014, 2). On an employee-health level, IDPs can provide consistent mentorship and support to help prevent burnout (Ko and Kimple 2018). Institutionally, IDPs are a useful tool because they allow writing center administrators to track how much work tutors conduct and how they prioritize and utilize their time. Such tracking is useful for making the case to upper administration for funding increases or additional staffing lines. Such documents can also be used to highlight professional development and workplace preparation, which is attractive to funding agencies and foundational giving. Because of these benefits, and because of the wide-ranging disciplinary and professional support for IDPs as a best practice for employee professionalization, we recommend writing center administrators adopt this support model.

CONCLUSION

Knowledge management is a critical practice, particularly in organizations that have as high a turnover rate as writing centers (or other academic organizations) do; leaders in the organization retire, others may leave, students graduate, and so on, and a number of different kinds of knowledge can get lost. This knowledge is incredibly valuable for maintaining the institutional consistency of the writing center, which may help in preventing making the same organizational mistakes multiple times over; however, it also helps to maintain coherence in staff experience and training and, ultimately, the broader mission(s) of the center. As King (2005) and Little (2010) note, there is both tacit knowledge and explicit knowledge in organizations. Tacit knowledge, for King (2005) is "usually not documented, but derived from expertise, collaboration, and field experience. This knowledge is often imparted from briefings, discussions, and first hand observation" (3). For Little (2010), tacit knowledge "exists within the actions and experiences" of employees and is therefore "challenging to disseminate via documentation" (1). Explicit knowledge, on the other hand, exists "in forms that can be communicated" and "can be presented in various printed or electronic documentations," such as personnel manuals (1).

These two kinds of knowledge—explicit and tacit—are dependent on each other. Any writing center administrator who struggles with sharing years of personal and collected tutoring and other organizational experience in a weeklong (or daylong) orientation or training understands the dilemma of capturing tacit knowledge and making it explicit for incoming tutors and administrators. Understanding the writing center as a managerial site and an organization helps to put into focus the need for knowledge management. The approach will certainly be multipronged and include both documentation that contains explicit knowledge and artifacts that aim to collect tacit knowledge. While it might be challenging, this is necessary for the longevity and success of the center, as well as for advocating for it to central administration.

While the documents that we discuss are not exhaustive, this process of examination and revision can be done on any number of documents endemic to writing center administration. We hope we have made the case for the work that our documentation does within an organizational framework, as we believe this model best articulates how we make sense of the work we do. To that end, we provide a starting heuristic for writing center documentation that provides guidance on assessing current documentation practices.

Heuristic for Writing Center Documents

1. How are my documents disseminated throughout my organization and external to my organization?
2. Do my documents support my mission and strategic plan?
3. Do my documents examine and address the needs of stakeholders?
4. Are my current documentation practices intentional and impactful?
5. How does central administration receive and understand my documentation?

Asking questions of your documents' purpose and use is a helpful starting point in considering your current writing center's sensemaking ecology and reimagining that ecology with and through new documentation.

In "The Writing Center as Managerial Site," Heckelman (1998) identifies the ways the field of writing center studies is not necessarily comfortable with understanding the nature of writing center work within managerial or organizational terms; he notes that "management need not be a dirty word for those of us who make our livings in the writing business" (1). Yet, over twenty years on from Heckelman's 1998 article, relatively little has been written regarding organizational theory or theories of management as they relate to writing center work (Heckelman 1998). Still, every day, we writing center administrators confront managerial challenges and seek to better our organization in terms of impact.

In this chapter, we have proposed that sensemaking ecologies for writing centers occurs through the copious amounts of data that we produce and the documentation that we create; however, at the moment, much of our sensemaking, like our documents, are inherited from those who've come before us—both in the field and in our respective center. It is time to look outside of our field for frameworks to assist in our sensemaking ecologies and to expand and refine our documentation practices. Learning to speak the organizational language of administrators, while also sensemaking independently of them, allows us to be better advocates of our centers and our field.

REFERENCES

Boquet, Elizabeth H. 1999. " 'Our Little Secret': A History of Writing Centers, Pre- to Post-Open Admissions." *College Composition and Communication* 50 (3): 463–482.

Brogle, Rob. 2013. "How to Avoid the Evils Within Customer Satisfaction Surveys." ISixSigma. https://www.isixsigma.com/methodology/voc-customer-focus/how-to-avoid-the-evils-within-customer-satisfaction-surveys/.

Buckland, Michael. 2013. "Document Theory: An Introduction." In *Records, Archives and Memory: Selected Papers from the Conference and School on Records, Archives and Memory Studies, University of Zadar, Croatia, May 2013*, Edited by Mirna Willer, Anne J. Gilliland and Marijana Tomić. Zadar: University of California, Berkeley. http://people.ischool.berkeley.edu/~buckland/zadardoctheory.pdf.

Buckland, Michael. 2017. "Encyclopedia of Knowledge Organization." *International Society for Knowledge Organization* 45 (5): 425–436. http://www.isko.org/cyclo/document.

Bugdal, Melissa, Kristina Reardon, and Thomas Deans. 2016. "Summing Up the Session: A Study of Student, Faculty, and Tutor Attitudes Toward Tutor Notes." *Writing Center Journal* 35 (3): 13–36.

Cardaro, Danielle. 2014. "Practical Uses for Session Reports Among Faculty: A Case Study." *Writing Lab Newsletter* 38 (9–10): 1–6.

Cogie, Jane. 1998. "In Defense of Conference Summaries: Widening the Research of Writing Center Work." *Writing Center Journal* 18 (2): 47–70.

Conway, Glenda. 1998. "Reporting Writing Center Sessions to Faculty: Pedagogical and Ethical Considerations." *Writing Lab Newsletter* 22 (8): 9–12.

Crump, Eric. 1993. "Voices from the Net: Sharing Records: Student Confidentiality and Faculty Relations." *Writing Lab Newsletter* 18 (2): 8–9.

Denny, Harry. 2010. *Facing the Center: Toward an Identity Politics of One-to-One Mentoring*. Logan: Utah State University Press.

Farazmand, Ali. 2002. "Introduction: The Multifaceted Nature of Modern Organizations." In *Modern Organizations: Theory and Practice*, edited by Ali Farazmand, xv–xxix. Westport, CT: Praeger.

Giaimo, Genie Nicole. 2017. "Focusing On the Blind Spots: RAD-Based Assessment of Students' Perceptions of A Community College Writing Center." *Praxis: A Writing Center Journal* 15 (1): 55–64.

Giaimo, Genie, Joseph Cheatle, Candace Hastings, and Christine Modey. 2018. "It's All in the Notes: What Session Notes Can Tell Us About the Work of Writing Centers." *Journal of Writing Analytics* 2:225–256.

Gitlin, Jonathan. 2008. "Establishing Career Platforms for Postdocs through Individual Development Plans." *Disease Models and Mechanisms* 1 (1): 1–3.

Goffnett, Sean P. 2014. "Steer Your Career: Employee Work Plans Feed into Organizational Success." *QP: Quality Progress The Official Publication of ASQ* 47 (1): 64–65.

Gofine, Miriam. 2012. "How Are We Doing? A Review of Assessments within Writing Centers." *Writing Center Journal* 32 (1): 39–49.

Hall, R. Mark. 2017. *Around the Texts of Writing Center Work: An Inquiry-Based Approach to Tutor Education*. Logan: Utah State University Press.

Harris, Muriel. 1990. "What's Up and What's In: Trends and Traditions in Writing Centers." *Writing Center Journal* 11 (1): 15–25.

Heckelman, Ronald. 1998. "The Writing Center as Managerial Site." *Writing Lab Newsletter* 23 (1): 1–4.

Henry, Nicholas. 2002. "Public, Nonprofit, and Private Organizations: Similarities and Differences." In *Modern Organizations: Theory and Practice*, edited by Ali Farazmand, 3–18. Westport, CT: Praeger.

Hernes, Tor, and Sally Maitlis. 2010. "Process, Sensemaking, and Organizing: An Introduction." In *Process, Sensemaking, and Organizing*, edited by Tor Hernes and Sally Maitlis, 27–37. Oxford: Oxford University Press.

Jackson, Kim. 1996. "Beyond Record-Keeping: Session Reports and Tutor Education." *Writing Lab Newsletter* 20 (6): 11–13.

Kalikoff, Beth. 2001. "From Coercion to Collaboration: A Mosaic Approach to Writing Center Assessment." *Writing Lab Newsletter* 26 (1): 5–7.

Kaye, Beverly. 2010. "IDP 2.0: The Future of the Development Dialogue." *T + D: Training and Development* 64 (1): 52–55.

King, Dennis J. 2005. "Humanitarian Knowledge Management." Paper presented at the Second International Information Systems for Crisis Response and Management Conference, Brussels, Belgium, April 17–20, 2005. http://citeseerx.ist.psu.edu/viewdoc/download?doi=10.1.1.455.913&rep=rep1&type=pdf.

Ko, Huaising C., and Randall J. Kimple. 2018. "The Resident Individual Development Plan as a Guide for Radiation Oncology Mentorship." *International Journal of Radiation Oncology, Biology, Physics* 101 (4): 786–788.

Krone, Diane, and Thomas Wenzel. 2016. "ChemIDP: Mapping Your Career." *Chemical and Engineering News* 94 (21): 36.

Larrance, Anneke J., and Barbara Brady. 1995. "A Pictogram of Writing Center Conference Follow-up." *Writing Lab Newsletter* 20 (4): 5–7.

Lerner, Neal. 2003. "Punishment and Possibility: Representing Writing Centers, 1939–1970." *Composition Studies* 31 (2): 53–72.

Little, Todd. 2010. "Understanding Knowledge Management: Developing a Foundation for Future Advising Practices." *NACADA Clearinghouse of Academic Advising Resources* para. 1–3. http://www.nacada.ksu.edu/Resources/Clearinghouse/View-Articles/Knowledge-management.aspx.

Lund, Niels Windfeld. 2011. "Document Theory." *Annual Review of Information Science and Technology* 43 (1): 1–55.

Lusthaus, Charles, Marie-Hélèn Adrien, Gary Anderson, Fred Carden, and George Pilinio Montalván. 2002. *Organizational Assessment: A Framework for Improving Performance*. Ottawa, Canada: International Development Research Centre.

MacNealy, Mary Sue. 1999. *Strategies for Empirical Research in Writing*. Boston: Allyn and Bacon.

Malenczyk, Rita. 2013. "'I Thought I'd Put That in to Amuse You': Tutor Reports as Organizational Narrative." *Writing Center Journal* 33 (1): 74–95.

Marcus, N. H. 2016. "The Individual Development Plan: A Tool to Help Graduate Students Assume Control of their Futures." *Oceanography* 29 (1): 31.

Mayer, Amy. 2011. "Easing the Transition." *BioScience* 61 (1): 14–17.

North, Stephen. 1984. "The Idea of a Writing Center." *College English* 46 (5): 433–446.

Pemberton, Michael. 1995. "Writing Center Ethics: Sharers and Seclusionists." *Writing Lab Newsletter* 20 (3): 13–14.

Reiff, Mary Jo, Anis Bawarshi, Michelle Ballif, and Christian Weisser. 2015. "Introduction." In *Ecologies of Writing Programs: Program Profiles in Context*, edited by Mary Jo Reiff, Anis Bawarshi, Michelle Ballif, and Christian Weisser. Anderson, SC: Parlor Press.

Rubens, Arthur, Gerald A. Schoenfeld, Bryan S. Schaffer, and Joseph S. Leah. 2018. "Self-Awareness and Leadership: Developing an Individual Strategic Professional Development Plan in an MBA Leadership Course." *The International Journal of Management Education* 16 (1): 1–13.

Salem, Lori. 2016. "Decisions . . . Decisions: Who Chooses to Use the Writing Center?" *Writing Center Journal* 35 (2): 147–171.

Schendel, Ellen, and William J. Macauley. 2012. *Building Writing Center Assessments That Matter*. Logan: Utah State University Press.

Sugarman, Nancy A. 2011. "Putting Yourself in Action: Individual Professional Development Plans." *YC Young Children* 66 (3): 27–33.

Sunstein, Bonnie. 1998. "Moveable Feasts, Liminal Spaces: Writing Centers and the State of In-Betweenness." *Writing Center Journal* 18 (2): 7–26.

Thompson, Isabelle. 2006. "Writing Center Assessment: Why and a Little How." *Writing Center Journal* 26 (1): 33–61.

Wallace, Ray, and Susan Wallace. 2010. "Growing Our Own: Writing Centers as Historically Fertile Fields for Professional Development." In *The Writing Center Director's Resource Book*, edited by Christina Murphy and Byron Stay, 45–52. New York: Routledge.

Weaver, Margaret. 2001. "Resistance is Anything but Futile: Some More Thoughts on Writing Conference Summaries." *Writing Center Journal* 21 (2): 35–56.

Weick, Karl E. 1995. *Sensemaking in Organizations*. Thousand Oaks, CA: SAGE Publications.

7
STORIES TO SUPPORT AND SUSTAIN A PROGRAM
Connections among the Library, WID, and the Writing Center

Susanmarie Harrington and Sue Dinitz

Writing programs exist as places, stories, and relationships. On our campus, the University of Vermont (UVM), the physical spaces for the writing programs are tucked in various buildings: tutoring and faculty development spaces in the library, TA and faculty offices in two different buildings, and classroom and other workshop spaces all over. We don't have a single formal writing program but, rather, a network of units, initiatives, and requirements that support writing, writers, and writing teachers: the graduate and undergraduate writing centers, a mentor program, a Writing in the Disciplines program, a foundational writing and information literacy requirement of courses in arts and sciences or honors, and librarians providing some instructional support for students and participating in faculty development. The faculty who oversee all these components don't all have common reporting lines or parallel titles; each of these features came into existence at a different moment in time. (Sue directed the Undergraduate Writing Center from 1983 to 2018, and Susanmarie has directed Writing in the Disciplines since 2008.) What unity exists comes from a common commitment to our disciplines, to our general education requirements, to UVM's teacher-scholar model, and the relationships we seek out and (re)forge among ourselves. This constant process of connecting and shaping relationships grows out of narration and interpretation of our experiences or a process of sensemaking. As we narrate our past and our present, we (re)interpret the institution and (re)create our path forward. Thus, our writing program is always creating and recreating itself: as one scholar of sensemaking notes, this process emphasizes "beginnings and emergings, which conveys a sense of ongoing forming and dissolving" (Weick 2012). Our writing program is always in process, and in this essay we

https://doi.org/10.7330/9781646424368.c007

explore why and how that happens. Our exploration highlights the role of stories in a writing program. Some other contributors to this volume—Genie Nicole Giaimo and Joseph Cheatle, who study documentation in the writing center, and Melissa Nicolas, who examines the role of union contracts in sensemaking—focus on texts as a vehicle for sensemaking; in this chapter, we look at the role of narrative and memory in the unfolding sense of our writing program.

LOCAL HISTORY: MAKING SENSE OF UVM'S PROGRAMMATIC EVOLUTION

While any writing program is likely to change over time, UVM's forming and dissolving of writing programs over time is somewhat unusual for a state institution. Unlike its peers in other states, UVM doesn't have a director of composition or a unit that unifies approaches to writing curricula. In that respect, UVM isn't that different from many smaller institutions (particularly those whose approach to first-year composition has centered on disciplinary writing seminars). Even in larger institutions, however, the very nature of writing across the curriculum depends on decentralization: when faculty in all departments are responsible for teaching writing, the program itself lives everywhere, and the simple fact of a large writing program doesn't immediately translate into a unified campus sense of what writing is or does. Thus, UVM's diffuse writing programs illuminate dynamics that are at work to some extent on most American campuses. People who teach writing in so many different contexts are likely to have very different understandings of what writing is and how it's learned, and there's a lack of clarity about how faculty responsibility for teaching writing can be systematically engaged. What's required in the face of such ambiguity is a process of making meaning, and so the concept of *sensemaking* becomes a valuable lens for looking at how such decentralized writing programs are sustained and transformed over time. Attention to sensemaking helps us see how networks of faculty and administrators make meaning of their past experiences, with an eye on future action. This chapter explores how UVM's writing initiatives have made sense of their roles through evolution by looking at three important moments in the evolution of UVM's writing initiatives: the creation of Writing Across the Curriculum at UVM, a shift in the administrative placement of the Writing Center, and the transitions necessary upon the retirement of a long-time writing director. Each of these moments offers insights into how UVM makes sense of writing.

Sensemaking is inherently retrospective, constituted of contextualized reflection. As Rita Malenczyk notes in the introduction to this volume, sensemaking concerns groups or organizations and the ways they come to understand the activities within them. Sensemaking concerns "the interplay of action and interpretations rather than the influence of evaluation on choice" (Weick, Sutcliffe, and Obstfeld 2005, 409). As we look back, "whatever is occurring at the moment will influence what is discovered" (Weick 1995, 26), and the present moment (both in substance and in emotion) affects what we see as we look back. In our current decentralized environment, in a budgetary era that struggles with tuition shortfalls and declining state funding, we see funding sources as a major element in UVM's storied WID/WAC history. UVM has twice sought to invigorate its formal writing programs through outside hires. In 1983, Toby Fulwiler left Michigan Tech for UVM, where he established the Faculty Writing Workshop, a cross between a faculty writing retreat and a WAC seminar. His work made UVM a WAC leader until his retirement in 2002. Six years later, Susanmarie came to UVM to establish the Writing in the Disciplines program, a successor to, but not a replacement for, the work that Fulwiler had established. As the Writing in the Disciplines program established itself in 2008, we looked to the past and asked, "What did the Fulwiler WAC program do?" We delved into stories of the past, learning what faculty development meant in the 1980s and 1990s.

At UVM, Fulwiler engaged faculty across campus to create both a community of scholars interested in supporting faculty writing practices as well as a community of teachers interested in exploring applications of WAC theory. The Faculty Writing Workshop offered two-day workshops, multiple times a year, that gave faculty the chance to write and reflect on their teaching and to learn about student-centered approaches to integrating writing in any discipline (these workshops are described in *Programs that Work* by Dickerson, Fulwiler, and Steffens 1990). Fulwiler's workshops focused more on expressive and informal writing—he was particularly known for his work on journals across the curriculum (Fulwiler 1987)—although the key point of his workshops was always that "it's hard to get improved *writing* without first (or simultaneously) getting improved *learning*. It simply cannot happen the other way around" (Dickerson, Fulwiler, and Steffens 1990, 54, emphasis in original). Participants in Fulwiler's workshops testify to the impact that work had on both formal and informal writing in the discipline.

When Susanmarie arrived at UVM, the thought of stepping into Toby Fulwiler's shoes was occasionally daunting. It can be hard to follow in the footsteps of such a well-known figure (that said, Fulwiler's legacy created a network of senior faculty who were quite interested in seeing what a new era of WAC/WID would bring, which was a wonderful welcome). Yet our current context leads us to look back and see the storied Fulwiler years with more nuance. Fulwiler's enormous achievements in the field masked a lack of institutionalized structure at UVM. Fulwiler had been hired in anticipation of a first-year composition requirement that never materialized. While he was known in the field of writing studies for his WAC work, Fulwiler's most consistently institutionalized (as in, predictably funded) role at UVM was as coordinator of the English Department's first-year composition course (required of about half the undergraduate degree programs) and as coordinator of the English TA practicum. A fully structured, regularly funded campus-wide writing program never happened.

Looking back at the Fulwiler era thus is both cautionary and inspirational. Its signature program was the Faculty Writing Project. This initiative introduced faculty to the theory and practice of writing processes with an eye toward influencing both pedagogy and faculty writing. Its main incentive was its inherent benefit: full-time faculty who were interested in writing gravitated toward the writing retreats and other programs that encouraged "writing to learn" with a host of strategies. The Faculty Writing Project's modest and inconsistent budget drew support from many units across campus, year by year, to offer WAC workshops on campus and writing retreats off campus. Those workshops, a hallmark of professional development at UVM from 1987 on, had a massive institutional impact. They were universally beloved, and they got faculty from all corners of campus involved in writing. They spawned pedagogical and scholarly collaborations. In a sense, the minimally funded Faculty Writing Project really was pure WAC: without funding, the only thing it could do was build a network of the willing. Even now, there are senior faculty on campus whose earliest professional experiences were transformed by their encounters with the FWP, and the stories they tell about that work has generated a lasting belief in the power of writing to learn. Given that there were few other outlets for faculty discussion of teaching across department lines, the FWP built an inspiring network in which faculty from history, psychology, English, and beyond joined Fulwiler in leading workshops. And that foundation, as we'll see, is what lifts up writing on campus today.

Looking around at other state institutions, it's easy to ask, "Why didn't UVM ever make more administrative structures around writing?" It's also easy to see the one-person WAC program that got erased upon

Fulwiler's retirement as an institutional failure. For seven years following his retirement, UVM had no formal WAC program. Yet sensemaking doesn't require continuous action for meaning to emerge. Weick (1995) reminds us that "the act that never gets done, gets done too late, gets dropped too soon, or for which the time never seems right is seldom a senseless act. More often, its meaning seems all too clear" (37). The Faculty Writing Project, definitely an act dropped too soon, is a clear precursor for understanding a writing program as constructed from faculty collaboration, not from formal administrative structures. In that light, UVM does devote considerable resources to writing, even if its formal administrative structures aren't cultivated. UVM today has a Writing in the Disciplines program, Writing Centers (both undergraduate and graduate), and a Foundational Writing and Information Literacy requirement that asks students to take one of three courses, depending on their degree plan. Students have a curricular requirement, but any sort of professional development around writing is wholly voluntary. Attention to writing—writing pedagogy and writing curriculum—draws together faculty and students who want to pay attention. And that attention is supported in large part because of stories that have circulated from the Fulwiler era. We might look back and wish that our institution's past attention to writing had set up larger and more permanent structures, but we see in the Fulwiler period the power of voluntary participation. What Fulwiler accomplished, in the words of one colleague who remembers attending the workshops, was "electric." As Bronwyn Williams notes in his chapter in this volume, emotions have a powerful force in the social work of sensemaking. "OMG I never thought of that before," one former department chair says Fulwiler workshops made him say, over and over. Those workshops "made me rethink the ways in which I wanted to present myself in the classroom" (another colleague says working with Toby made his life "more interesting and more fun"). The history of our writing program has an emotional core as well as an intellectual one—and what enabled that expansive fun to happen was precisely the lack of structure. In a sense, as Christy Wenger notes in her exploration of distributed leadership on campus, relational leadership, or the mutual influences of people in different roles, creates power. At UVM, WAC spread on the campus not because of a general education requirement, not because of a legislature mandating outcomes assessment, not because of preparation for accreditation, but simply because people wanted to come, and the Faculty Writing Project created space and time for people to retreat from campus and consider their pedagogy and their own writing. It was a time when *fun* or *pleasure* were key characteristics of the campus. There was a playful freedom in stepping back from the regular work of teaching—often stepping off-campus, in fact, for workshops by the lake or in the mountains—and thinking about cross-disciplinary strategies for writing to learn as well as making room for faculty's own writing.

Writing programs today exist in a different world, though. Financial pressures are different, publication requirements for tenure and promotion have increased, the scholarship of teaching and learning is valued unevenly in departmental promotion guidelines, the nature of our student body has changed, and the structure of the university itself has evolved. Indeed, reminiscences today about those lakeside retreats function to remind us how much things have changed. In this environment, a story about the faculty writing retreat up at Bolton Mountain or by the water is told to invite a negative comparison to today's environment, where an emphasis on publication alone seems to be putting pressure on UVM's teacher-scholar faculty model. Institutional priorities don't seem to welcome intensive attention on pedagogy, the comparison with the off-campus retreats implies. In the imagined past, faculty teaching writing and faculty writing were two sides of the same coin. Faculty could spend time with their colleagues and have that time recognized as valuable. Tempting as it might be to relocate our services to a mountain lodge and invite faculty to join us, that's not possible. But the institutional memories of those mountain writing retreats sustain our current work (since they have created a commitment to writing to learn that pervades our campus) even as they help explain the contrast in our current environment. They also guide a core principle of our current WID workshops: hospitality. We're not unique in using food as an incentive for workshop participants! But we strive to make our meeting room, which is named for Toby Fulwiler, a welcoming and hospitable place. With flowers on the table, well-chosen local lunches or snacks, and comfortable furniture, we strive to make even an hour-long workshop have an element of retreat. The top floor of the library may lack the views of Bolton Mountain, but it can provide respite from the busy campus routines and invite reflection and pedagogical attention. Stories of the Fulwiler era serve multiple functions as we make sense of our role on campus.

MAKING SENSE OF COLLABORATION

The story we tell most often about WID and the Writing Center emphasizes collaboration. Sometimes—despite Sue's long tenure as UVM's Undergraduate Writing Center director—faculty mix us up, and it's pretty common for faculty to be unsure whether WID (a relative newcomer, directed by Susanmarie for ten years now) and the Writing Center are one unit or two. These stories of momentary confusion of our units don't distress us, for they signal that other faculty recognize the close connections here. And, indeed, in our scholarship we have recognized the ways that collaboration between the Writing Center and WID makes every aspect of our work better. We've previously written about the collaborations between writing centers and writing in the disciplines, emphasizing the ways tutor stories can infuse the ways WID works with faculty (Harrington, Dinitz, et al. 2016). Working alone, the writing center amasses a great deal of knowledge about how students experience the curriculum, but that experience remains lore, accessible via anecdotes, shared perhaps randomly or erratically on an institutional level. Formal collaborations can help bridge knowledge gaps and are hugely valuable. But formal collaborations are only part of what makes decentralized writing programs work. Intellectual, practical, and emotional connections also play a role in creating the living web among sites of writing on our campus. What makes a network sustainable, as Cox, Galin, and Melzer note, is resiliency: the ability to respond to stresses and stimuli and change. They note that "curricular ecology," or the "relationship between social and curricular practices" (2018, 38) on a campus, have an enormous influence on the prospects for WAC/WID—and, we would add, the writing center. What creates and sustains resilience? The interplay between space, people, and structure.

Our main space is the Howe Memorial Library, home to writers of all types. It's April as we first draft this essay, and the end of the semester nears. Students in all kinds of courses are in the library studying for exams, consulting with librarians, and working on papers, projects, and presentations. Table space is harder to come by, as students spread out course materials and laptops. Computers in common work areas are busy into the evenings, and anyone walking through the library can feel the tension rising. There's an intensity to the work going on. As we walk to or from our office space up on the third floor, we'll pass students working in multiple languages, and we'll see graphing and writing and slides. We see librarians conferring with students and running classroom sessions, helping connect students with resources. Inquiry is happening all around.

So much of this inquiry involves writing, and the library is also home to spaces that offer support with writing. In ours, the ground floor is now home to the Writing Centers: a beautiful open reception area welcomes writers, who have their choice of more and less private tutoring spaces, for individuals or groups. Candy bowls and a tea cart offer sustenance. The Graduate Writing Center has its own vibe, with small consultation areas and more of an office feel. Large posters highlighting graduate students' own advice about writing processes center students in the space. Here, in the heart of the library, the space is for students talking to students, helping each other develop whatever sort of writing project is at hand.

Our office space is on the top floor of the library, and it includes three faculty offices for writing program administrators: the Undergraduate and Graduate Writing Center directors and the Writing in the Disciplines director, along with an office for our staff colleague. The biggest portion of our space is the Fulwiler Room, a large working space with comfy red chairs around the outside of the room and conference tables on wheels in the middle. Come during the day, and you'll see faculty working together in there, learning about writing; come in the evenings, and you may find group tutoring or WID mentors working with students in a space that works for workshops and meetings. With the mix of tables and soft chairs and the easy availability of coffee, tea, and snacks, it's a pretty comfortable working space, with large photographs of Vermont's landscape and Toby Fulwiler's gardens creating a pleasing backdrop in a space that works for large and small groups. Make a space, and they will come. Our current space calls back to the Faculty Writing Project days of the past, while literally bringing people into the library, where our proximity to the Center for Teaching and Learning creates a new hub for faculty development.

We're fortunate to be in the library, the intellectual crossroads of the campus. Our being here is an accident of timing: in 2007, the university decided to establish a WID program, reporting to the provost, in order to provide some focused attention to writing in the curriculum during a period of faculty expansion. Finally, UVM's WAC efforts would have a space, a budget (for both programming and a director). It so happened that faculty study carrels—great places for faculty on sabbatical to bring their typewriters for a year's leave—were sitting empty and a graduate student lounge nearby had been abandoned, and this space in the library became available for the new WID program. At the time of Susanmarie's hire, this was the only space available (a possibility in the administrative building didn't pan out), so into the library we went. In the library, but not of the library, we moved in. It took several months for locks to be put on the doors, but eventually, our space—with fresh paint, new carpet, and new furniture—opened for business.

We focus on the space because its location emphasizes an important aspect of writing on campus: it simultaneously belongs everywhere and nowhere. Our space here in the library is contained within the library, yet not planned and controlled in the library. So too is writing happening within classrooms and building, yet not fully planned and controlled in those spaces either. And it is our space that sponsors the stories.

In *The Everyday Writing Center*, Geller et al. (2007) emphasize "ways of acting with and for one another" as "ways of knowing . . . as a gift to be passed on and passed around" (9). They explore "the betwixt-and-between state in which so much of [their] work must be done" (9), and we find their emphasis on "everydayness" as a mode of producing knowledge to be inspirational. Their work reveals leadership that comes not from structural authority but from pragmatic action as an enactment of a mission (11). What is our mission? The Writing Center's mission statement emphasizes supporting students at any point, in any kind of writing project, supporting writers' development in an inclusive, productive environment. WID emphasizes making writing a significant part of students' experience beyond the first year. What we have in common is an interest in the whole writer and the whole faculty member—we want to encourage capacious approaches to writing. And our space is essential to the realization of these missions. It's the space that harkens back to the Fulwiler era—it may not offer lakeside calm, but it offers comfy furniture, it offers welcoming tea, and it invites faculty to rethink, for a moment, their relation to institutional culture as they collaborate with colleagues on pedagogy.

Our location in the library creates natural neighbors: we walk through the reference area on the way up to our own offices, and for many years the reference desk was directly in front of the Writing Center's main tutoring location. Another story that has become instructive concerns the location of the Writing Center: once upon a time, when a librarian retired, the library offered the space to the Writing Center. Sue eagerly accepted, as this gave the Writing Center an outpost in the center of campus, in its academic heart. This act by the library—a generous offer of support to an underbudgeted writing center—enabled the young Writing Center to develop a presence outside the tutoring space within student affairs. It also established a connection with the library that has grown over time. Sue cultivated relationships with the reference librarians in order to keep the space working smoothly—and fast-forward a few decades and the Writing Center and the library are partners in supporting a new general education initiative linking writing and information literacy. Information literacy work (led by librarian Daisy Benson) has changed the shape of our tutor training course as well as affected our annual tutor training program. The story of the library's gift of space similarly infuses the relationship between WID and the library, as it laid a foundation for mutual exchange of support and expertise. WID included librarians in its annual WID Institute from the start: Daisy participated in the first one and slowly grew into a cofacilitator of the weeklong workshop over time. The story of the library's offer of space reminds us that colocation is a gift. We've been able to take our space, and the casual conversations that happen within it, and grow programs together. The alignment of the Writing Center and the reference desk has led some librarians to consider the value of a research center, where librarians could do one-on-one consultations in the space vacated by the Writing Center. We've also begun to develop a peer-mentoring program focused on information literacy, inspired by the Writing Center. Being able to see each other work helps us find commonalities.

MAKING SENSE OF REPORTING LINES

Our shared space also helped shape a story at a crisis point we almost didn't realize was upon us. From its beginning, the Writing Center had been part of the student affairs side of campus. Opened in the early 1980s as a residential learning community in the dorms, the Writing Center was part of the Learning Annex, a tutoring space housed within a residence-hall complex. Its directors were originally hired as English Department faculty, whose Writing Center time was bought out by Student Affairs or other grant programs. The Writing Center operated relatively autonomously within the Learning Annex structure, reporting to the director of Academic Support Programs, who in turn reported to the dean of students. The Writing Center didn't have parallels in the Learning Annex—the other programs that hired students as subject-area tutors or as more general learning skills tutors didn't have as extensive a training as the Writing Center's two-course sequence, and the other programs were led by staff positions, not by a faculty director. The Learning Annex was a happy home for many years, and its infrastructure enabled the Writing Center's appointment calendar to be centrally managed (a boon given that the Writing Center had virtually no money for anything but tutor wages).

A 2009 reorganization of the Learning Annex into the Center for Academic Success created a different network of titles and reporting lines, and part of that process aimed to make all the tutoring services analogous—which meant that the new organizational chart would have to make the writing center director a staff position. The communication about this pending change happened over our heads, in communications at the deans' and chairs' levels. Our first inkling of the change came with a phone call from the English Department chair to Susanmarie: "Do you get along with Sue Dinitz?" The department chair, hearing of this proposed change, made up a story for what was motivating it. The only thing that made sense, he thought, was that the new WID program was somehow flexing its muscle to force a change in the Writing Center's place on campus. This story having nothing whatsoever to do with the working relationship between us specifically, and WID and writing centers in general, it took Susanmarie a few beats to realize that the chair had a serious concern.

We immediately realized this reorganization was a serious threat to the Writing Center. In many ways, the Writing Center didn't fit into the Learning Annex. Writing center work is an organized service-learning experience—from the two-course sequence to biweekly tutor meetings, the tutors are connecting their work with scholarly frameworks in writing studies. Writing center work focuses attention on making better writers, not better papers; course-based tutoring focuses more directly on completing assignments. Both sorts of support services are important for students, and both sorts of services require appropriate leadership. We feared that a switch to a staff directorship would threaten the Writing Center's ability to train its tutors through a two-course sequence (other changes were making it more difficult for staff to teach courses, and separating the director from the courses would weaken the director's connection to the daily work of the center). Overall, this seemed like a proposal that would threaten the Writing Center.

On the dean of students' side of campus, there was another story being told: budget reductions necessitated rethinking of the tutoring services and a reimagining of student services' hierarchy. This would create efficiencies and conveniences, as all tutoring services would be clearly and fairly connected in one structure. The problem with this story, of course, is that it treats writing center work as equivalent to subject-area tutoring. It treats expertise with a subject (e.g., calculus) as equivalent to expertise with tutoring skills and as equivalent to understanding of writing processes and theories. We set to work creating an alternative set of stories that would enable our administrative superiors to recognize WID and the Writing Center's work. We needed to be more than characters or resources in someone else's story.

Creating a story where there wasn't one before can be a challenge. We started listing everything we thought our supervisors needed to know about the relationship between supporting faculty teaching writing and supporting student writers:

- Peer learning is essential for students to progress in the disciplines.
- Writing centers support faculty too.
- WID work with faculty and writing center work with students all depend on the same assumptions, that
  - Writing is learned over time.
  - Writing is learned anew in each new context.
  - Writers need feedback.
  - Writers need good direction.
- Tutors and writing teachers alike need to be cognizant of the theories about writing that shape their actions.
- WID programs and writing centers are rooted in writing studies scholarship.

For each of these points, we had stories to tell—stories of faculty who'd called the Writing Center and ended up working with WID, stories of faculty who had come to WID workshops and ended up building projects with the Writing Center, and stories of faculty who developed new ways of talking with and about students as a result of their work with us. As we told these stories, we came to imagine a new structure, one in which the Writing Center could become part of Writing in the Disciplines.

This story made sense of our work in a new way: drawing on our spatial connections, we helped our chair see that the conversations the Writing Center was having with students could be advantageous for the WID program's work with faculty (and vice-versa). Our beginning plans for a WID mentor program, in which experienced tutors were placed in disciplinary courses, highlighted the need for close WID/Writing Center connections—and, in fact, the mentor program became key to others understanding these connections.

The negotiations around the move eventually revealed a structural weakness with the Writing Center budget: it didn't fully fund the director's salary (which, as it turned out, had been cobbled together from various funding streams on the student-services side, and changes in grant administration left the position only seven-eighths funded). The WID program's development of the mentor program became the final one-eighth of the director salary, as it moved over to the academic side of campus. And in this transition, support for writing—peer support and faculty support—became recognized as an intellectual part of the university's mission, rooted in the disciplines, and situated in the academic organization of the university.

LOOKING AHEAD: STORIES FOR THE FUTURE

We finish this essay in another era of transition: Sue has begun her well-earned retirement, there's a new Writing Center director, and we begin another era of making sense of where we've been and where we're going. Conscious that a new director must chart her own course and build new routines and relationships with WID and beyond, we consider this entire year a turning point. We find ourselves reaching for stories as reference points for tough transitions. For example, in making decisions about how to match writing center tutors with faculty in our writing fellows program, we have wrestled with balancing scheduling demands with disciplinary matches—which sometimes means evaluating how a close-but-not-exact match in a discipline can be a foundation for productive fellows work if the tutor with matching disciplinary expertise is unavailable at the class time. We look back to stories about how Sue solved similar problems; those stories function less as directions for us now than as a reminder that Sue developed what appeared to be an unerring ability to read faculty and tutors over time, with each interaction. Our Sue stories keep her influence alive as a happy inspiration, even as they remind us that a new director, making new choices, is right at home in the role. Stories are a core part of our sensemaking, and they keep us always reinventing ourselves.

So, what, in the end, is a writing program? Earlier in our careers, we would have offered a simple answer: a writing program is the living embodiment of a shared curriculum. Our experiences at UVM have led us to a different conclusion: what makes a writing program is an ongoing sensemaking process, in which stories guide the ways we see, and see again, our past—all the while allowing us to see our way forward too.

REFERENCES

Cox, Michelle, Jeffrey R. Galin, and Dan Melzer, eds. 2018. *Sustainable WAC: A Whole Systems Approach to Launching and Developing Writing across the Curriculum Programs*. Urbana, IL: National Council of Teachers of English.

Dickerson, Mary Jane, Toby Fulwiler, and Henry Steffens. 1990. "The University of Vermont." In *Programs That Work: Models and Methods for Writing across the Curriculum*, edited by Toby Fulwiler and Art Young, 45–63. Portsmouth, NH: Boynton/Cook.

Fulwiler, Toby, ed. 1987. *The Journal Book*. 1st ed. Portsmouth, NH: Boynton/Cook.

Geller, Anne Ellen, Michele Eodice, Frankie Condon, Meg Carroll, and Elizabeth H. Boquet. 2007. *The Everyday Writing Center: A Community of Practice*. Logan: Utah State University Press. https://doi.org/10.2307/j.ctt4cgmkj.

Harrington, Susanmarie, and Sue Dinitz, with contributions by tutors Rob Benner, Laura Davenport, Bronwen Hudson, and Kathryn Warrender. 2016. "Turning Stories from the Writing Center into Useful Knowledge: Writing Centers, WID Programs, and Partnerships for Change." In *Writing Programs, Collaborations, and Partnerships: Working*

Across Boundaries, edited by Lynee Lewis Gaillet and Alice Myatt, 141–160. London: Palgrave/Macmillan.

Weick, Karl E. 1995. *Sensemaking in Organizations*. Foundations for Organizational Science. Thousand Oaks, CA: Sage Publications.

Weick, Karl E. 2012. "Organized Sensemaking: A Commentary on Processes of Interpretive Work." *Human Relations* 65 (1): 141–153. https://doi.org/10.1177/0018726711424235.

Weick, Karl E., Kathleen M. Sutcliffe, and David Obstfeld. 2005. "Organizing and the Process of Sensemaking." *Organization Science* 16 (4): 409–421. https://doi.org/10.1287/orsc.1050.0133.

8
CASCADING TEXTS AND CAT'S CRADLES
An Institutional Ethnographic Approach to Understanding the Textual Production of Unionized Labor

Melissa Nicolas

INTRODUCTION

The following language appears in the University of California's (UC) union contract[1] governing the work of full-time faculty who are not in tenure-eligible positions:[2]

> The title Lecturer, whether used as an only title or as an additional title, shall be assigned to a professionally qualified appointee not under consideration for appointment in the Professorial series . . . whose services are contracted for certain teaching duties. (University n.d., Article 5, Section B #1, 11)

UC's lecturers are represented by a chapter of the American Federation of Teachers, and all ten campuses within the UC system are covered by the same contract, also known as the *Memorandum of Understanding* (MOU). While colleges and universities across the country have their local, institutionally specific definitions of the word *faculty*,[3] what is worth noting about UC's contract is that lecturers are defined by what they are not: lecturers are *not* considered for professorial (read: tenure-track) appointments. In regular campus and system-wide correspondence, lecturers are often referred to as non-senate faculty (NSF),[4] so even while the language of university business identifies lecturers as faculty, the "non" before their title is a constant reminder of what lecturers are not: they are *not* senate faculty.

I begin with the explication of just one sentence of a detailed contract to orient readers to the project of this chapter. Institutional texts, like labor contracts, affect the everyday work of writing programs by framing and shaping our labor in ways that we usually don't question because these "boss texts" construct the very parameters of the work we do. In

https://doi.org/10.7330/9781646424368.c008

terms of sensemaking, as Rita Malenczyk explains in the introduction to this volume, "much goes on in the working lives of . . . faculty" that we may not always be aware of but may impact "how writing is taught and delivered." In the above example, the MOU creates the category of non-senate faculty and then, for over two hundred pages, coordinates the work of these faculty in ways that naturalize the category so that non-senate faculty become a group in need of their own governance structure and rules and regulations that are set apart from those of senate faculty. Understanding how texts such as the MOU coordinate writing program work is a sensemaking project that foregrounds and exposes the ruling relations that are operant in our day-to-day activities. Through mapping ruling relations and understanding boss texts, we may be able, as Malenczyk explains, "to harness those interactions for more effective administration."

Ruling relations, according to Dorothy Smith (2005), are the "extraordinary yet ordinary complex of relations that are textually mediated, that connect us across space and time and organize our everyday lives" (10). Even though ruling relations play a central role in structuring our day-to-day work lives, they are often not visible precisely because of their ubiquity and capacity to naturalize what happens every day. Most frequently, ruling relations are codified in some sort of document: a memo, a policy, a form, or a job description. What gives these texts the capacity to shape individual experiences is that the texts themselves are replicable across sites, "coordinating someone's action *here* with someone else's' *there*" (Campbell and Gregor 2004, 33; Smith and Turner 2014). This replicability across sites gives texts the power to create facts, and facts often arise in response to texts (G. Smith 2014). The fact the MOU creates is that some faculty in the UC system will have tenure and voting rights, and some will not.

Another reason ruling relations can hide in plain sight is because the texts that carry them need to be activated by people using them before the ruling relations become operant. In other words, one cannot simply point to a text and say, "A-ha! I have discovered the ruling relationship here." Instead, one has to begin with how a real individual takes up a text in order to discover how that text works in the everyday by the people who use it. So, while ruling relations are "constituted externally to particular people and places" (D. Smith 2005, 13), they "are not done to people, nor do they just happen to people. Rather, people actively constitute [ruling] relations" (Campbell and Gregor 2004, 31). Ruling relations are powerful because they arise at the intersection of an institutional text and the activation of that text.

A university system's union contract is an example of a text that coordinates actions through its replicability. In the UC system, the MOU is reproduced across ten separate campuses and is taken up daily, hourly, and minute-by-minute, structuring the daily realities of not only the faculty covered by it but also the work of countless other university employees. Each campus is held to the provisions of the contract through the grievance process. No one really enjoys grievances: they are time-consuming, usually (though not always) adversarial, sometimes hostile, potentially expensive, and can be a death knell for morale—for all parties. Therefore, the contract necessitates a cascade of subsequent policies and procedures—that is, texts—to standardize the ways faculty are treated in order to avoid any real or perceived favoritism or the application of unequal or discriminatory evaluation criteria, among other potentially problematic situations. To accomplish this one-size-fits-all goal, the MOU requires specificity, clarity, and precision in creating policies and procedures, and one of the most important things to do to avoid grievances is to codify practices and employ them unilaterally (see Kahn 2013).[5]

In this chapter, I explore the ruling relations in one writing program in the UC system vis-à-vis the MOU by using concepts borrowed from institutional ethnography (IE). IE is a methodology that is concerned with relations, not with universalizing theories that turn people into "*objects* of investigation and explanation" (D. Smith 2005, 22; emphasis in original). The project of IE is understanding how people—as the doers of actions, with real, embodied, and lived experiences—participate in and make sense of institutional discourse. IE enables researchers to look at the material and ideological underpinnings of writing programs by focusing attention on how and under what conditions our everyday work gets done. As a tool for sensemaking, IE asks some critical questions: "What actually lies below our discourses? How do they gloss over or respond to the conditions that have produced them? How do our discourses actually mobilize the work of our programs?" (LaFrance and Nicolas 2012, 146)

In what follows, I attempt to answer these questions about my previous writing program by investigating the way that MOU functions as a boss text—a dominant frame—for structuring the everyday work in and of the program, much like the document analysis Genie Nicole Giaimo and Joseph Cheatle perform in their chapter on writing center ecologies (this volume). After offering examples of the utility of institutional ethnography as a methodology, I turn to a particular section of the MOU concerning personnel actions to illustrate how just one piece of this framing document reveals, in its activation, the way labor was constructed and counted in this program. In these ways, I hope to demonstrate how IE as a methodology can be a powerful tool for helping writing programs make sense of both their day-to-day activities as well as the institutional values that are embedded in their work.

INSTITUTIONAL ETHNOGRAPHY AND SENSEMAKING

Institutional ethnography is a situated methodology that is concerned with individuals and their relationships to the documents and texts that coordinate their work (Campbell and Gregor 2004; LaFrance and Nicolas 2012; Smith and Turner 2014). As such:

> [Texts] are never to be treated as objects of research in and of themselves nor as separate from how they coordinate people's doings. They [texts] must be conceived as occurring in definite actual settings of people's everyday/everynight living. . . . Institutional ethnographies exploring the complex and varied social relations are discovering and making observable just how texts enter into, organize, shape, and coordinate people's doings as they/we participate in the objectifying relations of ruling. (Smith and Turner 2014, 5)

An institutional ethnographer looks for "the interplay between structures and agency [as the] key to the social organization of lived experience" (Holstein and Gubrium 2011, 351). A foundational concept in IE is that, while texts exert tremendous influence on the everyday lives of individuals, the texts themselves are only understood by examining how real people take up, or "activate," them. In other words, an institutional ethnographer only considers texts *in relationship* to how those texts are operant (Holstein and Gubrium 2011; LaFrance and Nicolas 2012, 2013; Smith and Turner 2014).[6]

IE is pliable enough to help researchers uncover ruling relations from multiple activation points and, as such, is useful for mapping the many ways WPAs, writing faculty, and students make sense of this thing called a writing program.[7] After all, writing programs do not exist as atextual, disembodied sites. Without texts that bring writing programs into existence[8]—a general education curriculum, for example—and faculty, students, and writing program administrators taking up these texts through teaching, learning, and administrating, there would be nothing we would recognize or call the "writing program." (See Harrington and Dinitz, this volume, for an interesting discussion of the ways the lack of institutional texts erase programs.) In IE, some institutional texts such as the MOU are considered boss texts—that is, texts that govern and, in their activation, give rise to many other texts. Boss texts hold within them the ruling relations that situate people within an institutional framework.

In an institutional ethnographic study of her own writing center, Michelle Miley (2017) begins by considering the institutional documents—the boss texts—that were responsible for re-establishing her writing center, moving it into a visible and comfortable space, and creating her tenure-track position. In the neoliberal academy,[9] the allocation of physical space and a tenure-track faculty line for the new writing center could be interpreted, as Miley initially did, as an institutional acknowledgment of the importance of writing and support for that writing. However, despite the largesse[10] of Miley's institution, her new position and new writing center was far from utopian, even though on paper—in the language of neoliberalism—it should have been. It is in this dissonant moment that Miley decides to "look up," to "enlarge the scope of what is visible" (D. Smith 2005, 29), in order to map how those documents were being activated by the people doing the work. By looking up, what Miley calls "studying up," she begins to see the documents from the standpoint of the people whose work is organized by them. She begins to understand the ruling relations that are operant in the activation of these documents—relations that weren't exposed by traditional textual analysis. Indeed, it is once Miley starts asking the writing center's stakeholders how their work lives are structured by these documents that she starts to uncover a multilayered story that complicates the easy evolutionary narrative the official texts create. The story Miley uncovers is one of suspicion, fear, curiosity, resentment, confusion, appreciation, and generosity. Not all the writing center stakeholders, including those who publicly support its new form, align themselves with the institutional narrative of progress. Through IE, Miley is able to articulate moments of disruption, resistance, and pushback even as the stakeholders comply with the mandated changes to the writing center.

Like Miley, R. Mark Hall (2017) uses "the mundane documents of everyday writing center work" (Hall 2017, 14) to understand the "conceptual frameworks" operant in his writing center (Hall 2017, 4). In a chapter focused on session report forms, for example, Hall uncovers his tutors' attitudes about filling out these forms, and he is then able to have productive conversations about who should be filling out the forms and why, as well as what his tutors' beliefs are about confidentiality and tutor-student-teacher communication. The majority of Hall's study is a textual/rhetorical analysis of the efficacy of everyday documents and what data those documents might hold. While Hall's focus on ordinary texts and their usage is akin to the project of institutional ethnography, an institutional ethnographer would take her inquiry down a slightly different path, focusing on the way the texts under consideration actually shape the day-to-day work of the writing center. For example, an institutional ethnographer might ask: how do the tutor session reports forms construct, manage, and coordinate the work of tutors, clients, staff, and faculty?

Two studies, one by Geller and Denny (2013)[11] and the other by LaFrance and Nicolas (2013, 2012) do take the institutional ethnographic turn when looking at the everyday text of a job description for the ways that institutional rank designations (tenure track or administrative professional) impact the work lives of writing center professionals. Both of these studies begin in the everyday of real people working in actual writing center contexts. Looking up (or "studying up," as Miley (2017) says), these studies map out the ways that faculty and staff take up "writing center director" in particular ways. Research, for example, has a different weight and currency for faculty than for staff. Indeed, as LaFrance and Nicolas (2013) point out, the institutional rank designation in the job description even coordinates where someone's body is during the course of the day, with faculty directors being able to come and go as they please and professional administrators being expected to be physically in their centers for forty hours per week (LaFrance and Nicolas 2013, 11–12).

One of the greatest benefits of an IE approach is that institutional texts, such as those examined in these studies, "are not left standing or endowed with agency. . . . The focus is always on uncovering what people are actually doing, and the activity and coordination that are implicit in such terms" (Smith and Turner 2014, 8). By using IE, these studies showcase not only how texts structure everyday work but also how the work of those texts is carried out in real time, by real people, in their actual places of work. That is, instead of agency just being located in institutional texts, IE also call on us to look at the ways in which individuals working within the texts also are cocreating them. Specifically, in the next section I examine the ways activating the university's MOU reveals ruling relations in the writing program through the creation of a set of cascading texts.

CASCADING TEXTS

In my former writing program, lecturers (NSFs) are initially appointed to a series of one- or two-year renewable contracts. In their sixth year of employment, lecturers are eligible and must (per the MOU) undergo an excellence review, which, if successful, will grant them continuing lecturer status. According to the MOU, if as a result of the Excellence Review the NSF is deemed excellent, and the NSF has performed service in the 18th quarter, 12th semester or 24th fiscal quarter in the same department, program, or unit, the NSF shall have Continuing status[.] Conversely, if, as a result of this review, the University determines that the NSF is not qualified to perform anticipated responsibilities at an excellent level in the department, program, or unit, the NSF will be released at the end of her/his appointment. (University n.d, Article 7b, sect. A 4–5, 23)

The continuing lecturer rank is not tenure—although there are many misperceptions about this—but it does provide lecturers with reasonable assurance that, as long as there are classes to teach, they will have work. Additionally, continuing lecturers no longer need to reapply for their positions every year as they must before reaching continuing status. The continuing lecturer rank creates a "last-in, first-out" system wherein precontinuing faculty would be the first ones to lose their jobs if instructional need decreased. The excellence review, therefore, is a high-stakes employment action and, as such, is engaged with multiple (and sometimes contradictory) texts that strictly govern the process. In sum: the institution mandates, through the MOU, an excellence review process, and the review process is part of the institutional circuitry that coordinates the work of lecturers (NSFs).

Understanding boss texts and the other texts that govern the institutional circuits of our work is a way to make sense of our day-to-day. And, as Donna Haraway (2016), invoking Marilyn Strathern, reminds us, "it matters what matters we use to think other matters with; it matters what stories we tell to tell other stories with; it matters what knots knot knots, what thoughts think thoughts, what descriptions describe descriptions, what ties tie ties. It matters what stories make worlds, what worlds make stories" (12). The texts that are born of the MOU—as well as the MOU itself—are the matters, stories, knots, thoughts, descriptions, and ties that create and sustain our writing program. At the same time, when these texts are activated in the everyday of our work, they *become* the ways we—the doers of our writing programs—make sense of that work. It matters what these texts do because these texts *become* the work we do (see Giaimo and Cheatle, this volume).

The institutional circuitry surrounding the activation of the MOU in relation to the excellence review process is an example of the ways texts coordinate work. This review process produces a series of cascading texts in that the activation of one text triggers the creation of yet more texts to support the work of the first text, and so on. In mapping the cascading texts of the excellence review process, I will use Luisa (a fictional name) as a representative for faculty members undergoing review. Note that the boss text—the MOU—brings this process into being, and even in its most simplified form, the excellence review is carried out in many steps not necessarily covered in my narrative.[12]

During Luisa's tenth teaching semester, she receives official notification that she will be undergoing the Excellence Review in her twelfth semester. This review is not optional; if Luisa does not submit her portfolio, she will not be rehired. The material she must submit for her review is collated into what is called an excellence portfolio (EP). The contents of the EP are explained in detail in the writing program's faculty handbook (a separate boss text). Following these explicit instructions, Luisa puts together her EP and submits it in the appropriate format to the designated people at the appointed time. Once the EP has been received, Luisa is asked to sign a procedural safeguard statement that affirms she was notified she would be undergoing review and that she is satisfied that her EP contains all of the data she wants in it.

Once the EP has been submitted, it travels simultaneously to the peer personnel committee and the WPA. The peer personnel committee writes a recommendation back to the WPA, and the WPA reviews this recommendation before writing her own recommendation to the dean. Once the dean makes her decision, but before she writes her recommendation to the vice provost and sends Luisa's portfolio forward for the final review, Luisa and the WPA have a formal conversation (another form of an institutional "text"), wherein the WPA conveys the results of both the WPA's and the dean's recommendation and informs Luisa that she may provide a formal written response that will accompany these recommendations to the vice provost. Luisa then signs a second procedural safeguard statement acknowledging that all of these steps have been followed and submits a response letter if she so chooses.

Once Luisa signs off on the second safeguard statement, the dean writes a formal letter of recommendation to the vice provost, and Luisa's EP and the three recommendation letters are sent to the vice provost for the final decision. The vice provost informs the dean and the WPA of his decision via email, and the personnel specialist in the writing program writes a decision email to Luisa. Finally, Luisa receives an official memo, prepared by the personnel office and signed by the vice provost, that she has been promoted to continuing status. This entire process takes about nine months from start to finish.

As this makes clear, the excellence review process is carried out by and through faculty, staff, and administrators' performance of texts. These texts are best described as cascading because each step of the process is reliant on the execution of the one before it; each text coordinates work while simultaneously being created by that work. What that makes apparent is that the ruling relations in the excellence review process are both reactive and generative. The entire sequence is triggered by the need to conduct a personnel action. Each instance of take-up or activation generates a new text which then must be acted upon. What this cascading map reveals, among other things that I discuss later in this chapter, is the value the institution places on the bureaucratization and standardization of personnel decisions.

The way I have situated the cascading texts in this section implies a hierarchical process, but the reality is that while there is a certain linearity, the ruling relations embedded in the excellence review are anything but straightforward or monolithic. To further illustrate the interwoven complexity of the institutional circuitry of this personnel action, I turn now to another mapping technique: the cat's cradle.

CAT'S CRADLE

The graphic representation of the textual cascading of the review process is useful for understanding how the texts in the excellence review circulate but belie the complex web of relations—the institutional circuits—that enfold the process. According to Dorothy Smith (2005), institutional circuits are

> sequences of text-coordinated action making people's actualities representable and hence actionable within the institutional frames that authorize institutional action. In institutional circuits, institutional work comprises mining actualities selectively to identify aspects, features, measures, and so on that fit the governing frame (sometimes called a "boss text"). The textual representation then produced can be interpreted in terms of that frame and become, in this way, articulated to an institutionally mandated course of action. (10)

This writing program's faculty handbook, for example, is one piece of the cascading network, but it encodes many more ruling relations that organize and govern—much more than just personnel. Some topics covered in the seventy-five-page document include syllabus production, class cancellation procedures, plagiarism and attendance policies, and office space assignments.

For a visual representation of this institutional circuitry, I turn to Donna Haraway's (2016) thinking on string figures. While Haraway's project is not one of institutional ethnography, her use of string figures, popularly known in contemporary Western cultures as cat's cradles, is a productive metaphor for visualizing the complexity of ruling relations in this personnel process. Cat's cradles are string figures made on the hands or with pins and have patterns from the simplistic to the ornate; they signify different things to different people in different contexts and by how they are employed (Haraway 2016, 13–16).[13] A cat's cradle has an intricate pattern of overlapping and circulating strings.

It is possible to read this cat's cradle in several different ways. In one reading, the pins might represent the texts (the excellence portfolio, the memos, or the safeguard statements), while the strings would be the various individuals who need to take up and activate the texts (the WPA, the personnel specialist, the faculty member, the dean, etc.). In this first reading, the pins become their own boss texts as they coordinate the work of many different people from many different sites. From an institutional ethnographic perspective, having each pin represent a different text visually demonstrates the sheer scope of possible textual sites for a multilayered mapping (which is beyond the scope of this chapter).

In another reading, reversing the representations, the pins in the cat's cradle could be those individuals who take up the texts, and the strings would be the day-to-day work of those individuals creating the pattern of ruling relations. Returning to the excellence review process, then, if each pin represents one individual in the process—Luisa, the WPA, the dean, the vice provost, and so on—it is easy to visualize how this work is coordinated by the various interwoven strings (texts). As well, the tracing of these strings—the forms, documents, and letters of the review process—create the conditions of each different individual's work in relation to each other and the institutional texts. For example, the WPA is required by university policy (another boss text) to oversee the personnel processes in the writing program (the excellence review is just one of several processes including hiring, informal reviews, reprimands, and so on). The WPA's activation/participation in the excellence review process is just one piece of her job description, and her job performance is coordinated by the texts that govern her evaluation as an administrator and scholar. Much like the NSF review process, then, the WPA's performance review activates and coordinates the work of the dean, vice provost, provost, and academic senate, among others, and produces an entire new set of cascading texts that can similarly be plotted on another cat's cradle.

Yet a third use of the cat's cradle could be to illustrate how boss texts (the MOU) generate mini boss texts (or boss texts within boss texts) in the excellence review process. For this example, I turn to the EP. The EP is a lengthy document that can easily surpass one hundred pages in its entirety. Faculty bring the EP into existence because of the following language from the MOU:

Instructional performance is measured by the evaluation of evidence demonstrating such qualities as:

   a. Command of the subject matter and continued growth in mastering new topics;
   b. ability to organize and present course materials;
   c. ability to awaken in students an awareness of the importance of the subject matter;
   d. ability to arouse curiosity in beginning students and to stimulate advanced students to do creative work; and
   e. achievements of students in their field. (University n.d., Article 7b, E, 1 25)

While the MOU describes what criteria faculty will be evaluated on, it stops short of prescribing how those criteria will be demonstrated or evaluated other than announcing that these criteria must be deemed "excellent" to declare a successful review. Therefore, the writing program is tasked with articulating—making sense of—what the text(s) of the EP will look like.

The writing program provides these detailed guidelines in the program's faculty handbook, which, because of the importance of its contents, becomes a mini boss text within the personnel process because of the frameworks and institutional circuits it creates in its activation. According to the faculty handbook, the EP consists of:

1. self-statement artifact
2. CV
3. annotated syllabus
4. writing activity artifact
5. lesson plan
6. sample student work
7. class visit report (peer observation)
8. student course evaluations
9. teaching journal (optional)
10. letters of reference (optional) (Merritt Writing Program 2017, 68–69)

These ten texts are not necessarily produced in a cascading manner, because they can be worked on in any order, but the creation of these texts nevertheless orders and organizes the work of the faculty who need to produce the portfolio. Luisa, for example, is introduced to the idea of the EP during her first semester on campus and is given advice on how to prepare for it. She has participated in two optional, informal reviews (during her first and third years), and she has participated in program- and university-led workshops on portfolio preparation and university policy. Luisa has invited peers into her classroom, and they have written peer observations, and someone from the administrative team has done the same. Throughout her six years in the program, Luisa has been keeping a reflective teaching journal and annotating her syllabi to make her pedagogy transparent. While Luisa doesn't frequently teach from formal, daily lesson plans, she has written some for inclusion in the EP. She has amassed a trove of graded student work and has collected and reflected on course evaluations for about thirty courses. Finally, in the weeks before her summer portfolio submission deadline, Luisa has learned how to manipulate the required submission software package, chosen the most representative examples of each required EP element, and written a cover letter to persuade readers she has been an excellent teacher.

All the work of assembling and creating the portfolio is extra to Luisa's actual job of teaching; nevertheless, the EP coordinates much of Luisa's day-to-day work, even though "preparing excellence portfolio" is not stated anywhere in her job description nor is it something she (or anyone, really) would identify as taking up her work time. In this way, the EP is like a member of the writing program because of its need to be brought into existence by each and every faculty member; it is a constant presence in everyone's daily work lives. For example, in many conversations—both formal and informal—about service work, the question of how service will count toward the excellence review comes up. "Counting" really is a question about where committee service gets written into the EP—that is, where and how committee service is organized by the ruling relations of the EP and the MOU. Because there is no category for service in the excellence portfolio, and the MOU explicitly says that lecturers (NSFs) can only be evaluated on the materials submitted for review (only what is in the EP), then service, though palpable, recognizable, and vital to the sustained activities of the program, cannot be brought into the excellence review process and, therefore, doesn't count, raising all sorts of ethical and professional questions about the role of service work in the writing program.

In addition to defining what counts as work, the EP also organizes the relations between teaching and the evaluation of that teaching through the fuzzy lens of excellence. In particular, the EP forces teaching into a neoliberal project of quantification and legibility that is removed from the context of a real classroom with actual students and teachers performing the embodied work of teaching and learning. Nothing in the EP, with the possible exception of the self-statement, provides a forum for documenting the thousands of hours lecturers have spent in conversations with their students outside of class time about everything from their writing to their home life to their other classes to their roommates to the difficult subjects that often emerge in their writing. There is no place in the EP to account for the very real emotional labor of teaching writing, the kind of labor that most often falls to women and underrepresented groups.

The MOU (boss text) and the faculty handbook (mini boss text) that create the EP do not actually define what excellence means, so there is no rubric for differentiating a satisfactory portfolio from an excellent one. But even if that metric were defined, it would beg the question: can a portfolio be satisfactory but not excellent? In other words, to paraphrase Garrison Keillor, if all the portfolios demonstrated teaching excellence, wouldn't teaching excellence, by default become the baseline? Is excellence something that can be held by all faculty at all times, or does excellence have to be reserved for a select few? The ruling relations in the excellence review process seem to create this very scenario: all of the teachers must be excellent; therefore, all of the teachers are excellent, so the average rating for all teachers is excellent, rendering the category of excellent all but meaningless. It is a Kafkaesque situation that provides little room for variation or individual differences and forces uniformity—a condition of the MOU that coordinates the work.[14]

As someone who worked closely with faculty in the excellence review process, I was frequently at a loss to explain how the evidence gathered in the portfolio actually measured what it purported to measure. While I could and did use my professional experience and knowledge to make educated decisions about each EP, I really was only assessing whether the candidate put together a compelling set of texts. The leap from persuasive texts to teaching excellence is one that leaves much to be desired, but the boss texts that framed my work as the WPA coordinated my actions in such a way that this was a logical inconsistency I had to live with/in.

Despite my apparent consent in this process—after all, I did it!—I like to think that I was also performing Gunner's (2016) "creatively disruptive form of complicity" (154). So, even though I may have written multiple letters per year proclaiming the excellence of all faculty under review, I included phrases in letters such as "Since standardized course evaluations do not assess student learning and are problematic for multiple reasons" or "While the written feedback Luisa provides on student papers is limited, I know she spends an hour or more in one-on-one conversations with each student on each paper." In comments like these, I was complicit in acknowledging the quantifiable, locatable, point-at-able criteria I was supposed to, but I also was activating the required texts of my work to creatively disrupt the managed system by introducing criteria that were more situated and personal, closer to lecturers and their students. Lecturers also engaged in creative disruption when they "snuck" service contributions into their EP by framing them as teaching or using them as a form of professional development, both of which had an authorized place in the EP.

CONCLUSION

At the beginning of this chapter, echoing LaFrance and Nicolas (2012, 146), I asked "What actually lies below our discourses? How do they gloss over or respond to the conditions that have produced them? How do our discourses actually mobilize the work of our programs?" What I hope to have shown is that an institutional ethnographic approach to just two of the many texts that coordinate this one writing program uncovers rich, deep, and meaningful pathways for making sense of how ruling relations create the institutional circuits of our everyday. As is true with most institutional entities, writing programs exist within an ornate, complex cat's cradle composed of cascading texts. Understanding how these texts are activated by the people who use them, and who also create them in the process of using them, helps us better articulate what we want to focus attention on (also see, in this collection, Malenczyk; Giaimo and Cheatle; Wenger).

Being able to see the ruling relations of our work takes away some of the mystery surrounding how institutions operate. Most important, uncovering ruling relations and locating our boss texts and mini boss texts provide us with tools to make sense of the ways our work is organized and coordinated. Because much of the institutional circuitry of the work we do is hiding in plain sight, it is easy to overlook some of the mundane texts we activate. However, these everyday texts shape our writing programs and our work in specific and complex ways. By using institutional ethnography to make the hiding-in-plain-sight work of our programs visible, we gain greater insight into the ways our writing programs become legible to ourselves and others. This way of making sense of our work acknowledges the symbiotic relationship between text and agent, and in its explication, opens up spaces for complicit disruption in systems that we otherwise might not recognize.

NOTES

1. This chapter was written while the union contract from 2016–2020 was in effect. The contract language may have changed between the time this chapter was written and publication of this collection.
2. The UC system has three faculty tracks: ladder-rank, lecturers with security of employment (LSOEs), and non-senate faculty (NSF). The first two tracks are fully enfranchised and tenurable/tenured members of the academic senate. Non-senate faculty, on the other hand, are not members of the senate and, as such, have virtually no voting rights. Some individual programs or departments may elect to grant voting rights to NSF faculty within their program or department on specific matters. For example, with the creation of new bylaws to govern the new General Education curriculum, the General Education Subcommittee gave limited voting rights to representative NSF serving on several new GE committees.
3. For example, at some institutions, "faculty" are divided into "administrative faculty" and "teaching faculty." Administrative faculty include most of the professional (nonclassified staff) while academic faculty are professors.
4. Even as I offer this critique of the language used to describe my lecturer colleagues, I struggle to find the right words to describe their positions without using a negative or by privileging tenure-track positions. To say "non-tenure-track" puts those who are tenure-track in a one-up position. I have seen some clever attempts at tackling this problematic language with a term such as "tenure-free," which puts tenure in the one-down position, but this language has not yet become part of our lexicon. Therefore, for the sake of clarity and consistency, I consciously, though not thoughtlessly, use the same language as the program and university throughout this chapter.
5. Arguably, putting things in writing and employing them unilaterally is probably a good move for any administrator, provided they leave themselves room for exceptions. My point is that when working with unionized faculty, it is extremely important to have articulated what expectations and requirements are, in an effort to avoid a situation becoming grievable.
6. Because the MOU organizes much of my own day-to-day work, my project in this chapter is what Smith and Turner (2014) call an "experiential institutional ethnography," an approach that is "based on the ethnographer's own experience" and takes a different subject position from that of a participant-observer who still maintains a degree of removal or separation from what is being studied. The benefit of experiential ethnography is that because "major aspects of textual work are not spoken and are not in any simple way visible to an observer" (12), my own experience of the texts allows me to uncover these hidden aspects from an insider's point of view.
7. While there has been debate in the field over whether writing centers and writing center directors are "writing programs" and "writing program administrators" (see Ianetta et al. 2006), I come down firmly on the side of writing centers and writing programs being different slices of the same pie.
8. For an excellent discussion of the rhetorical construction of institutions see Porter et al. (2000). While IE is likewise concerned with how texts do work, unlike Porter et al.'s examination of rhetorical construction, IE's focus is on what people actually do with the texts that are written. IE is not as concerned with the ways texts bring institutions into existence as it is in what the texts are used for and how they organize the work that gets done.
9. In the process of conducting my study, I was quick to uncover the multiple ways that neoliberalism is a dominant frame, a boss text, in our writing program work;

10. however, that discussion is beyond the scope of this chapter. Readers can turn to Tony Scott and Nancy Welch's (2016) *Composition in the Age of Austerity* for a primer in the ways neoliberalism has impacted writing programs.
10. I use the term "largesse" with my tongue firmly in cheek. One result of the neoliberal turn, particularly in already-marginalized writing studies, is that most of us have been conditioned to believe that we are "resource rich" when we are simply given a physical place to do our work and the promise of being employed for more than one semester.
11. While Geller and Denny (2013) do not identify their study as in institutional ethnography, their focus on the connection between writing center professionals, their position in the university as faculty or staff, and the ways in which their work is coordinated by those position categories shares many of the goals and methods of IE.
12. IE's focus on individuals and their actions may make the use of a representative or composite character seem inappropriate; however, I have used this stylistic approach elsewhere (LaFrance and Nicolas 2012, 2013) to both protect identities and to cover a multitude of perspectives with the constraints of a condensed narrative. Interesting to note, within the context of IE, is how the texts governing the creation of text (publisher's guidelines) organize the work of producing the text (the narrative choices of the author).
13. In contemporary Western cultures, cat's cradles are often seen as simple child's games, but their use and signification predate Western imperialism and colonialism. Evidence has been found of cat's cradles being used along Asian trade routes as well as in other precolonial cultures. The Navajo and other Native American tribes use cat's cradles to tell stories and to pass along cultural information (Haraway 2016).
14. These questions of averages and baselines come to the fore much more prominently in the merit review process (a completely separate personnel action governed by another set of cascading texts caught in a cat's cradle). The merit process requires judgments of how meritorious someone's work is. Is it 6 percent merit worthy? 9 percent? And if the work isn't deserving of a merit increase, am I also saying that the teacher is no longer excellent, since surely if you have been labeled as "excellent" your work would be deserving of merit, right? The tension between excellence and merit is a real one in our program that has sparked many a heated debate, bruised some egos, and nicked a few friendships.

REFERENCES

Campbell, Marie, and Frances Gregor. 2004. *Mapping Social Relations: A Primer in Doing Institutional Ethnography*. Lanham, MD: AltaMira Press.

Geller, Anne, and Harry Denny. 2013. "Of Ladybugs, Low Status, and Loving the Job: Writing Center Professionals Navigating Their Careers." *Writing Center Journal* 33 (1): 96–129.

Gunner, Jeanne. 2016. "What Happens When Ideological Narratives Lose Their Force." In *Composition and the Age of Austerity*, edited by Nancy Welch and Tony Scott, 149–162. Logan: Utah State University Press.

Hall, R. Mark. 2017. *Around the Texts of Writing Center Work: An Inquiry-Based Approach to Tutor Education*. Logan: Utah State University Press.

Haraway, Donna. 2016. *Staying with the Trouble: Making Kin in the Chthulucene*. Durham, NC: Duke University Press.

Holstein, James A., and Jaber F. Gubrium. 2011. "The Constructivist Analytics of Interpretive Practice." In *The Sage Handbook of Qualitative Research*, 4th ed., edited by Norman K. Denzin and Yvonna S. Lincoln, 341–357. Thousand Oaks, CA: Sage Publications.

Ianetta, Melissa, Linda Bergmann, Lauren Fitzgerald, Carol Peterson Haviland, Lisa Lebduska, and Mary Wislocki. 2006. "Polylog: Are Writing Center Directors Writing Program Administrators?" *Composition Studies* 34 (2): 11–42.
Kahn, Seth. 2013. "What Is a Union?" In *A Rhetoric for Writing Program Administrators*, edited by Rita Malenczyk, 211–222. Anderson, SC: Parlor Press.
LaFrance, Michelle, and Melissa Nicolas. 2012. "Institutional Ethnography as Materialist Framework for Writing Program Research and the Faculty-Staff Work Standpoints Project." *College Composition and Communication* 64 (1): 130–150.
LaFrance, Michelle, and Melissa Nicolas. 2013. "What's Your Frequency? Preliminary Results of a Survey on Faculty and Staff Perspectives on Their Work in Writing Centers." *Writing Lab Newsletter* 37 (5/6): 10–13.
Merritt Writing Program. 2017. *Merritt Writing Program Faculty Handbook*. Merced, CA: Merritt Writing Program.
Miley, Michelle. 2017. "Looking up: Mapping Writing Center Work through Institutional Ethnography." *Writing Center Journal* 36 (4): 103–129.
Porter, James, Patricia Sullivan, Stuart Blythe, Jeffrey T. Grabill, and Libby Miles. 2000. "Institutional Critique: A Rhetorical Methodology for Change." *College Composition and Communication* 51 (4): 610–642.
Smith, Dorothy. 2005. *Institutional Ethnography: A Sociology for People*. Lanham, MD: AltaMira Press.
Smith, Dorothy, and Susan Turner. 2014. "Introduction." In *Incorporating Texts Into Institutional Ethnographies*, edited by Dorothy Smith and Susan Turner, 3–14. Toronto: University of Toronto Press.
Smith, George. 2014. "Policing the Gay Community: An Inquiry into Textually-Mediated Social Relations." In *Incorporating Texts Into Institutional Ethnographies*, edited by Dorothy Smith and Susan Turner, 17–40. Toronto: University of Toronto Press.
University Council American Federation of Teachers and the University of California. 2016. *Memorandum of Understanding: Non-Senate Instructional Unit*. Last modified January 31, 2020.
Welch, Nancy, and Tony Scott. 2016. "Introduction: Composition in the Age of Austerity." In *Composition and the Age of Austerity*, edited by Nancy Welch and Tony Scott, 3–17. Logan: Utah State University Press.

9
DISTRIBUTED LEADERSHIP FOR WPAS
Making Sense of Leadership Methods

Christy I. Wenger

When I was hired into my current position as the first-ever WPA for my small, public mid-Atlantic liberal arts university seven years ago, my graduate advisor told me to see the way my school separated developmental writing—taught via a Stretch model in the Academic Support Center (ASC)—and first-year writing—housed within the English Department and under my purview—as a boon to my position; in his view, without developmental writing I would have less responsibility, with fewer courses and faculty to manage. With his advice to stick to the duties listed in my job description, for the first few years on the job I occupied myself with questions about *who* I was as a WPA and how I could construct a professional identity that included first-year writing but not developmental writing; that involved training a pool of adjuncts with little formal expertise in writing instruction but who taught 88 percent of our writing courses; that situated me via my formal expertise in an authority position; and that earned me visibility across campus and respect among upper administrators at the same time that it kept me marginalized in my department of literature.

Eight years later and on the other side of tenure, my preoccupations have shifted, and I am most interested in *what* I'm doing as a WPA, in understanding the impact of my actions and how others are influenced and empowered by the work that I do. Of course, the who and the what of WPA-ing are interlocked, but the shift I aim to capitalize on here is significant. It's a shift that has me unpacking my WPA work these days as more than just another layer of my professional identity and as more than the service I provide my university or my students. I now see that work as academic leadership, actualizing Jane Detweiler, Margaret LaWare, and Patti Wojahn's (2017) recent call for us to problematize what counts as leadership in higher education. Understanding WPA

https://doi.org/10.7330/9781646424368.c009

work primarily as leadership and as distinct from identity, service, and management remains underexplored in our field. Despite a steady undercurrent of research on this topic (Phelps 2002; Kazan and Gabor 2013; Mirtz and Cullen 2002), there remains less scholarship on the topic than on other connected but distinct topics like power (White 1991), authority (Werder 2000), or management (Bousquet, Scott and Parasondola 2004; Strickland 2011).

Not surprisingly, then, the position of the WPA as leader remains foreign on many of our campuses; not once has my annual review cited my superior *leadership* skills, though it always notes my exemplary service to the university based on my work within the writing program. It has been my experience that "administering programs and launching student initiatives are generally not fully recognized as leadership nor credited toward promotion because they tend to be overshadowed by traditional emphases on scholarship and even service to the profession" (Detweiler, LaWare, and Wojahn 2017, 452). Because a lot of the leadership work that WPAs carry out on a daily basis, such as relationship-building, can remain either hidden or undervalued as so-called service, and because WPAs are often stuck in the ranks of middle management, where their responsibility tends to outweigh their power, they remain unable to challenge prevailing university hierarchies of service and leadership. To remedy this, Detweiler, LaWare, and Wojahn (2017) argue that we need to advocate for more inclusive models of leadership within higher education. We might also make those models publicly visible as Melissa Ianetta recommends when she suggests WPAs identify ourselves online through an institutional web presence and identify as leaders on our CVs, noting that our administrative vitas should look different than those of our teaching colleagues (2015, 146, 153).

Within this chapter, I look to leadership studies to supplement the commonplaces of category and parlance within WPA scholarship to more dynamically capture how leadership practices are constructed and shared within writing programs and to increase our leadership literacy in the field. In this chapter, I therefore approach sensemaking as a social and ongoing process that "enables leaders to have a better sense of what's going on," and as a way of creating a map for leadership action (Ancona 2011, 3). I theorize sensemaking from a feminist ecological perspective and enact it as a way of creating a framework for the unknown (Weick 1995, 4) and as a way of figuring out what can be. As Susanmarie Harrington and Sue Dinitz remind us elsewhere in this collection, the unknown confronts us, as WPAs, daily since writing programs are always in the process of being created and recreated.

In particular, my chapter seeks to productively discuss the kinds of leadership work that WPAs and full-time, contingent instructors do together. I examine the coalition I have formed with the full-time, non-tenure-track (NTT) instructors in the writing program and my campus's Academic Support Center and propose the value of applying models of distributed leadership, which defines leadership through interdependent interactions of leaders and followers, to WPA work. Ann Penrose (2012) claims that creating communities of practice within writing programs can position WPAs to become change agents and can empower NTT faculty. My chapter channels Penrose's activist exigency as it seeks to make sense of my group's coalitional work as distributed, borrowing from leadership studies' recent theories of distributed leadership. Like Courtney Adams Wooten in this collection, I am interested in how sensemaking helps us examine "how our writing program cultures are built and sustained, how instructors engage in underlife as they navigate institutional and programmatic structures," and how WPAs can productively intervene in these processes. Adams Wooten and I both look at marginalized instructors: she looks at TAs, and I look at contingent writing faculty, who may have even fewer job protections than graduate students. I join Adams Wooten's desire to incorporate these marginalized voices, so I turn to the personal testimony of the instructors in our working group collected through interviews and aggregated to preserve individual anonymity to explore how WPAs can use the theories and practices of distributed leadership to make sense of leadership "as not something 'done' by an individual 'to' others, [but instead as] a group activity that works through and within relationships, rather than individual action" (Bennett, Wise, and Woods 2003, 3). When approached as distributed, interactions, tools, and routines define the leadership situation as much as the leader-WPA herself, providing her new means of agency and problematizing her authority in useful ways. Examining how my campus divides basic and mainstream writing instruction and how these divisions work as a catalyst for creative leadership action, I turn to distributed leadership to explore how the relationships between WPAs and contingent instructors is increasingly the site where the economic, political, and interpersonal come together to shape the day-to-day work of our programs and the leadership options available to all of us within a program. As I will explore in the next section, distributed leadership allows me to enact feminist sensemaking because it values the interconnectedness of leadership and the relational well-being of everyone in a leadership network.

LIVING WELL TOGETHER: FEMINIST SENSEMAKING AND DISTRIBUTED LEADERSHIP

Joe Harris (2014) reminds us that "we do have real voices in a more symbolic economy [than the one of salaries and course loads], one in which we assign value to different kinds of intellectual work" (71) when he weighs in on the *College English* colloquium, "Off Track and On." Harris urges us to be more generous to our colleagues, both on and off the tenure track, and to work at creating an intellectual community all can share since none of us can "define good jobs in contractual terms alone" (2014, 70). Harris's comments resonate with what the NTT writing instructors in my program say about their experiences. In interviews, these writing instructors agree that they work above and beyond their contractual limits and remain in their positions precisely because they feel a part of a thriving intellectual community within the program, not because of their salaries or official job descriptions. Collectively, they mention a combination of the following factors that motivate them in the symbolic work economy Harris (2014) identifies: "Loyalty to and affection for the WPA, a feeling of ownership in the vision of the program, and the fulfillment that comes from [our] perceived ability to help change the writing program for the better."[1] My chapter is therefore driven by the aim of establishing new ways of talking about how writing program administrators and contingent writing instructors can work together without further disenfranchising those instructors. The resulting narratives are mindful of material conditions and equitable labor conditions yet hopeful of the real gains we can achieve collectively.

I'm drawn to thinking about these issues from an ecological perspective to reinforce the notion that my colleagues' livelihoods and my own are interconnected and dependent on the health of our work spaces. Theorizing what this ecological perspective might mean for feminist administrators, Kathleen Ryan (2012) proposes a feminist rhetorical ecological agency that strives toward an ethics of flourishing in an effort to help WPAs undertake their jobs in ways that are rooted and strategic while responsive to a seeming "endless stream of irresolvable dilemmas" (Leverenz 2002, 106, quoted in Ryan 2012, 80). Feminist rhetorical ecological agency is a method of sensemaking, then, as it strives to help WPAs structure the unknowns of their workplaces so that they may act and thrive within them. Through feminist rhetorical agency, the success of WPA work can be measured by its ability to create conditions where flourishing or living well together is made possible and desirable. In the shared paradigm of distributed leadership that I will propose, flourishing together is a central component of leadership, distinguishing it from management. Within my local context, my flourishing as a WPA is particularly linked to that of the full-time NTT writing instructors with whom I work closely, in part because of my positionality as the only tenured writing faculty member in a department of literature; conversely, the collective testimony I quote throughout this chapter points to the impact of my actions on my instructors' well-being and their ability to find meaning within their work.

Distributed leadership asks us to widen our attentive focus to include not only narratives of leaders themselves but also the situated practices that enable leadership to emerge within various local contexts. Distributed leadership considers who takes responsibility for leading, regardless of official titles or designated positions. Distributed models of leadership are a result of collective efforts of both macro leadership actions, such as making infrastructure decisions that affect a program or curriculum, and micro-level actions like monitoring implementation of program goals within one's own classroom and contributing to a larger mission or vision (Spillane 2006, 31–33). Because this method recognizes the interplay of a network of actors, "distributed leadership is not something 'done' by an individual 'to' others, or a set of individual actions through which people contribute to a group or organization . . . [it] is a group activity that works through and within relationships, rather than individual action" (Bennett, Wise, and Woods 2003, 3). What differentiates distributed leadership from more widely drawn-upon models like collaborative leadership are three central elements:

1. Leadership practice, or the "how" of leadership, is emphasized over the what or who;
2. leadership practice is understood through interactions of leaders, followers and situations which together make up more than the sum of their parts;
3. the situation both defines and is defined through leadership practice. (Spillane 2006, 4)

The process orientation of this paradigm can helpfully capture the work of leadership executed by those outside of formal leadership structures, such as contingent faculty, and the emphasis on the ecosystem at work between all members of a writing program faculty underscores the interconnectedness of effort and collective action within a program that is driven by human relationships.

Because it impacts the ways individuals relate to one another, from a distributed viewpoint, the material situation is seen "not simply [as] a context within which school leaders practice; it is a defining element of practice" (Spillane 2003, 22). This viewpoint enables me to see my leadership practice as more than a testament to my identifications as a WPA, though, of course, those remain significant but as borne from the collective labor of the writing faculty on my campus and myself as we work together to increase our individual and collective well-being by providing each other support we cannot find elsewhere. This shift to recognize relationality is meaningful since much of what is written about WPA leadership focuses on the individual actions of the WPA who shapes her program, leaving less said about how the program itself and how the people within it shape the WPA in turn.

The sensemaking that a distributed leadership perspective on WPA work provides is an ecological understanding of leadership less focused on the individual agency of the WPA (positional leadership) and more focused on networked relationships and the co-influence of leaders and followers (relational leadership): "Sensemaking is inherently collective; it is not nearly as effective to be the lone leader at the top doing all the sensemaking by yourself. It is far better to compare your views with those of others—blending, negotiating, and integrating, until some mutually acceptable version is achieved" (Ancona 2011, 8). Because distributed leadership can help us to focus on the relational ecosystems within writing programs, it helps me to make sense of how we might productively share leadership in mixed faculty groups of full-time contingent and tenured faculty—to say nothing of adjunct labor, a topic for another article. The sharing of leadership I examine here is not as much lateral among my fellow tenured literature colleagues as it is vertical between the contingent writing faculty and myself. Though challenged by institutionalized hierarchies and status differences, we have found shared leadership sustainable when it is built first on primary identifications with writing, regardless of official titles or campus designations. Conscious focus on what connects WPAs and NTT faculty doesn't mean we don't keep calling attention to the fact that "current [university] labor conditions undervalue the intellectual demand of teaching," as Seth Kahn (2015, 120) points out, but it does validate the need to find more inclusive understandings of leadership that give agency to followers and enable multiple leadership positionalities within our programs—one way of attending to the labor of leading.

I was hired into my job with the appointed positionality of caretaker, a positionality I have actively refused in my quest to make other positions from which I might lead more visible. My hire as the first official WPA on my campus was ostensibly to provide university leadership in all matters of writing and pedagogy, what my interdisciplinary colleagues refer to as a means of caring, of "taking care of writing" on campus, which minimizes my leadership role by feminizing it under a caring ethos. As general caretaker, my colleagues look for me to be what Eileen Schell (1998) has deemed a "composition evangelist," or one who transforms everything from curriculum to instruction by spreading the good word (70). As the sole resident compositionist on my campus, I am expected to be a zealous and caring expert so that everyone else is freed to invoke the "myth of the novice" (Gunner 2002, 12), a sustainable way of not caring so that they might avoid responsibility for writing and the guilt that might accompany this avoidance. At the same time, my evangelism can be disregarded at any point, given its associations with fanaticism: like the friendly evangelicals who go door-to-door in my neighborhood, I find that departmental doors mostly remain closed when I come around with flyers. Very few of my tenured colleagues regularly attend the professional development trainings I offer through the writing program, for instance. The ones who I can really "share the news" with are the contingent instructors who do attend those trainings and cannot shut me out for fear of losing their jobs. My departmental colleagues, on the other hand, are ultimately free to teach composition as they wish—if they teach it at all—because they have "power equal [to mine as] the WPA's and greater than any non-tenure track instructor's" (Gunner 2002, 13). As for the writing instructors themselves, they cite my tenured colleagues' ceding of ownership over writing in the program as creating a "gulf between literature and untenureable writing faculty" that makes them feel more like "distant cousins" to the tenured faculty and "less like colleagues."

The result is an ecosystem of sustainability between those of us who align ourselves closely to writing so that intersectional marginalization serves as a uniting factor despite our mixed positions on and off the tenure track. The NTT instructors recognize, as one instructor put it in a voluntary survey of community and leadership experiences conducted to formalize responses for this article, that "the writing program as a whole has been just as marginalized by the university and the department as the faculty who teach these classes. We feel that the mutual recognition (if not appreciation) of our shared experiences has made the collaborations and connections between WPA and NTT faculty much stronger." In my program, then, primary alignment with writing is itself a binding agent and a catalyst, opening novel spaces for shared leadership and collective action that destabilize traditional academic hierarchies and understandings of agency and power, spaces where my NTT faculty claim they have a "voice and the ability to make positive changes."

As a result, sensemaking is, for me, an ecological leadership strategy that arises from "thoughtful practice" (Cuomo 1998, 143), informed by lived experience, an embodied quest of making sense of our local contexts and our material place(s) within them, and as understanding how "people can live well together and respectfully with and within the physical/natural world" (Code 2006, 19). Sensemaking means that I approach leadership pragmatically: I want to make sense of my influence over others at my university and understand the interconnection of knowledge and action, leading to responsible knowing and willingness to accept things as they are even while working to change them. "Sensemaking involves not only trying out new things but also trying to understand your impact on a system as you try to change it" (Ancona 2011, 11).

For instance, the very existence of the NTT writing instructors in my program is the result of my advocacy. It's easy to get caught up in arguments against this additional tier of contingent labor, to see my advocacy as shortsighted and not particularly thoughtful, especially because my NTT colleagues all share with me wishes that they could be working with me to improve the writing program from the position of tenured colleagues with job security. Despite the limitations of their positionality within the university and academic superstructure, within the more local context of my program and the historical overuse of adjuncts in my program, I see their NTT lines as a great stride toward more equitable labor conditions in my program and as a move in the right direction. When I started my position, my program relied on adjuncts to teach 88 percent of its courses; now, that number is closer to 40 percent. As Karl Weick et al. have noted, sensemaking is "being thrown into an ongoing, unknowable, unpredictable streaming of experience in search of answers" (Weick, Sutcliffe, and Obstfeld 2005, 410), which is an eerily accurate job description for most WPAs.

So, as I attempt to understand the influence of actions such as these, I make sense of my WPA leadership by harnessing a "rhetorical ecological feminist agency [that] is socially constructed, ecologically located and enacted, ethically responsible, rhetorically directed, and pragmatically oriented. It values experiential alongside disciplinary knowledge and recognizes that place and situation constitute knowledge" (Ryan 2012, 80). From this perspective, I see the impact of these teaching positions within the writing program as transformative to my practice and understanding of WPA action and agency. Distributed leadership provides a useful lens to recognize the place-based, ecological interdependence among a WPA and her NTT writing faculty to see how they can endeavor to "live well together," because it helps move us away from looking at the

WPA as a solitary figure of leadership solely responsible for establishing the social and structural conditions through which her program can flourish and toward a more ecological perspective that accounts for followers and environments and how these enable shared infrastructures to work. Distributed leadership "highlights leadership as an emergent property of a group or network of interacting individuals . . . where people work together in such a way that they pool their initiative and expertise, the outcome is a product or energy which is greater than the sum of their individual actions" (Bennett Wise, and Woods 2003, 7). This method resists the "add leader and stir" recipe for administration and instead views leadership as a collective effort cultivated by our interactions together and dependent on the ways those who are not in official leadership positions take on leadership roles in flexible, dynamic, and provisional ways, especially if they are supported and encouraged.

My NTT instructors describe a shift away from power to empowerment to define how this distribution works: the shared "leadership within the program shows how the WPA is confident in her ideas and her vision for the program and in establishing authority as opposed to wielding power . . . [and is] confident in her ability to hire people who can be trusted to make good judgments." In interviews, these instructors credit their leadership abilities to my leadership: "You give us opportunities and space to lead in ways we see fit and at times that seem right," they note. Distributed leadership thus begets more and better leaders and more engaged followers who move flexibly between these roles.

The widening of our perspective to include more leader figures than the solitary WPA is a benefit of distributed leadership over more traditional understandings of collaborative leadership. Feminist administrators often turn to collaboration as a potentially potent political strategy to de-emphasize power and to create networks of support for the WPA's professional and emotional well-being. But collaborative leadership discussions often end up focusing primarily on the WPA(s) and not the larger writing program ecology. Jeanne Gunner's oft-cited definition of collaborative leadership is instructive: "Where labor and responsibility are shared, where administrators have some degree of authority over their particular duties, and where the various 'heads' meet to consider the program as a whole rather than individually reporting 'up' to a single person in charge" (2002, 255). Gunner's definition illustrates the emphasis on the individuals who "head" up the work, not on the followers or on the lived social and place-based networks that make administrative collaboration possible. We can see this focus on formal administrators in Anne Aronson and Craig Hanson's (1998) reflective piece on cochairing a writing department when they describe themselves as "equals in every sense" because "there is no visible or hidden hierarchy that determines who really is in charge" (29). Even when we approach the WPA position as dynamic "in terms of multiple subject positions" and not a "totalizing unity" (Gere 1996, 127), as an amalgamation of "I's" (Malenczyk 2012), we tend to get stuck on the level of the individual administrator(s). Those who work together collaboratively within writing programs often have similar amounts of institutional power, as in the case of the cochairs, and therefore have the luxury of ignoring the structural expectations of their university culture; they can, in other words, create safe spaces for experimentation not afforded to others in more vulnerable positions.

While momentary erasures of hierarchy may be possible some of the time in some academic workplaces, these common conceptions of collaboration in contrast to distributed leadership tend to rest on overly simplistic notions of how challenging it can be to enact genuine collaboration in university environments, especially when your closest colleagues are graduate assistants or contingent full-time or part-time instructors. As a result, many discussions of collaboration tend to de-emphasize that while labor may be shared, power often is not. Lynn Meeks and Christine Hult (1998) open their article about collaborative administration with a detailed description of the beginning of a semester when the electricity goes out in the English Department. While no WPA is present, graduate student instructors are, and they take charge, reassigning campus classroom space to those who need it and supporting teachers who need to find other campus locations to teach online. Meeks and Hult describe this scenario to show how they "power share" with graduate students and enact a "collaborative relationship in which all parties contribute equally to the relationship" (1998, 9–10). I admire the collaborative spirit and the *espirit de corps* in their example and fully believe that the same scenario would play out similarly in my own program but worry over the slippery way shared responsibility is equated to shared power.

Within my program, contingent instructors and I, too, "work together to fix what needs fixing" (Meeks and Hult 1998, 11), but I hesitate to describe my active and persistent efforts to involve my writing instructors as first and foremost being a collaboration—shared labor *and* power toward a common goal—and not conjoint activity—united action that doesn't necessarily entail equal power sharing or even common goals.[2] My efforts to involve instructors in curriculum planning, assessment and programmatic reviews are quite successful in sharing responsibility, and the NTT instructors in my program note that "our WPA has created an atmosphere in which faculty are consistently encouraged to take ownership of a larger collective program space. Ownership in this instance is what brings us all together, rather than what sequesters us apart." However successful this move toward collective ownership has been on a program level, it has not been as successful in mitigating our hierarchical university to allow for genuine power sharing. These challenges guide me as I attempt to apply sensemaking not only to the ecological environment of the writing program but also to the larger university in order to enable shared action. They also remind me of the importance of seeing our work together through the wider lens of distributed leadership and not the more focused lens of collaboration.

A recent email sent internally to the school of arts and humanities by our dean became a reminder of how difficult it is to work together as "equals in every sense" with my NTT colleagues, a marker of success traditionally associated with the collaborative models of administration that I am here arguing are problematic. The email asked faculty to weigh in on an *Inside Higher Ed* article, "What Students Write," by Colleen Flaherty (2014). Flaherty reviews Dan Melzer's book, *Assignments Across the Curriculum* (2014), which analyzes assignments across the university curriculum and finds that they tend to overemphasize lower-order writing concerns such as grammar and lack consistent focus on writing as a process and higher order concerns like analysis. A flurry of responses from colleagues within the School of Arts and Humanities ensued, all of which took issue with the idea that teachers may place too much emphasis on grammar. Grammar was of prime importance, several loud voices argued. Many others chimed in, and a general consensus formed over-against the ideas in the article. Consensus formed around the idea that correct grammar is *the* key to good writing and that students who had the most correct sentences often showed the most amount of critical thinking. I carefully weighed in to share the kinds of discussions we have in the writing program about how grammar is best taught in context and how students who are learning new writing styles and developing critical thinking skills will often make grammar and style mistakes in their writing until they can begin to remap what they know. I mentioned the importance of communicating what we really want from our students' work in our assignments, reinforcing the main point of Flaherty's review and encouraged continued conversation among faculty in this space and beyond.

Despite keeping my tone light and inviting more conversation, I received no responses, not even from my departmental and program colleagues. Troubled, I approached the NTT instructors for their take on the emails and found that they were not included in the school listserv. That my coauthors were not welcomed into this intellectual forum effectively interrupted the collaborative moment engendered by this school discussion, one where productive dialogue and action could have been born. Likely, had one of them been on the email list, they would have responded to me and more productive discussion could have followed. It's no surprise that my NTT instructors note in interviews that they feel a "greater sense of obligation to and alignment with the writing program and their WPA" than the humanities college or English department, which houses the program and by which they feel largely ignored. The tone for this division is even set during campus interviews for these positions, when none of my literature colleagues attend teaching discussions or lunch with our candidates, a few citing their absence due to a lack of expertise in writing.

Accordingly, I take Ilene Crawford and Donna Strickland's (2010) warning that we must not efface the real differences in status and institutional power of those working in collaborative teams. They note, "In practice . . . collaborative teams must often include members who are asked to work with the program as if they have the same power as tenured faculty, even when that sharing of power materially benefits the tenured faculty more" (79). To address these dangers, these authors recommend that "as we work collectively—even collaboratively—with contingent faculty, we consider it a feminist duty to be ever attentive to interruptions, to moments when status differences interrupt, reminding us over and over again to reconsider the material limitations of our practices" (Crawford and Strickland 2010, 91). To address these limitations and to be better attentive to moments of interruption, I go to theories of distributed leadership, as I have been arguing. Distributed leadership practice is dependent on the interaction of leaders and followers within these social and material situations, creating a true leadership ecosystem. This ecosystem is not necessarily the result of sharing leadership equally between individuals of similar power: this is a key difference in the distribution of leadership in contrast to collaborative leadership. "While collaborative leadership is by definition distributed," according to leadership theorist James Spillane, "all distributed leadership is not necessarily collaborative" (2006, 23).

Despite my university's commitment to a hierarchical structure that problematizes how effectively I can carry out genuine collaboration with my NTT colleagues, evidenced by their omission from important emails, we can understand our collective efforts through theories of distributed leadership, which better reflect situated realities on our campus. While there are many factors to our local environment that allowed distributed leadership to form organically and thrive within my program, the situational context I focus on for the remainder of this chapter is the split instruction of basic writing and first-year writing at my institution. The ways first-year and basic writing were managed separately was the catalyst that drove me and my writing colleagues to think about and enact distributed leadership dynamically and organically within our local culture.

BASIC WRITING INSTRUCTION: A CASE STUDY OF DISTRIBUTED LEADERSHIP

As I note in my introduction, years before my arrival, my campus moved basic writing instruction to the campus's Academic Support Center (ASC) and adopted a Stretch model of instruction for these classes, especially popular in the late 1990s and early 2000s (Glau, 1996). Effectively, the ASC staff, who did not hold faculty positions and were not credentialed in writing or another related humanities field, were in control of those classes, including hiring and supervising instructors and overseeing the Stretch courses. Once Stretch students passed their two-semester "stretched" out 101 that included a first-semester 101A and a second-semester 101B course, they enrolled in English 102. Because they would eventually mainstream into 102 sections with other first-year writers, Stretch students were best served by being exposed to the same concepts and curriculum as their peers in the 101 sections, which I oversaw and for which I set the curriculum. This meant the ASC staff were required by their dean to adopt my curriculum and to enforce its use among instructors. In consequence, it did not take long for the writing instructors in the ASC (at that time, all adjuncts) to flock to me to take part in the formal writing training and mentoring I offered all writing program faculty through writing workshops and professional development seminars, roundtables, and reading groups. Spurred by my arrival on campus and my leadership within the writing program, the ASC realized they needed a content expert who could translate this curriculum to Stretch students and who could serve as a head teacher for the adjuncts; they soon hired an NTT instructor for their program. Without meaningful support for writing instruction in the ASC, however, this NTT instructor eagerly accepted my invitations to attend the professional development trainings I offered through the writing program.

This professional development was especially attractive since the Stretch program offered no such training and consequently lacked community among its instructors. The sole NTT Stretch writing instructor noted in interviews that hers was a "lonely island" before I invited her to create inroads into the writing program and to share in our intellectual community and (albeit limited) resources. A few years into my position, citing desperate need, precedent from the Stretch instructor hire, and statistics regarding reduced adjunct use, I was given permission to hire two NTT writing instructors for the writing program. The NTT Stretch instructor and NTT writing program instructors quickly bonded. I provided them direction and leadership, identifying their desire to connect with each other across departments and providing inroads to allow for frequent connection and sharing. What resulted was a natural alliance between myself as WPA and all the NTT writing instructors on my campus, both those who served the program from "inside" 101 and 102 and those "outside," teaching 101 through a Stretch model from the ASC and feeding students into the 102 courses. This alliance has stood in sharp contract with the tension the NTT writing instructors describe between themselves and the other departmental faculty who they feel treat them like "distant cousins you catch up with during the holidays," according to their interviews, and not "close family with whom you can collaborate," how they collectively described our writing community in an interview. As these instructors engaged in sensemaking to map out their workspaces, they repeatedly noted they felt the opportunities to work collectively with other instructors and myself as "endless," while the opportunities to work conjointly with other tenured faculty were "limited to nonexistent." The ways we have actively reshaped our workplace environment together is a direct factor in how these instructors view their agency within the writing program. And their reflections here are a means for them to engage in sensemaking and the negotiation of their leadership identities in my program, as Adams Wooten notes in her chapter in this volume on TAs and sensemaking.

What began with informal meetings in my office before and after we taught our classes to discuss what worked and what didn't in our lessons soon evolved into more organized meetings to review and discuss changes to the writing program's curriculum and assessment structures. Echoing the roundtable style of these meetings, distributed leadership breaks up the leader-follower division, insisting that leadership is a coperformance of all actors, an ecological understanding of how agency works within a writing program. In academic environments, distributed leadership can support already-entrenched values of collegiality and autonomy, leading to instructor satisfaction and increased well-being, as my instructors attest. Of course, I have the luxury of constructing theory from our experiences, not easily available to my instructors: I write this chapter as a WPA sharing a professionally recognized and published "WPA narrative" and fully cognizant that my positionality gives me the time and mental space to research and write, much harder for my instructors who have larger teaching loads and lower salaries that don't permit summers devoted to writing. Distributed leadership can capture these various positionalities while equalizing our focus, since within the paradigm, the role of official, designated leaders like WPAs isn't overlooked, just complicated. Similarly, we can still recognize how WPAs propel concertive action even as we also simultaneously understand leadership actions within our situational contexts and recognize the leadership potential of all actors within a networked community.

My actions as a WPA following distributed leadership methods have consequently been directed at creating a formal infrastructure that will allow for the sharing and distribution of leadership roles as well as creating official learning environments that support individual action. My formal leadership can be traced through the implementation of professional development in the form of workshops and roundtables I hold each semester to discuss topics like fostering metacognition through reflection, assessment, and strategies for scaffolding writing. Carefully constructed professional development engenders shared responsibility by creating learning environments that encourage dialogue and collective action toward program goals. As a leader striving for concertive action, I provide energy and direction for my instructors so they feel enabled to take the reins. The instructors noted in interviews that my direction provides "a sense of connection and responsibility to the program that helps us organize our courses, values our voices and, more importantly . . . makes us feel like we are contributing meaningfully to a larger educational project through curricular decision making and program wide policies." According to them, my efforts at shared leadership are reinforced in the structure of these professional development opportunities. Instead of using these solely, or even primarily, as times to review the nuts and bolts of teaching writing or of delivering our specific curriculum—what they called "staff meetings" and talked about despairingly from their teaching experiences at other schools—they felt our trainings were "invitations to taking the lead within the program" because of the ways I used carefully chosen themes and readings to think "about important, complicated questions related to pedagogy and writing theory, [and] also more general critical inquiries about higher education and its social and cultural contexts." Such testimony highlights distributed leadership's potential to empower others and thereby strengthen the WPAs own leadership.

Trainings are just one part of a larger ecosystem of distributed leadership; committee work is another. From my instructors' and my initial meetings, I created a Writing Advisory Board, which democratized the decision-making of the writing program and established regular meetings with both the full-time NTT and the adjunct faculty who could freely volunteer to serve on the board and/or attend all meetings, which I made open to the entire writing staff. It soon became clear that while this mixed setting instituted transparency and encouraged collaboration between adjuncts, full-time NTT instructors, and me, the NTT instructors and I needed additional, formalized administrative spaces; we were still finding ourselves in my office, talking for hours about program changes, reviews, and improvements. As a result, I established the Writing Steering Committee, on which sit the two NTT writing instructors in my department as well as the one NTT instructor in the ASC and myself. These instructors testify that because of these committees and their active involvement in the writing program, "it feels like there is a difference between the more prominent 'voice' that [we] are afforded in writing program meetings concerning program direction, curriculum and so on versus the larger departmental meetings and discussions covering global issues impacting all English department instructors. On the writing side, [we] feel like [we] have a voice and a vote, while on the departmental side [we are] allowed to *participate* but have less of a voice. For instance, we are not allowed to officially vote on departmental or university matters that directly impact us." As we meet outside of university-sponsored events and around course schedules and formal obligations, we actualize the principles of distributed leadership wherein "the material situation does not simply 'affect' what school leaders do, it is constitutive of their practices" (Spillane, Halverson, and Diamond 2004, 26). It's not so much that distributed leadership helps us to overcome our professional boundaries (a viewpoint that would see those only as obstacles) but that these boundaries have marked and shaped our leadership efforts so that we cannot define our practice without them.

While these committees are tolerated by my department chair and colleagues, they are not recognized as official, and the NTT instructors' involvement in them is viewed by my departmental colleagues, chair, and dean with some disapproval since the terms of their contracts specifically note that they have no service obligations. My campus's insistence that our NTT instructors do not take on so-called service roles is understandable, in one sense, from the perspective of equitable working conditions—they teach more, so service expectations are removed to account for this extra work—but does not fairly consider these instructors' abilities and desires to take on leadership roles from within their positions, regardless of how these roles are ultimately considered optional. This predicament shows the dangers of collapsing leadership under the category of service: taking away such leadership opportunities for NTT instructors denies them skills they may call upon for career advancement and denies them a voice in creating workplace conditions that guarantee their well-being and success. While they do not believe they should be required to maintain the same service expectations as tenured faculty, my instructors report that "NTT positions are often staffed by instructors with PhD degrees (and the result of national searches) who do not have any interest in separating their own personal interests, service, training, and scholarship from their roles [as] teachers."

Similar to how collapsing WPA work to service devalues that work by keeping it invisible to university reviews and annual evaluations, denying our full-time NTT instructors institutionalized access to leadership roles may limit their meaningful engagement in work environments and negatively threaten their well-being and the sustainability of our programs. My experience distributing leadership throughout my program and sharing it with my writing faculty has convinced me that we need to start taking more seriously the development of leadership skills important to work in higher education and the formalization of leadership roles for more individuals within our programs, including NTT faculty. One way I have given this traction in my own program is by distributing leadership over program implementation and review.

For instance, in addition to conducting classroom observations of my NTT instructors each semester myself, I ask them to also observe each other (and I invite them to observe me), using the same classroom observation form I use when I visit, to provide constructive criticism. Their evaluations of each other are used genuinely: theirs and mine will get combined and together will provide specific documentation of their teaching for program annual reviews and university performance reports. They will also be used to shape discussions of curriculum in workshops, which themselves inform program reviews and ongoing revisions. Again, I am forbidden to make such observations mandatory or to create a schedule which would officially document them, since this would formalize "service" for these NTT positions. Yet, by sharing this leadership practice with my instructors, they become active contributors to summative and formative evaluation, creating a situational coperformance of teacher evaluation. This coperformance exists together with my vertical leadership; as I request they set up such observations of each other, I generate the observation report form they use to collect and share feedback, and they receive a copy of their observations of each other.

In a traditional understanding of leadership, the actions of the writing instructors to observe each other and provide feedback might be seen simply as an extension of my leadership actions as WPA, a natural consequence of my program policy regarding classroom observations, or maybe even as simply service in line with my superiors' fears. Distributed leadership instead allows us to recognize that while the exigence of leadership action may be autocratic decree, which compels leader-followers with varying power differentials to work together, the exigence does not invalidate multiple levels of leadership action within specific contexts. In no way do my leadership actions undercut my instructors; distribution illustrates how material situations are constitutive elements of leadership practice, shaping the forms such leadership takes, a central tenant of distributed leadership theory.

Put in relief by my earlier email example, my testimony of coperforming teacher evaluation again illustrates how distributed leadership is more than collaborative leadership; it may or may not be collaborative in execution depending on the situation. Collaborative leadership models may widen the network of leaders to include multiple players rather than a single figurehead, but it may also invest too much in those individual leaders while minimizing the shaping role of followers and the situational context. Instead, distributed leadership accounts for the shaping role of the leadership actions of my writing instructors in concert with my own. Distributed leadership allows us to see variances in the sharing of leadership to account for gradients of collaboration and the dynamism of collective effort. The sharing of leadership under this paradigm need not be equally distributed; appointed leadership is not assumed to eclipse other vertical or hierarchical structures of leadership precisely because it is leadership *interactions* and not individual actions that are understood to be paramount.

Because of our power differentials and official positions on and off the tenure track, the work of our group has not always been collaborative, but it has always been interdependent and coconstitutive. What initially brought us together—the desire to bridge our efforts across departments and programs in the ASC and writing program to connect basic writing and first-year writing—has since disrupted unquestioned norms at our university that separated us to begin with. Recently, my university requested that I attend a workshop on corequisite writing instruction hosted by Complete College America (CCA). My purpose at the workshop was to review the ways our university delivered developmental writing instruction and to provide an action plan to my dean that would allow us to comply with a new statewide allegiance to CCA that mandated all developmental education be able to be completed within one academic year for undergraduates, effectively challenging the Stretch model of instruction. Because of my strong working relationship with the writing instructor in the ASC, who was teaching a large percentage of our Stretch classes, I was able to convince my dean that she also needed to attend this workshop because we already had a conjoint curricular project underway through our committee work. While he had little knowledge of our Writing Steering Committee's actions, I could point to several curricular changes on which our group had worked together, such as the ways we had recently digitized the basic writing curriculum, and provide reasons for our dual attendance at the workshop.

What resulted from this initial CCA workshop was a months-long alliance between me, the NTT instructors within the writing program, and the NTT instructor of writing in the ASC to research, develop, and test new course structures that would move our basic writing courses to a corequisite model of instruction. Because neither I nor my writing instructors within the program could actually teach basic writing based on its location within the ASC rather than the writing program, we worked together to read, discuss, and brainstorm new course structures that the ASC instructor could apply to her classroom. And because none of us could access the power to change course structures, much of this work happened without acknowledgment. In turn, what resulted was a true ecosystem of distributed leadership wherein "leadership [was] about learning together and constructing meaning and knowledge collectively and collaboratively. It involve[d] opportunities to surface and mediate perceptions, values, beliefs, information and assumptions through continuing conversations. It mean[t] generating ideas together; seeking to reflect upon and make sense of work in the light of shared beliefs and new information; and creat[ing] actions that grow out of these new understandings" (Harris, 2003, 314). We learned together, brainstormed together, conducted experiments within the limits of our individual classrooms, and reported back. Slowly and together, we discovered sustainable corequisite models for our local context. The product of distributed leadership is concertive action, which is the product of conjoint activity in which initiative and expertise are pooled and "the outcome is a product or energy, which is greater than the sum of [the group members'] individual actions" (Bennett, Wise, and Woods 2003,

7). What this means in pragmatic terms is that distributed leadership attempts to account for many types of expertise beyond subject matter or official titles or degrees to include experience, passion, and drive and the consideration that expertise is always dependent on contextual relevant skills as enacted; individuals with relevant expertise may start an initiative or project that others will adopt and adapt in ways that benefit the group and the individual.

In the end, an outcome of our collective actions became much greater than the sum of our individual ones. The decree to change our basic writing curriculum, which was brought to me to manage as the "writing expert" and official leader on my campus, drew attention to our working group in a way citations in our annual review documents didn't. As our dean became aware of our ability to work against the institutional boundaries that divided us for years, he also began an administrative conversation that questioned those boundaries. While it's been a long road with many challenges, our distributed efforts have ultimately resulted in a merging of our programs effective in fall 2018 so that all writing will be centrally administered by me, and all of our writing faculty will be able to contribute equally to the development and instruction of developmental *and* first-year writing. Additionally, as a result of our efforts, our dean granted us two new NTT lines to help stabilize the program and further decrease our demand on adjuncts.

Distributed leadership is, for me, a feminist sensemaking pragmatic because it captures the significance of interactions and offers a heuristic for thinking about WPA leadership differently—indeed, in thinking that administration is leadership at all and not just service. It allows for power differentials between group members without negating the impact of the relationality of leading. Our efforts illustrate how distributed leadership is defined by "interacting component parts in relationships of interdependence in which the group has distinct properties over and above the individuals" who comprise it (Spillane 2006, 16). It was our combined interactions that broke down artificial barriers that impeded our work, and our results would not have been achievable had we not worked together collectively and taken on various micro- and macro-leadership actions individually as necessary. While there is certainly no one right way to administer writing within a university, we are excited by our new combined model because it will institutionalize our collective labor and make it easier for us to find official, institutionalized spaces to interact. Our sensemaking will be therefore driven by and accountable to this interactive map. And our collective resilience is brought about by this interaction: "What creates and maintains resilience?" ask

Harrington and Dinitz in this collection. "The interplay between place, people, and structure," they answer.

Of course, there is a risk of distributing leadership in programs comprised of untenured and untenurable faculty. My instructors know that, despite how much they value it, "shared leadership could be a burden for non-tenured track faculty . . . [if] it leads to the exploitation of non-tenured track faculty." Exploitation is a very real danger that should drive us to continue communicating openly with all of those participating in shared leadership structures, respecting the relational process of distributing leadership. Like any other, these structures can be corrupted. Even so, practicing distributed leadership as a feminist ecological means of sensemaking means we define success by efforts to attain mutual well-being and engagement, so I can address labor inequalities in my program as I also try to change them. In the end, I continue to distribute leadership because my instructors believe it is worth it: "Ultimately, we value a leader who is willing to share leadership because it gives us non-tenure track faculty a voice and the ability to make positive changes." Together, we can all flourish.

NOTES

1. All instructor testimony is IRB-approved and collected through both in-person and emailed interviews. Instructor responses have been aggregated and are referred to collectively to preserve the anonymity of responses. Testimony includes the viewpoints of both past and present full-time, non-tenure track writing faculty at my university.
2. The difference between collaboration, which functions as a measure of equality and interchangeable power as defined by Gunner (2002), and conjoint activity, which highlights emergent and interdependent action between varied and unequal power positions as defined by Spillane (2006), is significant and can help us deepen our thinking about Meeks and Hult's (1998) example and explore the limits of collaboration within a hierarchical university. While their example is seemingly collaborative as presented, we can also imagine an unexplored subtext by undertaking a thought experiment: the same graduate students who were lauded by Meeks and Hult's department for their creative thinking to reassign classes to new rooms may have circumvented a classroom reservation system and, in turn, irritated a secretary who oversees those rooms. The secretary was irritated because she was approached by a tenured faculty member who wanted a room in which the now-reassigned writing class was meeting—a confrontation that might not have happened had the WPA, a fellow colleague, been the one in the room. Perhaps that faculty member or involved secretary even complained to the WPA that the graduate students were overstepping their bounds. And, perhaps the dean, who got wind of the reassignments, though not the complaints, was so impressed that no classes were missed that he congratulated the WPA for her management of the TAs, thereby giving credit to the WPA and not the graduate students. Such a thought experiment, while necessarily brief, illuminates the possible ways graduate students may be denied

equal power as the WPA, even if they assume and work toward common program goals in collaborative spirit. What is exposed by the experiment is the range of role interdependencies and situational interdependence among the leaders—factors distributed leadership can better account for than can collaboration.

REFERENCES

Ancona, D. 2011. "Sensemaking: Framing and Acting in the Unknown." In *The Handbook for Teaching Leadership*, edited by S. Snook, N. Nohria, and R. Khurana, 3–19. Thousand Oaks, CA: Sage Publications. https://www.sagepub.com/sites/default/files/upm-binaries/42924_1.pdf.

Aronson, Anne, and Craig Hanson. 1998. "Doubling Our Chances: Co-Directing a Writing Program." *WPA: Writing Program Administration* 21: 23–32.

Bennett, Nigel, Christine Wise, and Philip Woods. 2003. *Distributed Leadership: A Review of Literature*. National College for School Leadership. http://oro.open.ac.uk/8534/1/bennett-distributed-leadership-full.pdf.

Bousquet, Marc, Tony Scott, and Leo Parasondola. 2004. *Tenured Bosses and Disposable Teachers: Writing Instruction in the Managed University*. Carbondale: Southern Illinois University Press.

Code, Lorraine. 2006. *Ecological Thinking: The Politics of Epistemic Location*. Oxford: Oxford University Press.

Crawford, Ilene, and Donna Strickland. 2010. "Interrupting Collaboration: Feminist Writing Program Administration and the Question of Status." In *Performing Feminism and Administration in Rhetoric and Composition Studies*, edited by Krista Ratcliffe and Rebecca Rickly. Cresskill, NJ: Hampton Press.

Cuomo, Chris J. 1998. *Feminism and Ecological Communities: An Ethic of Flourishing*. London: Routledge.

Detweiler, Jane, Margaret LaWare, and Patti Wojahn. 2017. "Academic Leadership and Advocacy: On Not Leaning in." *College English* 9 (5): 451–465.

Flaherty, Colleen. 2014. "What Students Write." *Inside Higher Ed*. https://www.insidehighered.com/news/2014/08/21/study-examines-professors-writing-assignments-students.

Gere, Anne Ruggles. 1996. "The Long Revolution in Composition." In *Composition in the Twenty-First Century: Crisis and Change*, edited by Lynn Z. Bloom, Donald A. Daiker, and Edward M. White. Carbondale: Southern Illinois University Press.

Glau, Gregory. 1996. "The 'Stretch Program': Arizona State University's New Model of University-level Basic Writing Instruction." *WPA* 20 (1–2): 79–91.

Gunner, Jeanne. 2002. "Collaborative Administration." In *The Writing Program Administrator's Resource: A Guide to Reflective Institutional Practice*, edited by Stewart C. Brown, Theresa Enos and Catherine Chaput, 253–262. Mahwah, NJ: Lawrence Erlbaum Associates.

Harris, A. 2003. "Teacher Leadership as Distributed Leadership: Heresy, Fantasy or Possibility?" *School Leadership and Management* 23 (3): 313–324.

Harris, Joseph. 2014. "Places at the Table." In "Symposium: Off Track and On: Valuing the Intellectual Work of Non-Tenure-Track Faculty." *WPA* 77 (1): 69–72.

Ianetta, Melissa. 2015. "Absence and Action: Making Visible WPA Work." *WPA* 38 (2): 141–158.

Kahn, Seth. 2015. "Towards an Ecology of Sustainable Labor in Writing Programs (and Other Places)." *WPA* 39 (1): 109–121.

Kazan, Tina S., and Catherine Gabor. 2013. "Magic, Agency and Power: Mapping Embodied Leadership Roles." *WPA* 37 (1): 134–160.

Malenczyk, Rita. 2012. "Kitchen Cooks, Plate Twirlers, and Posers; or, the I's Have It." *WPA* 35 (2): 184–189.

Meeks, Lynn, and Christine Hult. 1998. "A Co-Mentoring Model of Administration." *WPA* 21: 9–22.

Melzer, Dan. 2014. *Assignments across the Curriculum: A National Study of College Writing.* Logan: Utah State University Press.

Mirtz, Ruth M., and Roxanne M. Cullen. 2002. "Beyond Postmodernism: Leadership Theories and Writing Program Administration," In *The Writing Program Administrator as Theorist: Making Knowledge Work*, edited by Shirley K. Rose and Irwin Weiser, 90–102. Portsmouth, NH: Boynton/Cook.

Penrose, Ann. 2012. "Professional Identity in a Contingent-Labor Profession: Expertise, Autonomy, Community in Composition Teaching." *WPA* 35 (2): 108–126.

Phelps, Louise Wetherbee. 2002. "Turtles all the Way Down: Educating Academic Leaders." In *The Writing Program Administrator's Resource*, edited by Stuart C. Brown and Teresa Enos, 3–39. Mahwah, NJ: Lawrence Earlbaum.

Ryan, Kathleen J. 2012. "Thinking Ecologically: Rhetorical Ecological Feminist Agency and Writing Program Administration." *WPA* 36 (1): 74–94.

Schell, Eileen. 1998. "Who's the Boss? The Possibilities and Pitfalls of Collaborative Administration for Untenured WPAs." *WPA* 21: 65–80.

Spillane, James P. 2006. *Distributed Leadership*. San Francisco, CA: Jossey-Bass.

Spillane, James P., Richard Halverson, and John Diamond. 2004. "Towards a Theory of Leadership Practice: A Distributed Perspective." *Journal of Curriculum Studies* 36: 3–34.

Strickland, Donna. 2011. *The Managerial Unconscious in the History of Composition Studies.* Carbondale: Southern Illinois University Press.

Weick, Karl E. 1995. *Sensemaking in Organizations*. Thousand Oaks, CA: Sage Publications.

Weick, Karl, Kathleen M. Sutcliffe, and David Obstfeld. 2005. "Organizing and the Process of Sensemaking and Organizing." *Organization Science* 16 (4): 409–421.

Werder, Carmen. 2000. "Rhetorical Agency: Seeing the Ethics of It All." *WPA* 24 (1–2): 9–26.

White, Edward M. 1991. "Use It or Lose It: Power and the WPA." *WPA* 15 (1–2): 3–12.

10
SENSEMAKING AS ANTIRACIST WRITING PROGRAM ADMINISTRATION
Reappropriating Activity and Actor-Network Theory

Brian Hendrickson

Despite their significant impacts on how we understand writers and writing, both activity theory (AT) and actor-network theory (ANT) have not been adequately explored as means for writing program administrators (WPAs) to make sense of their work. By examining their historical appropriation within writing studies more generally, I will demonstrate how we as a field have abstracted these methodologies from their original intents, and I will further argue that we have neglected recent developments that have rendered these methodologies more effective tools, particularly for antiracist WPA sensemaking—AT for transforming racist organizational dispositions and ANT for interrogating them. I will conclude by providing examples of how I am beginning to use each of these in my work to interrogate and transform racist organizational dispositions at my own university.

From my early teaching experiences in majority-minority elementary schools, community colleges, and correctional facilities to my doctoral studies at a Hispanic-serving institution, I have spent my career in education exploring—and oftentimes stumbling through—what it means for me to be a white ally in a racially, culturally, and linguistically diverse classroom, institution, and community. Since accepting a position at Roger Williams University, a private, predominantly white institution whose main campus is located in the predominantly white town of Bristol in Rhode Island, a predominantly white state, I've been forced to rethink what it means for me, a white person, to commit myself to antiracist writing program administration; in continuing to learn how to be what Neisha-Anne Green (2018) describes as an accomplice to people of color (POC), I've been trying to make sense of this new challenge of working with a predominantly white faculty, administration, and student body to interrogate and transform racist organizational dispositions in and beyond my university's writing programs.[1] In the process, I have begun to interrogate the racist organizational dispositions that appropriate our sensemaking as writing studies scholars. Before delving deeper into that interrogation, I first want to explicate what I mean by organizational sensemaking, racist organizational dispositions, and the combined explanatory power these concepts afford antiracist writing program administration.

ORGANIZATIONAL SENSEMAKING AND RACIST ORGANIZATIONAL DISPOSITIONS

The concept of organizational sensemaking affords WPAs a useful framework through which to consider how writing programs perpetuate racism despite and even because of best intentions and how white WPAs in particular might better account for racializing dissonance in the way that we make sense of our organizational contexts. Social psychologist Karl E. Weick (1995, 2000) contends that strategic planning is not as formative of organizations as are their recursive attempts to offer plausible accounts of dissonance arising between the tidier stories they tell about themselves and their encounters with the unexpected. Sensemaking as a collective act of organizing isn't inherently reactionary or revolutionary. It might attempt to explain away dissonance, or it might account for dissonance as a characteristic of organizational identity. Weick (2009) does, however, identify productive sensemaking as occurring in what he terms high reliability organizations, which are less worried about strategic decision-making and "more worried about enacting a structure that makes sense of the unexpected" (7).

When an organization places too much value on strategic decision-making, it tends to make sense of failures to plan for the unexpected by constructing a plausible account of how the unexpected did not happen at all, was inconsequential, or was, upon closer inspection, already accounted for in the organization's strategic plan. The plan—the principal way the organization makes sense of itself—never changes in response to the unexpected. In the same way, writing programs can focus too much on standardizing what they perceive as best practices at the expense of remaining responsive to unexpected changes within the larger institutional context; recent pedagogical and administrative developments in the field; shifting student demographics; and racial, cultural, and linguistic differences among students. As an organizational theory, sensemaking helps us see that when WPAs drink our own Kool-Aid, our attempts to standardize best practices mutate into plausible accounts of how we have done the right thing for our writing programs, despite the myriad ways in which we and our programs are still complicit in racializing practices.

So, racism presents itself first as a dissonance to be explained away by our sensemaking and, again, as a result of it. Hence, in his plenary address at the 2016 Council of Writing Program Administrators (CWPA) Conference, Asao B. Inoue (2016) insists, "We must do violence to the CWPA and our own writing programs if we are to address racism" (134). Anticipating his audience's resistance, Inoue concedes, "Many of you might be saying to yourselves, 'yes, but not me. I'm fair. I'm not racist.' Let me be clear. I ain't talkin' 'bout people *being* racist. I ain't talking 'bout intentions. We are all good people trying to do what's right. I'm talking about our programs and organization being racist. I'm talking about our dispositions toward language and its judgement being racist" (135). Then Inoue doubles down on the grounds of his initial assertion: "But this is not completely true. I *am* talking about how in unconscious ways *all of us are racist*" (135). Inoue reminds us that our very dispositions toward sensemaking as WPAs—that is, our organizational mindsets, habits of mind, habitus—color and are colored by the way our organizations perpetuate racist language, values, beliefs, and practices and, yes, racist characterizations of our students.

Our individual intentions, Inoue implies here, are not nearly as deterministic as our organizational dispositions, which he links to the concept of whiteness as a racialized habitus, or "a set of structuring structures, durable, transposable, and flexible" (2016, 145). Individuals can inhabit dispositions, but dispositions themselves are hardly individual characteristics. As Elizabeth Wardle (2012) notes, drawing upon Bourdieu's characterization of disposition as habitus, "Institutional habitus creates and recreates orthodox discourse and attempts to push the social world to the status of doxa—beyond question or even recognizable as anything other than natural and inevitable. Individual dispositions toward finding and answering and moving on, rather than asking questions and exploring problems, might be directly linked to dispositions of fields or educational habitus that have a vested interest in maintaining dominant structures, beliefs, and practices (doxa)" (under "Can Dispositions Change?"). In creating and recreating whiteness, writing programs make sense of dissonant practices such as evaluating students on their Standard Edited American English proficiency as natural and inevitable (this despite also acknowledging the inherent racism in such practices).

It is exactly this sort of racist organizational sensemaking that Alba Newmann Holmes describes elsewhere in this collection as circumscribing "open communications about race and privilege . . . by assertions of positive intent." As such, a writing program's racist organizational disposition feeds on and is fed by racist organizational sensemaking that enables WPAs to *act* in ways we concede are racist while still claiming not to *be* racist, that is, not to hold explicitly racist individual intentions.

Racist organizational sensemaking aligns with Wardle's articulation of habitus as an answer-getting, as opposed to problem-exploring, disposition. Wardle (2012) suggests that individual as well as institutional answer-getting dispositions can be transformed into problem-exploring dispositions, but doing so in either case appears to involve a synthesis of individual motives and social action. That's why Inoue (2016) "ain't talking 'bout intentions," which are much easier to change, yet alone are highly unlikely to effect change in a self-replicating, answer-getting disposition toward sensemaking such as whiteness (135). It is therefore necessary but ultimately insufficient, Frankie Condon (2007) tells us, that white WPAs critically and intentionally reflect upon, check, and correct our individual racist dispositions toward our work: "Commonsense and past practice have led to a shared conceptualization of anti-racist process as beginning with the self and extending outward to an analysis of institutions, then systems. Too often, however, this trajectory has been interrupted when whites, overcome by a fascination with the personal, are unable to extend ourselves beyond what has been done to us, through us, and in our name with regard to racism" (22). Nor does it suffice, Inoue (2016) warns us, that we relegate our antiracist activism to our teaching, tutoring, and training: "Writing programs cannot leave a white racial *habitus* at that, at just critical discussions of language and texts, without also using those discussions in some way to change the program, to change the dispositions toward language that drive judgment in the program" (150). This is what Inoue means by doing violence to our writing programs: we must reappropriate our organizational sensemaking toward transformation of our racist organizational dispositions.

Before white WPAs can develop the sorts of problem-exploring dispositions, we need to transform our organizational dispositions; we have to admit that we have a problem that needs exploring. Doing so requires that we pay attention to what scholars of color have to say about racism in writing programs, because as Genevieve García de Müeller and Iris Ruiz (2017) report, POC often have different perceptions from their white peers regarding the racial climates of their writing programs. In articulating "the precise role of blackness as its own cultural epistemological framework" in writing program administration, Staci M. Perryman-Clark, Collin Lamont Craig, and their contributors evidence just how much writing program administration stands to gain by perceiving itself through a problem-exploring, antiracist, nonwhite lens (Perryman-Clark and Craig 2019, 3). Unfortunately, much of the story of racism in writing programs is told by the absence of voices of scholars of color. As Sherry Craig (2016) points out, "For emergent WPAs of color, the stories shared inside and outside [CWPA] do not often portray our experiences. The few examples available are woeful tales of loss and critique" (17). That's not to say that critique can't still be useful. Scholars of color remind us that the changes that need to be made are far from superficial. Through his analysis of the history of writing center scholarship, Romeo García (2017) demonstrates how an "incoherent narrative of 'diversity' and 'collaboration' is evidence of the degrees in which whiteness shapes the imagining of both centers and practices as 'safe' and 'inviting'" (34). As an answer-getting disposition, whiteness reproduces whiteness through buzzwords that, like other plausible accounts generated by our sensemaking, obscure even as they acknowledge racism in writing programs.

The answer-getting disposition of whiteness renders necessary but insufficient that white WPAs acknowledge the personal accounts, theoretical insights, and empirical research findings upon which scholars of color base their assertions that writing programs are racist. White WPAs must also employ that acknowledgment in efforts to reappropriate our field's ways of sensemaking—our methodologies—which have come to inhabit whitely dispositions that sever them from their potentially antiracist uses and our own best intentions.

REAPPROPRIATING ACTIVITY THEORY

AT is foundational to our understanding of learning transfer, an increasingly significant factor in how writing programs affect and assess student learning, yet scholarship in writing program administration has not employed AT to make sense of how writing programs construct and conceptualize themselves in order to transform racist organizational dispositions. In particular, developments in AT over the past ten years are primed for doing this difficult work, and reappropriating AT in this way would constitute a radical reclamation of the antiracist motives that introduced it to the United States.

Michael Cole (1988) provides a concise history of AT as originating in the work of sociohistorical psychologists Alexander R. Luria (1928), Lev S. Vygotsky (1929), and Alexie N. Leontiev (1932) and elaborated by a broadly interdisciplinary and international range of scholars, many of whom became associated at one point during the 1970s and 1980s with Cole's Laboratory for Comparative Human Cognition (LCHC). According to Cole (1988), the LCHC was established to provide "a systematic alternative to cultural deprivation theories" exploited to blame communities of color for the poor school performance of students of color and subsequently support policies that treated cultural difference as a problem requiring a solution (145). Cole notes that early Soviet AT attempted to disprove fascistic theories of racial/genetic differences in human development by studying the influence of macrocosmic sociohistorical forces on individual human development, but it made the mistake of using experiments modeled on Western cultural practices to measure cognitive development in so-called primitive cultures. The LCHC sought to correct this error by focusing on how subjects develop culturally enriched ways of knowing, learning, and doing within particular sociohistorical contexts. In doing so, this new wave of scholarship grounded in AT refined its underlying principle, which Cole (1988) defines thusly: "Tool use implies both mediation and context specificity, while context-dependence implies that mental processes are historical phenomena" (148). In other words, the tools we use, such as writing, and the contexts in which we use them, such as particular cultures or disciplines, affect the way we think and learn; schools therefore have an obligation to teach in ways that are culturally responsive, or else risk teaching in ways that pretend to be culturally neutral but are actually racist.

Over a decade prior, the influence of Soviet AT is evident in Janet Emig's foundational argument for understanding writing as a situated learning/learned technology (Emig 1977). Later, Charles Bazerman (1988) draws upon Vygotsky (1929) to theorize genres as social facts within particular disciplinary activity systems. Carol Berkenkotter and Thomas Huckin (1995) then draw from AT to develop a sociocognitive theory of genre knowledge. But David R. Russell (1995) is likely the first in writing studies to adopt not only AT's theoretical insights but also the associated interventionist methodology of expansive developmental research put forward by Yrjö Engeström (1987) to assist groups of learners in working through iterative stages of expansive learning—from indiscriminately performing isolated operations to coordinated concept and goal formation and collectively transforming and assessing the transformation of a particular organization's rules (norms and values) and divisions of labor—with the aim of collectively overcoming the isolating forces of capitalist labor relations and assuming agency over the means of economic and epistemic production.

Using Engeström's mapping of the cycles of expansive learning, Russell (1995) critiques first-year writing programs that don't empower students to assume agency over their own learning within particular disciplinary contexts, and he leverages this assertion to make what is likely one of the earliest cases for a writing-about-writing pedagogy, largely informing Douglas Downs and Elizabeth Wardle's (2007) argument for the same on the basis that the knowledge students acquire in first-year writing doesn't transfer to later coursework. Elsewhere, Wardle (2007) draws upon scholarship collected in Terttu Tuomi-Gröhn and Yrjö Engeström's (2003) *Between School and Work* on learning at the boundaries between activity systems to make two key recommendations: focus on teaching metacognition in first-year writing and work with other disciplines toward increasingly shared instruments and objectives in the teaching of writing. These recommendations continue to impact the field, as evidenced in the teaching-for-transfer pedagogy advocated by Kathleen Yancey, Liane Robertson, and Kara Taczak (2014) in their 2015 CCCC Research Impact Award- and 2016 CWPA Best Book Award-winning work, *Writing Across Contexts: Transfer, Composition, and Cultures of Writing*, to provide just one noted and far-reaching example.

Despite its influence on writing program administration, the literature does not document AT being used by WPAs as a means of enacting and assessing organizational transformation, yet the lessons from Engeström's (1987) theory of the stages of expansive learning are pertinent in particular to antiracist administration. Whiteness, as a habitus symbiotically enmeshed with capitalism, is an isolating force. At its most fundamental level, it is meant to assign power and privilege to some by denying it to others, even as it renders the means of that assignation and denial invisible. Although white WPAs benefit from this arrangement, Inoue (2016) makes clear in his inventory of the features of whiteness as a discourse in the classroom that the habitus of whiteness comes at a cost for all who inhabit it. The hyper-individualized, hyper-rational mindset of whiteness constrains all subjects' operations to its conditions. Most of us are, at best, aware of those conditions and are employing our best intentions to transform our immediate circumstances. AT reminds us that our best intentions are insufficient. As Genie Nicole Giaimo and Joseph Cheatle point out in this collection regarding writing center documentation, we must look beyond our immediate circumstances for instruments—conceptual, semiotic, and material—capable of transforming them. White WPAs must risk the transformation that we invite by working toward increasingly shared objects with other systems, especially racialized Others. However, AT also reminds us that antiracist institutional transformation is, at best, an iterative endeavor, because, like capitalism, the habitus of whiteness resists transformation.

Nevertheless, in employing the instrument of AT toward the object of antiracism, WPAs can pursue the boundary work that promises to be the most transformative for their particular programmatic contexts. Consider, for instance, the description Genevieve García de Müeller (2016) provides for "the migrant activist WPA," who, in recognizing that the migrant student activist appropriates "the genres and rhetorical moves of the dominant institution with non-assimilationist methods . . . seeks not to use these transference of skills as a mode of assimilation into the academy but as a path for migrant undocumented students to change academic discourse and to combat racist structures on and beyond the university" (36). Changing academic discourse and combating racist structures on and beyond campus is an expansive object shared in the boundary work of two activity systems: the writing program and the migrant student activist organization. Each contributes a transformative element to the instrument of transformation: the genres and rhetorical moves appropriated by migrant student activists. García de Müeller (2016) predicts that such boundary work can lead to "self-interrogation in WPA that focuses on the intersections between administering writing programs and race, ethnicity, linguistic diversity, and citizenship" while repositioning "the migrant activist . . . at the center" (41). As an assessment instrument, AT asks WPAs to account for how such partnerships reposition stakeholders within a programmatic activity system, transforming not only the curricular instruments and objectives but the rules and divisions of labor that form the system's base, as well as the WPAs themselves—in García de Müeller's (2016) example, from an administrative agent to a migrant activist.

From a methodological perspective, García de Müeller's (2016) example reminds us, too, that delineating the boundaries of an activity system—part of the work that goes into what Engeström (1987) labels preliminary phenomenological insight—can be a messy and often imperfect affair. Are the migrant student activists already a part of the programmatic activity system or not? Can the WPA ever become a fully integrated subject in the activity system of the migrant activist community? Through their longitudinal ethnographic study of a dual immersion elementary school classroom, Kris D. Gutiérrez, Patricia Baquedano-López, and Carlos Tejeda (1999) reveal how the activity system of the classroom operates as a hybrid space in which official and unofficial discourses productively collide to create a Third Space in which learning occurs—an explanation consistent with AT's account of contradictions within an activity system as catalysts of learning. Gutiérrez, Baquedano-López, and Tejeda's scholarship urges those of us making sense of writing programs with AT that even the most rigidly structured activity systems are inherently hybrid spaces, and that accurately delineating boundaries between systems is less important than actively cultivating productive Third Spaces. Doing so is consistent with Weick's (2009) assertion that attuning to the unexpected is more important in sensemaking than developing strategies aimed at reducing it.

Gutiérrez (2008) attends to what it means to attune to the unexpected in articulating the objective and instrument of teaching and learning in the Third Space as sociocritical literacy, "a historicizing literacy that . . . emerges in discursive and embodied practices including writing, reading, and performative activities with transformative ends," and that attends "to contradictions in and between texts lived and studied, institutions (e.g., the classroom, the academy), and sociocultural practices, locally experienced and historically influenced" (148–149). What Gutiérrez (2008) articulates, in effect, is AT employed as antiracist sensemaking, that is, a performative, collective activity with the transformative institutional aim of making space for racial, cultural, and linguistic difference. Cultivating Third Spaces in writing programs therefore involves analyzing how WPAs make sense in response to the unexpected contradictions between our best intentions and our complicity in administering racist programs. As such, Kris D. Gutiérrez and Lynda D. Stone explain, our sensemaking must account not only for the organizational rules, divisions of labor, and objectives that shape the instruments we use to make sense of and administer writing programs but also our organizational dispositions (Gutiérrez and Stone 2000).

In his more recent work, Engeström (2010) employs the trope of mycorrhizae to describe how, in increasingly fluid organizational settings, organizational dispositions enable seemingly discrete, improvisational teams to execute goal-oriented actions toward a shared objective. The term *mycorrhizae* refers to the vast belowground structures of filamentous roots that plants grow and that fungi inhabit and extend, or, more accurately, the catalyzing symbiotic relationship. Engeström (2010) explains mycorrhizae as "simultaneously a living, expanding process (or bundle of developing connections) *and* a relatively durable, stabilized structure; both a mental landscape . . . and a material infrastructure" (229). What Engeström appears to be describing here is a problem-exploring organizational disposition. Within this metaphor, the more stable plants are the organizational activity systems, the mushrooms are the more impromptu teams, and the process is the disposition. "Without these 'plants' and 'mushrooms,'" Engeström (2010) elaborates, "the knotworking mycorrhizae will not take shape. If anything, careful analyses of the dynamics of the activity systems involved are more important than ever before" (229). As important as such analyses may be, and as apt Engeström's trope, mycorrhizae is more of a concept of what organizational dispositions look like and how they function and less an analytical tool for tracing them out, and so it can only really serve as a generic metaphor that helps us understand how racism takes hold of and circulates through organizational dispositions.

AT appears well equipped to help WPAs transform the racist, answer-getting dispositions that manifest in our writing programs. White WPAs can use AT as a tool for cultivating Third Spaces in which racialized Others from across and beyond the university can assume agency over our writing programs' economic and epistemic means of production, leading to new, antiracist conceptualizations of our writing programs and their objectives. Furthermore, we can use AT as a tool for assessing just how comprehensively we have transformed our writing programs and their whitely dispositions through transformed rules and divisions of labor and increasingly shared instruments and objectives.

REAPPROPRIATING ACTOR-NETWORK THEORY

Nevertheless, AT seems ill-equipped to map out the subterranean mycorrhizae, or dispositions, themselves, so that we might better attune to racializing dissonance as a constant variable in our organizational sensemaking. Clay Spinuzzi (2008) comes to a similar conclusion regarding AT in his analysis of emergent telecommunications organizations. In an attempt "to develop a deeper account of how AT deals with the interplay among multiple activities" (29), Spinuzzi employs both AT and ANT in his study, ultimately concluding that AT is better suited to studying how organizations develop communication practices, but that its account of that development is too rigid, vertical, and dialectical, and requires a more dialogic flexibility to trace how communication practices develop in dispersed and highly dynamic organizational settings. With this recommendation, Spinuzzi (2008) positions himself within a tradition in writing studies that appreciates certain elements of ANT but ultimately rejects its more radical methodological constraints—a tradition with which white WPAs will have to contend if they are to effectively reappropriate ANT as antiracist sensemaking.

As a means of studying the social construction of scientific facts, ANT arose out of the sociology of science (or science and technology studies), especially the work of Bruno Latour and Steve Woolgar (1979), and collected into a set of theoretical and methodological assumptions in Michel Callon, John Law, and Arie Rip (1986; Law 1986) and Latour (1987). Spinuzzi (2015) points out that ANT's raison d'être is avoiding begging the question, that is, studying some social formation through the lens of a theory that already explains it. To avoid this trap, Latour (2005) lays out the five principles that outline ANT's methodological commitment to uncertainty: focus not on group formations but the controversies that give rise to them; interpret facts as matters of concern; trace effects, not causes; treat anything that produces an effect as an actor; and recognize the limitations in any textual account of an actor-network. In effect, ANT is an approach to sensemaking that is radically attuned to the unexpected.

ANT initially receives a warm reception in writing studies, appearing as a frequent point of reference in Bazerman (1988) and throughout Charles Bazerman and James Paradis (1991); Greg Myers (1996) also makes an extensive case for the relevance of ANT to writing studies research. But Bazerman (1997, 1999) begins to lose interest in what he perceives as ANT's stubborn insistence on symmetry, which he claims counterintuitively heroizes certain actors while downplaying the influence of history. Although Russell (1997) admits a number of points of convergence between AT and ANT, he contends that ANT's decentering of the human subject is incompatible with AT's placement of humans as the principal agents of all activity, a criticism later echoed by Tony Scott and Nancy Welch (2014). Taken together, these criticisms paint a portrait of ANT as ahistorical and disembodied, and thus about as incompatible a methodology as one could imagine for studying racism as a sociohistorical and embodied phenomenon.

In response to objections that ANT obscures the role of human agency and inhibits materialist critique, I point back to Inoue's insistence that to transform our racist organizational dispositions, we must see past the primacy of individual intentionality (Inoue 2016). Furthermore, whiteness may operate within particular sociohistorical contexts, but as an answer-getting disposition, it also denies its own historicity. Like capitalism, the habitus of whiteness is parasitic; it subsists on history even as it devours it. Keeping within Engeström's metaphor of mycorrhizae, capitalism and whiteness are similar to the parasitic genus of fungus known as *Amarillia*, one particular species of which, *Amarillia ostoyae*, covers nearly four square miles of Oregon's Malheur National Forest, holding the title of the largest living organism ever known (Engeström 2010; Zhang 2017). Rather than initiating the symbiotic process Engeström

(2010) describes, the *Amarillia ostoyae*, or honey mushroom, instead injects its rhizomorphs up into the tree itself. It develops, but not through dialectical synthesis; its only calculus is accumulation and decay.

Understanding this basic developmental principle of whiteness is insufficient to explaining how whiteness infects particular organizational dispositions, but this is exactly what recent methodological developments in ANT have inclined it to do. Those developments arise out of Latour's attempt to develop an anthropology of modern Western civilization. "Moderns," as Latour refers to the denizens of modern Western civilization, are coming to realize that our attempts at emancipation from social and natural constraints through reason and objectivity have only produced more oppressive social and natural constraints. As such, we've begun to question reason and objectivity, and subsequently, just how modern we really are or have ever been. Now our disciplines, institutions, and values require revaluation to determine if they can, or should, be reconstituted within a new, amodern ontology, which requires an anthropology designed not for western moderns to study other so-called primitive cultures through a modern lens, but to study ourselves and modernity itself through an avowedly amodern lens that we are in the collective process of forming. In their critiques of Latour (1993), writing studies scholars have largely ignored this inherently sociocritical mission, and thus the antiracist potential of ANT, for interrogating the unique contours of racist organizational dispositions within particular organizational contexts.

To accomplish his anthropology of modern Western civilization, Latour (2013) develops a methodological extension of ANT indicated by the code tag [PRE], which signifies the unique *preposition* for a particular actor-network's (code tag [NET]) values. Latour (2013, 57) draws upon William James (1884, 1905) in explaining, "There exists in the world no domain of 'with,' 'after,' or 'between' as there exists a domain of chairs, heat, microbes, doormats, or cats. And yet each of these prepositions plays a decisive role in the understanding of what is to follow, by offering the type of relation needed to grasp the experience of the world in question." Putting it in other terms writing studies scholars will appreciate, Latour (2013) compares the notion of preposition to that of J. L. Austin's felicity and infelicity conditions, the idea being that different networks, such as the law, possess felicity conditions by which legal practitioners discursively arrive through *legal means* at a peculiarly legal account of what is true or false, which is not at all the same account as the account of truth and falsehood according to the felicity conditions of scientific proof (Austin 1962). Equally complementary to our discipline is

Latour's comparison of preposition to genre. Like the concept of a novel, a preposition establishes one's expectations for what's to come, yet proclaiming that one is going to write a novel doesn't necessarily determine that what one composes will become a novel (Latour 2013). To a greater extent, the explanatory force of a genre label materializes through the dialogically connected acts of composing and interpreting the text as a generalization, but one that is nevertheless specific enough that the label of novel can't just be applied to an expense report and retain any of its explanatory force. What Latour recommends is following the methodological protocol of ANT in order to trace the associations through which a particular actor-network extends itself, then identify the preposition according to which that network develops its own peculiar account of what counts as true and false.

I want to draw a parallel here between an actor-network's preposition and a writing program's organizational disposition. As a tool for interrogating the grounds for what counts as a plausible account in WPA sensemaking, ANT and its [NET · PRE] extension can help white WPAs render racist organizational dispositions more visible, which can in turn open up opportunities for transforming them through an interventionist protocol such as AT.

EMPLOYING AT AND ANT AS ANTIRACIST WPA SENSEMAKING: TWO BEGINNINGS

In the preceding sections, I have sought to reconnect AT and ANT as we understand them in writing studies to their historically intended uses and their more recent methodological developments. In so doing, I have also sought to demonstrate the utility of reappropriating each methodology for antiracist writing program administration through the overlaid lenses of organizational sensemaking and dispositions. By honoring AT's historical use as a tool for combating racism and its current use in creating a productive Third Space between dominant and non-dominant discourses, WPAs can enact and assess how their work assigns administrative agency to racialized Others and creates space in writing programs for racial, cultural, and linguistic difference through increasingly shared and equitable instruments, objectives, rules, and divisions of labor. Meanwhile, ANT's development into a tool for interrogating Western value systems lends itself to use by WPAs in interrogating the manner in which whiteness operates in accordance with the contextually peculiar organizational dispositions of particular writing programs and institutions.

At my own institution, I do not yet serve as a WPA, though our stand-alone writing department takes a very deliberative approach to administering our core writing program and writing minor, which we are currently planning to develop into a major, and eventually, I will rotate into one or more associated administrative positions. For the moment, I am focused on cultivating the sorts of antiracist community partnerships around which I hope we will continue to develop our writing programs. To that end, I have been employing AT to implement and assess the community-engaged teaching and writing partnerships I have been developing. Over the course of the 2018–2019 academic year, one of those partnerships involved a local police department's community relations unit working with neighborhood associations and community organizations representing communities of color. The goal of the partnership was to develop a website that reflected the combined efforts of community and police stakeholders to improve community-police relations—especially among Hispanic, Black, and LGBT communities—and enacted community-based approaches to public safety that reduce both crime and arrest rates in those communities.

Overseeing the community relations unit were two Hispanic (white and Columbian) officers from predominantly Hispanic and historically working-class, immigrant neighborhoods in the city and with extensive backgrounds in community policing and teaching college-level cultural competency courses for police officers, as well as an African American civilian community engagement specialist with an extensive background in community development.[2] The community engagement specialist recounted to my classes how her experience partnering with the police department on a community revitalization project proved to her that constructive community-police relations were possible. However, after Michael Brown, a Black eighteen-year-old, was killed by Darren Wilson, a white police officer, in Ferguson, Missouri, she began to worry that children of color in her neighborhood were at increasingly greater risk of being shot by police. When first recruited for her new position, she was reluctant to take it, having spent her career advocating not for the police but for those most at risk of being victimized by them. Ultimately, she decided she couldn't refuse; from her perspective, the stakes were too high for her community.

Hearing this story from an African American woman willing to risk complicity in a racist institution in order to better advocate for her community eased some of my own initial reservations toward developing a partnership with a police department that, like many throughout the nation, had invited criticism for its policing particularly of POC.

Furthermore, the Hispanic (white) captain overseeing the unit stressed that part of our mission was to help the community relations unit persuade the rest of the department of the value of community policing. When the community engagement specialist first proposed the partnership to me, my greatest concern was becoming complicit in circulating propaganda for a department that wasn't interested in fundamentally transforming its policing practices, but her and the captain's remarks helped me to understand that as a white, tenure-track faculty member at a predominantly white institution, I was already operating from a position of complicity in racist organizations, and my principal obligation was to put whatever privilege my whiteness granted me to use in interrogating and transforming that complicity. I therefore began to envision the community engagement project as user-experience (UX) research aimed at designing instruments (digital tools and content) that facilitated increased motive and objective sharing between community and police stakeholders.

Beyond my hopes for contributing to the transformation of a racist organization in the community, I began this project with an interest in how a community-engaged teaching and writing project with antiracist objectives could work to transform our own writing programs' curricula and student learning outcomes. In fall 2018, my first-year writing students researched best practices in effective community policing, community engagement, and UX design, all with consideration toward racial justice, and completed the Collaborative Institutional Training Initiative's (CITI) certification course in the responsible conduct of social and behavioral research in preparation for conducting IRB-approved UX research. Students then analyzed websites of police departments across the country with robust community policing programs and designed and conducted interviews with seven lieutenants and captains (three Hispanic and five white) involved in community policing. Students then synthesized their findings into a report read by students enrolled in my spring 2019 special topics course, Community-Based Writing in a Digital World, who conducted their own IRB-approved UX interviews with twelve community stakeholders (three African American, one Hispanic, and three LGBT) to develop a web content strategy that informed the designs created by students working concurrently in another professor's web development class. Students in my predominantly white spring 2019 course went out of their way to achieve diverse representation among interview participants and take their input into account, using it to develop content around themes of community-based problem solving and recommending interactive features that would allow community members to share information and tell their own stories. Meanwhile, in their reflective journals, students wrote about better understanding community concerns about police and using UX research and design principles to decenter themselves and their own opinions about what would make for an effective web design in order to instead center the perspectives of community members. These outcomes suggest that establishing courses such as my spring 2019 special topics course as permanent fixtures of our writing programs would go some way toward foregrounding the motives and objectives of communities of color and thus transforming our programs' racist organizational dispositions.

Under the right circumstances, the partnership with the community relations unit would have transformed over time as well, through the work of generating and updating web content, to further partnerships with neighborhood associations and community organizations. But that didn't happen. Although out of the three web designs created by the web development course, the one chosen by the community relations unit and approved by city and police department leadership was clearly the one most informed by my class's strategy, the design was never implemented. Flash forward to the summer of 2020, and, following the murders of George Floyd and Breonna Taylor as with many other police departments across the nation, the one in question is facing calls for defunding and abolishment from some of the same community organizations included in my spring 2019 class's UX research. I would never venture so far as to say that our website would have prevented that outcome, but as a potentially expansive instrument of antiracist institutional transformation, failing to implement it couldn't have helped.

Despite the less-than-ideal outcome of this particular partnership, the connections I developed through that community engagement project informed other ones I've since pursued around digital storytelling and issues of equitable housing, for instance. What's more, in planning to publish on this work, I began asking around about whether our university had an Indigenous land acknowledgment that I could include in any forthcoming publications. This led me into conversation with Taino J. Palermo, Cacique Ama' Guatu' of the Baramaya Guainia clan, and Raymond Two Hawks, Ketasœt of the Mashapug Nahaganset chiefdom, who coauthored the initial draft with me. But those conversations immediately evolved into strategizing how to use the land acknowledgment as an expansive instrument of antiracist transformation at the institutional and even state levels. Via the subsequent drafting and institutional adoption process, we formed an Indigenous Land Acknowledgement Working Group comprised of undergraduate student leaders, faculty, administration, and Indigenous community leaders enrolled in Roger Williams University's Law School (the latter including Palermo and Two Hawks). Together, we solicited and received feedback from culture bearers of two tribal nations with historic and contemporary claims to the land upon which Roger Williams University's Bristol and Providence campuses are located, resulting in the following statement:

> We acknowledge the peoples of the Narragansett and Pokanoket Nations as the original inhabitants and enduring stewards of the lands and waters upon which Roger Williams University is located. We recognize that our presence on this land implicates us in the legacy of our namesake, who strove in ways to respect the sovereignty and humanity of Indigenous peoples but in others actively contributed to their genocide. In becoming the university the world needs now, let us commit to reconciling and partnering with the Narragansett and Pokanoket, and all Indigenous peoples whose lands and waters we benefit from today.[3]

Within the larger activity system of the university, the circulation of this statement immediately exposed racist institutional dispositions as they manifest in resistance, as the statement was not received well by some in upper administration, who feared the language was too divisive, as our university prefers to remember Roger Williams as one of the progenitors of modern Western values such as religious tolerance, civil discourse and disobedience, and multiculturalism, and not as one of the architects and prosecutors of the genocide perpetrated against the Indigenous nations of southern New England. Furthermore, due to Brown University's poor handling of the Pokanoket Nation's request for access to ancestral lands currently owned by Brown, the Pokanoket are now pressing for the land to be transferred over to them, and, as it just so happens, the land in question is just a few miles down the road from our Bristol campus. Therefore, the statement's language of acknowledgment, recognition, and reconciliation has our university's legal counsel jittery. Nevertheless, the work of drafting the acknowledgment led to the formation, or in some cases reaffirmation, of working relationships with tribal nations and Indigenous-led community organizations, including a community engagement project in my writing classes that involves digital storytelling as part of a larger cultural tourism initiative. Through an AT lens, the Indigenous Land Acknowledgement Working Group evolved into a Third Space within which a network of activity systems connected around the expansive object of centering Rhode Island's unique Indigenous history and living culture as part of a broader cultural equity agenda. And that evolution produced a new expansive instrument: a proposal for a three-prong (engaged learning and scholarship, legal education and advocacy, and community and economic development) initiative we're calling Wutche Wame: A Living Culture Collaborative at Roger Williams University.[4]

At present, our pitch for Wutche Wame has been received by upper administration far more warmly than the acknowledgment itself, and there are already some promising signs of institutional impact in the form of a prospective faculty development program for our freshman seminar faculty. Right now, though, in the midst of the COVID-19 pandemic, our WPAs have been reluctant to take on a program-wide community engagement initiative, which I understand sounds like a heavy lift, but it is really only the beginning of the antiracist work to which we must commit ourselves if we ever expect to transform our racist organizational dispositions.

The question remains as to whether Wutche Wame's expansive object of cultural equity centered on Indigeneity is capable of doing just that. What makes AT a useful tool in organizational sensemaking is that it enables us to strategically design and assess the impact of this institutional intervention as we move forward. I don't expect that Wutche Wame or any other network of activity systems committed to antiracist work and based in or serving communities of color will eliminate all traces of racism from a writing program's organizational disposition any more than I should expect such work to absolve me of my own implicit cultural and racial biases, but AT provides at least an interventionist means of making sense of racialized dissonance in a way that doesn't explain it away. That hopefully will hold as much if not more influence over our program development as do our university's and region's political economies, which by any objective measure have historically disenfranchised POC and continue to do so.

This remains true, despite our university's efforts to center diversity, equity, and inclusion in its strategic planning. It is easy enough to provide a plausible account of this dissonance with appeals to racism as a universal, structural problem, but I believe that to do so is insufficient in that it makes sense of dissonance without actually demanding that its causes and effects within a particular institutional context be accounted for. To avoid accepting the most generic plausible account, I've begun to explore the potential of ANT for studying what could be taken at face value to be racist institutional policies at my university, beginning with our policy on academic integrity, which acts as a kind of social fact or habitus—what in ANT is called a black box. And contained within the black box of academic integrity—a virtue we do not question and so do not open, peer into, or pick apart—are our university's plagiarism policies and practices. Scholars in and beyond writing studies have for some time warned that plagiarism is a largely modern Western social construct grounded in assumptions about individual autonomy, rationality, and proprietorship, and that, if treated without nuance, can lead to the institutionalization of racially, culturally, and linguistically discriminatory practices (Canzonetta and Kannan 2016; Howard and Robillard 2008; Saltmarsh 2005; Scollon 1995; Vie 2013; Zwagerman 2008). It didn't take me long to pick up on the ways in which the general discourse around plagiarism at my university—at least in spaces beyond the bounds of writing department meetings—lacked nuance in exactly this way.

I can't claim to know the original motivations for drafting our plagiarism policy, but I can, with the help of ANT, begin to trace out the network of effects that lead into and out of it. One of my first exposures to the policy was at convocation, where incoming students are led in a recitation of the university's academic integrity pledge. From there, students encounter the university's academic integrity policy as a required component of all syllabi, sometimes accompanied by a boilerplate passage for courses in which the faculty have chosen to use the university's plagiarism-detection software. The blurb explains that by taking the course, students agree to their work being included in the university's plagiarism-detection repository. Notably, just below this passage in the university's syllabus guidelines is a suggested clause reminding students that all course materials distributed by a faculty member remain that faculty member's personal intellectual property. The virtue of intellectual property is again defended in the language surrounding breaches of academic integrity, which warns that plagiarism in particular "is sometimes a form of intellectual theft and is always a form of intellectual fraud." What's more, the immediately preceding sentence explains that "plagiarism fails to engage in civil, scholarly discourse." It's hard not to discern these two virtues as being in conversation with one another, just as the English colonial conception of civility was inherently tied to English colonial conceptions of property ownership, thereby forming the base rationale for displacing, enslaving, and exterminating Indigenous peoples (Lepore 1998). Within our particular institutional context, it might not be coincidental that this very conception was formulated by Roger Williams's mentor, Sir Edward Coke (Barry 2012).

Unsurprisingly, then, I would continue to encounter conversations surrounding plagiarism at faculty gatherings, both formal and informal, where it was obvious that the focus of attention was on efficiently identifying and prosecuting plagiarizers as if one were attempting to stop the spread of a virus. This led me to wonder just how many cases of plagiarism were actually being reported, by whom, to what end, whether racially and linguistically diverse students were overrepresented in that population, and how those cases were being documented. Since consulting with our provost and vice presidents for equity and inclusion and institutional research, I've been invited to further pursue the matter of analyzing our records on breaches of academic integrity as part of the team participating in a regional institutional research consortium devoted to racial equity. It's encouraging to be among faculty and administration actively working toward institutional transformation, yet no one has any illusions regarding how deeply entrenched racism is at our university.

Disaggregating by race the as-yet-raw data on breaches of academic integrity is one step toward better understanding how the detection and prosecution of plagiarism operates in accordance with our university's own peculiarly racist organizational disposition, but that's just one node in the actor-network, and a potentially misleading one, given the low numbers of students of color historically enrolled at our university; what might be more telling is the language used to describe each instance in the report form submitted by the faculty member and in whatever documentation is generated by the academic integrity committee that oversees the appeals process. The pledge, policy, syllabi requirements, sanctions protocols, and formal and informal enculturation of faculty each represent separate but interconnected nodes that require a tracing of the effects that lead into and from them. Also requiring tracing is our own writing program's approach to training faculty how to interpret and address suspected instances of plagiarism. ANT as a means of organizational sensemaking can trace out these effects and their associations and identify the uniquely corresponding [PRE] for our particular [NET], which will hopefully cast in starker relief the dissonances between our writing programs' and university's best intentions and the racist organizational dispositions that lead to plausible deniability of our complicity in the reification of white hegemony that continues to define our university's relationship to students and communities of color.

These examples I've provided of employing AT and ANT as antiracist WPA sensemaking are of course just beginnings, but I hope they sufficiently illustrate the associated affordances of each methodology. In Hendrickson (2016), I contend that writing studies' pragmatist foundations incline our discipline toward pluralistic approaches to utilizing AT and ANT to integrate and interrogate writing in the disciplines, and I hope here to have invited further consideration as to their complementarity in pursuing antiracist objectives in writing program administration, which as a subfield of writing studies is itself just beginning to make sense of how to go about interrogating and transforming its own racist organizational dispositions. In the same way that sensemaking is both retrospective and active, reappropriating AT and ANT toward antiracist objectives reconnects them with their original methodological intents while also pushing WPAs to make sense of racializing dissonance in our writing programs and scholarship, and in ways that do not ignore it or explain it away with appeals to our individual or collective best intentions.

NOTES

1. Relatedly, I want to acknowledge the help Al Harahap provided me in thinking through my own positionality in writing this chapter.
   In this chapter, I intend "writing program" to include first-year writing programs, writing degree programs, WAC/WID programs, writing centers, and so forth.
2. Descriptions of participants' race/ethnicity reflect the language provided by the participants themselves.
3. For their counsel on and coauthorship of this acknowledgment statement, and for the conversations we've shared along the way, which have helped me think through what antiracist writing program administration means, I am additionally grateful to Sachem Po Pummukaonk Anogqs (Tracey Brown) and Sagamore Po Wauipi Neimpaug (William Guy) of the Pokanoket Nation; Lorén M. Spears, traditional name Mukhasunee Pashau (Narragansett Tribal Nation), executive director of Tomaquag Museum; all the leaders at other institutions who graciously shared their stories and strategies with me; and the rest of the Indigenous Land Acknowledgement Working Group at Roger Williams University.
4. The name Wutche Wame (woo-chee' wah'-me), or "for all" in Eastern Algonquian languages, indicates an intentional emphasis on Indigeneity in working toward cultural equity, as well as an acknowledgment of cultural difference as the cornerstone of a vibrant community.

REFERENCES

Austin, J. L. 1962. *How to Do Things with Words*. 2nd ed., edited by J. O. Urmson and Marina Sbisá. Cambridge, MA: Harvard University Press.
Barry, John M. 2012. *Roger Williams and the Creation of the American Soul: Church, State, and the Birth of Liberty*. New York: Penguin Group.
Bazerman, Charles. 1988. *Shaping Written Knowledge: The Genre and Activity of the Experimental Article in Science*. Madison: University of Wisconsin Press. http://wac.colostate.edu/books/bazerman_shaping/shaping.pdf.
Bazerman, Charles. 1997. "Discursively Structured Activities." *Mind, Culture, and Activity* 4 (4): 296–308. https://doi.org/10.1207/s15327884mca0404_6.
Bazerman, Charles. 1999. *The Languages of Edison's Light*. Cambridge, MA: MIT Press.
Bazerman, Charles, and James Paradis. 1991. *Textual Dynamics of the Professions: Historical and Contemporary Studies of Writing in Professional Communities*. Madison: University of Wisconsin Press.

Berkenkotter, Carol, and Thomas N. Huckin. 1995. *Genre Knowledge in Disciplinary Communication: Cognition/Culture/Power*. Mawhah, NJ: Lawrence Earlbaum.
Callon, Michel, John Law, and Arie Rip. 1986. *Mapping the Dynamics of Science and Technology: Sociology of Science in the Real World*. New York: Palgrave MacMillan.
Canzonetta, Jordan, and Vani Kannan. 2016. "Globalizing Plagiarism and Writing Assessment: A Case Study of Turnitin." *The Journal of Writing Assessment* 9 (2). http://journalofwritingassessment.org/article.php?article=104.
Cole, Michael. 1988. "Cross-Cultural Research in the Sociohistorical Tradition." *Human Development* 31: 137–152.
Condon, Frankie. 2007. "Beyond the Known: Writing Centers and the Work of Anti-Racism." *The Writing Center Journal* 27 (2): 19–38. https://www.jstor.org/stable/43442270.
Craig, Sherry. 2016. "A Story-less Generation: Emergent WPAs of Color and the Loss of Identity through Absent Narratives." *WPA: Writing Program Administration* 39 (2): 16–20. http://www.wpacouncil.org/archives/39n2/39n2all.pdf.
Downs, Douglas, and Elizabeth Wardle. 2007. "Teaching about Writing, Righting Misconceptions: (Re)Envisioning 'First-Year Composition' as 'Introduction to Writing Studies.'" *College Composition and Communication* 58 (4): 552–584. https://www.jstor.org/stable/20456966.
Emig, Janet. 1977. "Writing as a Mode of Learning." *College Composition and Communication* 28 (2): 122–128. https://www.jstor.org/stable/356095.
Engeström, Yrjö. (1987) 2015. *Learning by Expanding: An Activity-Theoretical Approach to Developmental Research*. Helsinki: Orienta-Konsultit Oy. Reprint, 2nd ed. with a new introduction. New York: Cambridge University Press.
Engeström, Yrjö. 2010. *From Teams to Knots: Activity-Theoretical Studies of Collaboration and Learning at Work*. New York: Cambridge University Press.
García de Müeller, Genevieve. 2016. "WPA and the New Civil Rights Movement." *WPA: Writing Program Administration* 39 (2): 36–41. http://www.wpacouncil.org/archives/39n2/39n2all.pdf.
García de Müeller, Genevieve, and Iris Ruiz. 2017. "Race, Silence, and Writing Program Administration: A Qualitative Study of US College Writing Programs." *WPA: Writing Program Administration* 40 (2): 19–39.
García, Romeo. 2017. "Un-Making Gringo Centers." *The Writing Center Journal* 36 (1): 29–60. https://www.jstor.org/stable/44252637.
Green, Neisha-Anne. 2018. "Moving beyond Alright: And the Emotional Toll of This, My Life Matters Too, in the Writing Center Work." *The Writing Center Journal* 37 (1): 15–34. www.jstor.org/stable/26537361.
Gutiérrez, Kris D. 2008. "Developing a Sociocritical Literacy in the Third Space." *Reading Research Quarterly* 43 (2): 148–164. https://doi.org/10.1598/RRQ.43.2.3.
Gutiérrez, Kris D, Patricia Baquedano-López, and Carlos Tejeda. 1999. "Rethinking Diversity: Hybridity and Hybrid Language Practices in the Third Space." *Mind, Culture, and Activity* 6 (4): 286–303. https://doi.org/10.1080/10749039909524733.
Gutiérrez, Kris D, and Lynda D. Stone. 2000. "Synchronic and Diachronic Dimensions of Social Practice: An Emerging Methodology for Cultural-Historical Perspectives on Literacy Learning." In *Vygotskian Perspectives on Literacy Research: Constructing Meaning through Collaborative Inquiry*, edited by Carol D. Lee and Peter Smagorinsky, 150–164. New York: Cambridge University Press.
Hendrickson, Brian. December 26, 2016. "Studying and Supporting Writing in Student Organizations as a High-Impact Practice." [Special issue on WAC and high-impact practices]. *Across the Disciplines* 13 (4). https://wac.colostate.edu/docs/atd/hip/hendrickson2016.pdf.
Howard, Rebecca Moore, and Amy Robillard, eds. 2008. *Pluralizing Plagiarism: Identities, Contexts, Pedagogies*. Portsmouth, NH: Boynton/Cook.

Inoue, Asao B. 2016. "Friday Plenary Address: Racism in Writing Programs and the CWPA." *WPA: Writing Program Administration* 40 (1): 134–154. http://www.wpacouncil.org/archives/40n1/40n1inoue.pdf.
James, William. 1884. "On Some Omissions of Introspective Psychology." *Mind* 9 (33): 1–26. https://www.jstor.org/stable/2246788.
James, William. 1905. "The Thing and Its Relations." *The Journal of Philosophy, Psychology and Scientific Methods* 2 (2): 29–41. https://www.jstor.org/stable/pdf/2011699.pdf.
Latour, Bruno. 1987. *Science in Action: How to Follow Scientists and Engineers through Society.* Cambridge, MA: Harvard University Press.
Latour, Bruno. 1993. *We Have Never Been Modern.* Translated by Catherine Porter. Cambridge, MA: Harvard University Press. Original work published in 1991 in French by La Découverte.
Latour, Bruno. 2005. *Reassembling the Social: An Introduction to Actor-Network Theory.* New York: Oxford University Press.
Latour, Bruno. 2013. *An Inquiry into Modes of Existence.* Translated by Catherine Porter. Cambridge, MA: Harvard University Press. Original work published in 2012 in French by Éditions La Découverte.
Latour, Bruno, and Steve Woolgar. 1979. *Laboratory Life: The Construction of Scientific Facts.* Beverly Hills, CA: Sage. Reissued in 1986 as a 2nd ed. with a new preface by Princeton University Press.
Law, John. 1986. *Power, Action, and Belief: A New Sociology of Knowledge?* Boston: Routledge and Kegan Paul.
Leontiev, Alexie N. 1932. "Studies on the Cultural Development of the Child: III." *Pedagogical Seminary and Journal of Genetic Psychology* 40: 37–51.
Lepore, Jill. 1998. *The Name of War: King Philip's War and the Origins of American Identity.* New York: Vintage Books.
Luria, Alexander R. 1928. "The Problem of the Cultural Behavior of the Child." *Pedagogical Seminary and Journal of Genetic Psychology* 35: 493–506.
Myers, Greg. 1996. "Out of the Laboratory and Down to the Bay: Writing in Science and Technology Studies." *Written Communication* 13 (1): 5–43. https://doi.org/10.1177/0741088396013001003.
Perryman-Clark, Staci M., and Collin Lamont Craig, eds. 2019. *Black Perspectives in Writing Program Administration.* Urbana, IL: Conference on College Composition and Communication and National Council of Teachers of English.
Russell, David R. 1995. "Activity Theory and Its Implications for Writing Instruction." In *Reconceiving Writing, Rethinking Writing Instruction,* edited by Joseph Petraglia, 51–78. Hillsdale, NJ: Lawrence Erlbaum.
Russell, David R. 1997. "Rethinking Genre in School and Society: An Activity Theory Analysis." *Written Communication* 14 (4): 504–554. https://doi.org/10.1177/0741088397014004004.
Saltmarsh, Sue. 2005. " 'White pages' in the Academy: Plagiarism, Consumption and Racist Rationalities." *International Journal for Educational Integrity* 1 (1). https://www.ojs.unisa.edu.au/index.php/IJEI/article/view/17/10.
Scollon, Ron. 1995. "Plagiarism and Ideology: Identity in Intercultural Discourse." *Language in Society* 24 (1): 1–28. https://doi:10.1017/S0047404500018388.
Scott, Tony, and Nancy Welch. 2014. "One Train Can Hide Another: Critical Materialism for Public Composition." *College English* 76 (6): 562–579. https://www.jstor.org/stable/24238203.
Spinuzzi, Clay. 2008. *Network: Theorizing Knowledge Work in Telecommunications.* New York: Cambridge University Press.
Spinuzzi, Clay. 2015. "Symmetry as a Methodological Move." In *Thinking with Bruno Latour in Rhetoric and Composition,* edited by Paul Lynch and Nathaniel Rivers, 23–39. Carbondale: Southern Illinois University Press.

Tuomi-Gröhn, Terttu, and Yrjö Engeström, eds. 2003. *Between School and Work: New Perspectives on Boundary-Crossing.* Boston: Pergamon.
Vie, Stephanie. 2013. "A Pedagogy of Resistance toward Plagiarism Detection Technologies." *Computers and Composition* 31 (1): 3–15. https://doi.org/10.1016/j.compcom.2013.01.002.
Vygotsky, Lev S. 1929. "II. The Problem of the Cultural Development of the Child." *Pedagogical Seminary and Journal of Genetic Psychology* 36: 415–434.
Wardle, Elizabeth. 2007. "Understanding 'Transfer' from FYC: Preliminary Results of a Longitudinal Study." *WPA: Writing Program Administration* 31 (1–2): 65–85. http://wpacouncil.org/archives/31n1-2/31n1-2wardle.pdf.
Wardle, Elizabeth. 2012. "Creative Repurposing for Expansive Learning: Considering 'Problem-Exploring' and 'Answer-Getting' Dispositions in Individuals and Fields." *Composition Forum* 26. http://compositionforum.com/issue/26/creative-repurposing.php.
Weick, Karl E. 1995. *Sensemaking in Organizations.* Thousand Oaks, CA: SAGE.
Weick, Karl E. 2000. *Making Sense of the Organization.* Malden, MA: Blackwell.
Weick, Karl E. 2009. *Making Sense of the Organization: The Impermanent Organization.* Chichester, UK: John Wiley and Sons.
Yancey, Kathleen Blake, Liane Robertson, and Kara Tacsak. 2014. *Writing across Contexts: Transfer, Composition, and Cultures of Writing.* Logan: Utah State University Press.
Zhang, Sarah. 2017. "The Secrets of the 'Humongous Fungus': How One of the Biggest Living Organisms in the World Got So Big." *The Atlantic*, October 30, 2017. https://www.theatlantic.com/science/archive/2017/10/humongous-fungus-genome/544265/.
Zwagerman, Sean. 2008. "The Scarlet P: Plagiarism, Panopticism, and the Rhetoric of Academic Integrity." *College Composition and Communication* 59 (4): 676–710. http://www.jstor.org/stable/20457030.

AFTERWORD
A 2×2 REVIEW OF *SENSEMAKING FOR WRITING PROGRAMS AND WRITING CENTERS*

Karen Keaton Jackson

In 2021, notions of diversity and inclusion can refer to any number of things, depending upon the context and the speaker using the terms. In some settings, it refers heavily to ideas surrounding race and cultural backgrounds. In other contexts, diversity and inclusion have much broader implications, drawing in attributes such as socioeconomic status, gender identity, religious preferences, age, and more. While these general categories surrounding diversity certainly are helpful and needed, particularly as we evolve more into this space of awareness and inclusion of diverse people, the categories do not necessarily articulate all kinds of diversity needed in all types of situations.

I'm going to call my conversation here a 2×2 review, for I plan first to bring together *two primary observations* I see in terms of what makes *Sensemaking for Writing Programs and Writing Centers* so relevant. I will then bring those observations in conversation with the *two non-academicians* who are influencing my academic thoughts and behaviors quite heavily in this moment. My goal, through this conversation, is to highlight the importance of this edited collection and why I believe more like these are needed.

When I consider Rita Malenczyk's work, I realize she has demonstrated inclusion in two essential ways, both of which are necessary for propelling our discipline of composition studies forward. First, she intentionally calls for works that include participants' outside experiences into the learning spaces on campus. While this concept is not brand new, what is novel is how she has embraced all participants as active beings in these learning spaces. Much of our field's previous research, including my own, if I'm being honest, has focused on the students' outside experiences and how those events shape who they are in the classroom.

We can easily find a plethora of research that talks about embracing the whole learner before we move to engage in academic tasks. Abraham Maslow's *Hierarchy of Needs*, first published back in 1943, is evidence of educators' longstanding recognition of the need to address external issues before engaging in classroom activity.

Traditionally, though, the discussion focuses solely on the students' lived experiences, as if we, the educators, have standard, or uniform, experiences that don't influence our interactions with students and each other, which just is not true. All of us are people outside of the classroom; therefore, it is beneficial for us all to reflect upon our own experiences and how they shape who we are as professionals. By including chapters written by a variety of educators at different points in their careers and educational journeys, Malenczyk breaks down the silos that often impede our ability to most effectively communicate with each other: teacher versus student; tutor versus tutee; administrator versus professor; faculty versus staff. In fact, even as I write this piece, I'm struggling to find a comprehensive term that accurately identifies all of us who occupy the academic space and are represented in these chapters. Yet, I can't do it. The term *educator* does not most accurately describe the teachers, tutors, and staff, for though they all educate students in their own ways, the term itself does not connote those who teach students outside of the traditional classroom. And, of course, the term *educator* omits students all together (though if we're being real with ourselves, our students definitely teach us a lot, if we are paying attention), which I guess goes to show how rare such a comprehensive conversation is. I think I'm likely rambling a bit and perhaps confusing myself. But the fact that there truly is no all-encompassing term that refers to all of us who occupy higher education in an equivalent way perhaps is evidence of how necessary a conversation such as this one is.

When I directed our Writing Studio at North Carolina Central University from 2005 to 2019, I resurrected a graduate course that had been on the books but not taught in years: Composition Theory and Pedagogy. Upon reenvisioning the course, I used an especially effective assignment: the literacy autobiography. The purpose was for students, most of whom were writing consultants in our Writing Studio, to self-reflect upon their own literacy experiences, both within and outside of the classroom, and then consider how those experiences shaped the way they approached their writing tutorials and ultimately the kind of instructors they wanted to be. This assignment led to some extremely personal and insightful conversations about how they were socialized as children through literacy practices in various familial and community relationships. In addition, they reflected upon many of their K–12 and higher education learning environments and the role that writing and speaking played in them. Ultimately, I think it lent itself to the type of metacognitive awareness that Malenczyk is encouraging us to engage in by reading her collection.

The second aspect of inclusiveness that comes to mind when reading *Sensemaking* is the variety of institution types represented here. So often, and for so many reasons, R1 voices dominate the conversations in our field. For many HBCUs in particular, "full teaching loads (a 4/4 or 4/5 teaching load compared to our RI counterparts with a 2/1 or 2/2 load), heavy committee work, and decreased funding assistance for conferences, combined with minimal collaborative efforts with our RI colleagues, mean that currently our voices are rarely heard on a national level" (Jackson, Jackson, Tafari 2019, 191). Some of those same attributes describe conditions at smaller teaching institutions and community colleges, voices who also are heard less often in our field's scholarship. And yet, we miss so many valuable perspectives when other institutions are excluded. Thus, the authorship of the various chapters alone guarantees this conversation will be broader than we have traditionally seen. Represented in this edited collection are authors from large, state R1 schools with nearly thirty thousand students and from small private institutions with approximately two thousand students. Additionally, in reviewing the past institutions of some of these authors, we see even more variety, such as multicampus community colleges to private institutions with a primary student population of Orthodox Jews. Those past experiences inform who those authors are today and are a part of their journeys.

The second part of my 2×2 review involves me grounding Malenczyk's ways of inclusion within discourse from my two current primary sources of inspiration: Coach Deion Sanders and Dr. Martin Luther King Jr. Yes, I know. On the surface, it appears that it would be difficult to relate these two people to composition studies, and certainly hard to relate them to each other. Yet these two pioneers—and yes, I am calling them both pioneers—are influencing my mindset, my conversations, and my short- and long-term strategies on a daily basis.

In a brief column I recently wrote for *Praxis*, I speak a great deal about how NFL Hall of Famer and current college football coach, Deion "Prime Time" Sanders, gets me excited about the work I do with my HBCU (historically Black college or university) students each day:

> While he dominated professional football far more than professional baseball in the 1990s and early 2000s, [Deion Sanders] remains the only athlete who has competed in both an MLB World Series and an

> NFL Super Bowl. . . . In 2019, Deion Sanders accepted a position as the head football coach at Jackson State University (JSU), a public HBCU in Jackson, Mississippi. Many questioned his decision, noting that he had been a commentator on CBS and the NFL Network and certainly had many options to go to larger programs for his coaching career. And yet, he chose a historically black university in a small town in Mississippi. In several interviews, he has noted that for him, this is not just a job, but a calling. He sees it as a mission beyond helping the student athletes just at JSU, but as a way to provide exposure for all HBCU athletes who often are overlooked because they do not get as much airtime on television and because NFL teams rarely send scouts to these institutions. . . . Overall, his goal is to give voice, recognition, and tangible opportunities to those who often are excluded from mainstream athletic conversations. Connected to that, his broader goal is to give respect to the spaces, HBCUs, that create these athletes. (Jackson 2022, 139)

While my reason for bringing Deion Sanders into this conversation may not be immediately obvious, I see his intentions regarding sports teams as similar to Rita Malenczyk's approach to writing studies. Just as Sanders wants more than just large "Power 5" football programs and their players represented in the NFL, Malenczyk "recruited" (to keep with the sports theme for a moment) contributors from contexts, such as writing centers or special population institutions, that often are excluded from the R1-dominated field of scholarship. In both instances, the target programs—the NFL and writing studies—stand to benefit greatly as they will have talent from a variety of schools that they likely would have never encountered had they maintained more traditional images of authority and success.

My second source of influence, Martin Luther King Jr., fits in here, as well. While often King is touted for his notions of nonviolence, which some mistakenly perceive as passivity, he actually spoke with great passion, urgency, and certainty. In his 1963 text, *Why We Can't Wait*, King discusses the Civil Rights Movement, including why it was important and the strategies that made it successful. In 2020, in the height of the COVID-19 pandemic and protests sparked by the death of George Floyd, I invited my students to read King's text as a way to contextualize and make sense of the activism and social unrest they were experiencing versus that activism of the 1960s. One particular idea King explores is that of tokenism:

> [H]e who sells you the token instead of the coin always retains the power to revoke its worth, and to command you to get off the bus before you have reached your destination. . . . With tokenism, the solution was simple. . . . A judge here and a judge there . . . three Negro children admitted to the whole high school system of a major city—all of these tokens

were used to obscure the persisting reality of segregation and discrimination. . . . Those who argue in favor of tokenism point out that we must begin somewhere. . . . This position has a certain validity. . . . [But] there is a critical distinction, however, between a modest start and tokenism. . . . Its purpose is not to begin a process, but instead to end the process of protest and pressure. (2000, 22–24)

Granted, the context in which King (2009) is speaking is far more intense and serious than our topic here of writing studies. Yet, I think the ideas expressed still hold true. This edited collection is a great start in terms of having a variety of voices included and heard in many ways. However, we all must do our part to make sure this work is not a token, but rather an inspiration for others to be sure that their future works are just as diverse.

For Malenczyk to even attempt making sense of composition studies and writing programs is nothing short of amazing! Writing programs are so diverse, and so institutionally specific, that trying to make sense of them is difficult and complicated. Moreover, the field of composition studies itself is hard to make sense of in any succinct way. I've always thought of it as the blessing and the curse of composition studies. The positives are that, with it still being a fairly new-ish field (new as in the 1970s), the rules are still being formed. The discipline is still being established. It is broad and includes so many aspects of written communication and literacy practices. That, to me, is part of what makes it so innovative and engaging. Subjects of study in the field vary greatly to include literacy practices between doctors and patients in medical trials to how word choice in military files code or covertly identify the race of officers to effective pedagogical approaches in the writing classroom. And yet, that same strength often is our weaknesses when it comes to scholars in more traditional fields such as literature: we are seen as too scattered, ill-defined, and not structured with a lack of quality texts to analyze and critique.

However, as a die-hard compositionist myself, I am going to stick with the latter perspective—that our appeal is we can look at literacy practices and written communication from multiple perspectives and in multiple spaces. This edited collection works to give us some structured ways of reflecting on our contexts, yet in a manner that still respects our layers of diversity. More specifically, what makes this collection so unique is that it gives voices to and insights from writers with a range of titles and positions and experiences and from a variety of institution types and sizes. So often, graduate teaching assistants and student-tutors are talked about rather than talked to or talked with, yet these student workers often are more visible to or interacting directly with undergraduate students than the actual professors or administrators. Years ago, when I was a graduate student in a feminist theory class, we read Indian literary theorist Gayatri Spivak's groundbreaking 1988 article, "Can the Subaltern Speak?," in which she questions colonial practices and whether or not those in subjective positions can give power to their own voices. I also loved to flip the question and instead ask, "Can the superiors listen?" In other words, even if those in marginalized positions do speak, if no one is listening, then what is the purpose of their words? Those in higher positions must be able to hear and validate those voices so they can effectively bring about reform when needed. And sometimes, those in higher positions need to be taught how to listen to a voice that is different than their own.

I feel like that is what is happening here in this edited collection. All of these authors are placed on an even playing field, teaching readers to take in a variety of perspectives as a way of helping us to rethink our own pedagogies and practices.

REFERENCES

Jackson, Karen Keaton. 2022. "Coach Prime and Me: Deion Sanders's Impact on My Academic Self." *Praxis: A Writing Center Journal* 19 (1): 139–141.

Jackson, Karen Keaton, Hope Jackson, and Dawn Hicks-Tafari. 2019. "We Belong in the Discussion: Including HBCUs in Conversations About Race and Writing." *CCC*. December 2019.

King, Martin Luther Jr. (1963) 2000. *Why We Can't Wait*. New York: Signet Classic. First published 1963.

INDEX

academic cleaning services, 59
academic integrity policy, Roger Williams University, 199–200
Academic Support Center (ASC), 158, 160, 176; Stretch model instruction, 170–71
Academic Support Programs (UVM), 136
activity system, classroom, 188–89
activity theory (AT), 6, 181, 190, 191, 193; antiracist work, 187–88, 200–201; history of, 185–87; Third Space, 188–89
actor-network theory (ANT), 5, 6, 181, 200; antiracist work, 200–201; origins of, 190–91; preposition in, 192–93
Adams Wooten, Courtney, 160
adjuncts, visibility of, 96–97
administrators, 5–6; collaboration, 166–67; and staff relationships, 96–100. *See also* writing program administrators
advice columns, for teaching assistants, 25
advice seeking, by teaching assistants, 29–31
affect, affective practice, 12, 86, 95; intersubjectivity, 89, 98
African Americans, community engagement specialists, 194
agency, 42, 165, 191
Alex, 28, 35; underlife negotiation, 31–32
Amarillia ostoyae (honey mushroom), 191–92
American Federation of Teachers, and University of California faculty, 141
American Handbook of Psychiatry, on microaggression, 68–69
Anna, 28, 30; on teacherly identity, 35–36
antiracist work, 7, 64, 67, 184, 195; in breakout meetings, 71–75; community partnerships, 194–95; institutional transformation, 187–88; mentoring, 67–68; resistance to, 76–77; scenarios, 70–71; white privilege and, 65–66; writing program administration, 181–82
anxiety, 86
Aronson, Anne, 166–67
Around the Texts of Writing Center Work: An Inquiry-Based Approach to Tutor Education (Hall), 115
ASC. *See* Academic Support Center
Assignments Across the Curriculum (Melzer), 168

assumptions, white, 62
asynchronous online sessions, affordances and constraints, 52–53
Austin, J. L., 192
authority, white, 64

Baquedano-López, Patricia, 188
Bazerman, Charles, 186, 191
Benson, Daisy, 135
Berkenkotter, Carol, 186
Between School and Work (Tuomi-Gröhn and Engeström), 187
biological systems, and memory, 88–89
blame, 29; teaching assistants and, 32–34
bodily responses, 88
Boquet, Elizabeth H., 11
boss texts, 147–48, 153; generation of, 150–51; MOUs as, 143, 144–45
Bourdieu, Pierre, on habitus, 183
bracketing, 26
brainstorming, 58
breakout groups, 66; antiracist work, 71–75
Brooke, Robert, 24
Brown, Michael, 194
Brown University, 197

Callon, Michel, 191
"Can the Subaltern Speak?" (Spivak), 210
caretaking, vs. leadership, 163–64
cascading networks, in union contracts, 146–49
cat's cradles, institutional structure as, 149–50
CCA. *See* Complete College America
Center for Academic Success (UVM), 136–37
Center for Teaching and Learning (UVM), 134
CITI. *See* Collaborative Institutional Training Initiative
Civil Rights Movement, 208
classroom: activity system, 188–89; narrating events, 31–32
clients, surveys, 116–19
Coding Manual for Qualitative Researchers, The (Saldaña), 28–29
Cogie, Jane, 72
Coke, Edward, 199

INDEX

Cole, Michael, 185; Laboratory for Comparative Human Cognition, 186
collaboration(s), 6, 20, 185; administrative, 166–68; hierarchical structure and, 169–70, 178–79n2; vs. individualism, 78–79; in tutoring, 56–58; University of Vermont programs, 132–33
Collaborative Institutional Training Initiative (CITI), certification course, 195
collaborative leadership, 166, 169, 175
collective actions, 177
committee work, 173–74
Complete College America (CCA), 176
conflicts, 79, 81n7
common standards, 54
communication, 27, 209; access to, 168–69
community, 5, 103, 194; membership in, 19–20; problem solving, 195–96
Community-Based Writing in a Digital World, 195
community colleges, 207
community engagement specialists, 194
community partnerships, antiracist work, 194–95
complaints, responses to, 97–98, 100
composition studies, 209
Composition Theory and Pedagogy (North Carolina Central University), 206
Condon, Frankie, 184
confidence, 86
conflict, interpersonal vs. task, 77–78
contracts, excellence reviews, 146–47
conversation, stories in, 4–5
Cooper, Marilyn, 46
coperformance, leadership and, 174–75
Council of Writing Program Adminstrators (CWPA), 185; "Framework for Success in Postsecondary Writing," 85
Council of Writing Program Administrators Conference, 183
course evaluations, 102, 151–53
Craig, Collin Lamont, 185
Crawford, Ilene, 169
cross-disciplinary strategies, 132
crosstalk, tutor, 21, 59
cultural deprivation theories, 186
culture, writing center, 42–43
curriculum development, 87

"Defense of Conference Summaries: Widening the Reach of Writing Center Work, In" (Cogie), 115
"Detour Spotting for White Antiracists" (Olsson), 70
Detweiler, Jane, 158

Dewey, John, 48
Diane, 28, 30, 32, 34, 37
discomfort, antiracist work and, 70, 71–72
discourse community, 16–17
discovery learning, 59
discursive framework, 17–18, 21
disidentification, 70
dispositions, emotional, 91
disrespect, 66
dissonance, racism as, 182, 183
distributed leadership, 131, 160, 161–63, 165–67, 169, 173, 174, 175; as feminist sensemaking, 177–78; professional development, 170–72
diversity, 62, 65, 72, 185, 205; institutional, 69–70
Dobrin, Sidney I., 23
documentation, documents, 5, 57, 58; excellence review process, 150–52; organizational capacity, 114–15; in union contracts, 141, 143–45, 147–48, 155n1; writing center, 6, 123–24, 145–46; writing center ecologies, 109–11
Downs, Douglas, 187

ecological interdependence, WPA-NTT faculty, 165–66
ecologies: rhetorical, 46–47, 161–62; writing centers, 109–11
educational harmony, 47–48
effectiveness, of organizations, 112
embodied meaning-making, 88
Emig, Janet, 186
emotions, 12, 93, 94; and experience, 89–90, 99–100; frustration, 91–92; grading and, 101–2; and knowledge, 87–88; as meaning-making, 85–86; in writing programs, 90–91, 96–99, 103–4
empathy, 86, 94
engagement, 75–76; tutor-to-tutor, 68
Engeström, Yrjö, 186; *Between School and Work*, 187; mycorrhizae trope, 189–90, 191–92
English Department, first-year composition, 130
entitlement, lack of, 66
environment, organizational, 116
epistemological pluralism, 13
essays, teaching assistants, 25
Estrem, Heidi, 24
ethnography. *See* institutional ethnography
evangelism, compositionist, 164
events, and emotional experiences, 101
Everyday Writing Center: A Community of Practice, The (Geller), 11, 135

excellence portfolio (EP), 148, 150, 154; components, 151–52; purpose of, 152–53
excellence review process, 146–49, 156n14; documents in, 150–52; drawbacks to, 153–54; quantification in, 152–53
expansive learning, 186, 187
expectations, 38, 66
experience(s), 95; emotional, 89–90, 100–101
explicit knowledge, 122–13
extracurricular literacies, 3

face-to-face interactions, 62
Facilitators Guide to Courageous Conversations About Race (Smith and Tuck), 71–72
faculty, 141, 155n2, 155n3, 155n4, 160
faculty handbook, 153; in excellence portfolio, 151–52
Faculty Writing Project (FWP), University of Vermont, 130, 131
Faculty Writing Workshop (UVM), 129, 131
failure, student, 33–34
false rules, 50, 56
family issues, focus on, 36, 37
feedback practices, values and goals, 53–54
feedback sessions, 58
feminist ecology, 6
feminization, 164; of sensemaking, 177–78
Ferguson, MO, 194
figurative language, 5
first-year composition, University of Vermont, 130
Flaherty, Colleen, "What Students Write," 168
Floyd, George, 196, 208
Foundational Writing and Information Literacy requirement (UVM), 131
Four Agreements, 71–72
framework, organizational theory, 111–12
"Framework for Success in Postsecondary Writing" (Council of Writing Program Administrators), 85
frustrations, 102; of resistant students, 92–93; talking about, 90–92
Fulwiler, Toby, 132; Faculty Writing Workshop, 129; Writing Across the Curriculum program, 130–31
FWP. *See* Faculty Writing Project

Gabriel, Yiannis, 27
García, Romeo, 185
García de Müeller, Genevieve, 184–85, 188–89
gatekeeping, 59
Geller, Anne Ellen, *The Everyday Writing Center: A Community of Practice*, 11

genuine interaction, 65
goals, 120; and online protocols, 52–54
grading, emotional responses to, 101–2
graduate teaching assistants (GTAs), 5, 23, 91, 98, 209–10
grammar, and good writing, 168
Grammarly, 51
Green, Neisha-Anne, 64, 181
grievance process, 143
Grimm, Nancy, 70
ground rules, antiracist work, 71
group membership, 19
growth, emotional response, 102
GTAs. *See* graduate teaching assistants
Guatu', Ama', 196
guidelines, tutor-to-tutor, 79–80
guilt, 16
Gunner, Jeanne, 166
Gutiérrez, Kris D., 188, 189

habits, avoiding unhealthy, 36
habitus, 183; racial, 184
Hall, R. Mark, 145
Hanson, Craig, 166–67
Haraway, Donna, 147, 149
Harris, Joe, 161
HBCUs, 207, 208
Hewett, Beth, *The Online Writing Conference*, 44
hierarchy, collaboration and, 169–70, 178–79n2
Hierarchy of Needs (Maslow), 206
higher education, 87, 206
hiring, Stretch model instructions, 171
hiring process, writing center staff, 65
hospitality, in tutor and teacher relationships, 94–95
Howe Memorial Library, Writing Center at, 133–36
Huckin, Thomas, 186
Hult, Christine, 167
human agency, 191

Ianetta, Melissa, 159
idea-exchange meeting, 51
identity, identities, 5, 21, 59, 63, 86, 101, 158, 163; intersectional, 75, 76–77; shared religious, 18–19, 20; teacherly, 34–36, 39; teaching assistants, 24, 26–27
identity construction/formation, 24, 29, 70
identity kit, 15–16
IDPs. *See* individual development plans
IE. *See* institutional ethnography
inclusion, 205–6
inclusivity, 72
Indigenous land acknowledgement, 196–97

Indigenous Land Acknowledgment Working Group, 196–97; Wutche Wame, 198
individual development plans (IDPs), 111; writing center, 119–22
individualism, vs. collaboration, 78–79
information literacy work, University of Vermont, 135–36
Inoue, Asao B., 66, 183
institutional disposition, 66
institutional ethnography (IE), 143, 146, 155n6, 155n8, 156n11, 156n12; ruling relations, 144–45
institutional politics, 87
institutional review board (IRB), 13
institutions, 21, 169; antiracist work, 187–88; cat's cradle structure, 149–50; diversity, 69–70
instructors, 165; collaborative construction, 167–68; committee work, 173–74; professional development, 170–72
intent, intentionality, 16
interaction, as reciprocal, 73
International Writing Centers Association (IWCA), 64
interpersonal conflict, 77–78, 81n7
intersubjective meaning, 74
interventionist methodology, 186
intra-institutional relationships, 6
invisibility, 66, 68, 78
IRB. *See* institutional review board
"I Thought I'd Put That in to Amuse You" (Malenczyk), 115
IWCA. *See* International Writing Centers Association

James, William, 192
Jennifer, 28; advice seeking, 29–30
Jewish college, all-women's, 13–14
Jewish Modern Orthodoxy, 20; lived experience of, 17–18
Johnson, Michelle, "Racial Literacy and the Writing Center," 72
job descriptions, 146, 158
Jones-Walker, Cheryl, 76

kavanah, 15, 16, 17
King, Martin Luther, Jr., 209; *Why We Can't Wait*, 208
knowledge, 19, 72, 112, 186; and emotion, 87–88; explicit and tacit, 122–23; writing center, 42–43, 58–59

labeling, 26–27; positive and negative, 32–34
labor, 12, 40n20, 167

Laboratory for Comparative Human Cognition (LCHC), 186
labor contracts, 141–42
land acknowledgment, Indigenous, 196–98
language, 21, 54, 74, 77; and discourse community, 16–17
Latour, Bruno, 191; on preposition, 192–93
Law, John, 191
LaWare, Margaret, 158
LCHC. *See* Laboratory for Comparative Human Cognition
leadership, 6; vs. caretaking, 163–64; collaborative, 166, 169, 175; committee work, 173–74; coperformance, 174–75; distributed, 131, 160, 161–63, 166–67, 169, 170–73, 177; writing program administrators as, 158–59, 165
learning, 48, 102, 129; course evaluation and, 153–54; environment for, 207; expansive, 186, 187; theories, 6; Third Space, 188–89
Learning Annex (UVM), 136
"Learning to Teach: Letter to a New TA, On" (Reid), 25
lecturers, contracts, 146–47
Leontiev, Alexie N., 185
Lerner, Neal, "Punishment and Possibility," 112
"Letter to a New TA: Affect Addendum" (Saur and Palmeri), 25
Liggett, Sarah, 23
Lily, 28, 30; teacherly ethos, 34–36; work-life balance, 36–37
listening, 54, 57, 94, 98
literacy, 93, 100, 127, 189, 209
lived experiences, 13–14, 17–18, 206
lower order concerns (LOCs), 49
Luria, Alexander R., 185

Macauley, William J., Jr., *Standing at the Threshold*, 25
Malheur National Forest, *Amarillia ostoyae* in, 191–92
marginalization, 69, 112, 160
marshmallow teacher, 34–35
Maslow, Abraham, *Hierarchy of Needs*, 206
McKinney, Jackie Grutsch, *Peripheral Visions for Writing Center Work*, 11
meaning-making, 85, 110; embodied, 88–86, 87–90
medachtic, 15
Meeks, Lynn, 167
Melzer, Dan, *Assignments Across the Curriculum*, 168

Memorandum of Understanding (MOU), 152; as boss text, 143–45, 153; excellence reviews, 146–47; University of California faculty contracts, 141, 142, 147–48
memory, social context of, 88, 89
mentoring, mentors, 22, 30, 55; writing center, 67–68
metaphors, 4, 5, 11, 12; within organizations, 12–13; religious, 14–17, 21
"Metaphors and Ambivalence: Affective Dimensions in Writing Center Studies" (Lawson), 12
Michigan State University Writing Center, 116
microaggressions, 66, 68–69, 74, 78, 81n2
microinteractions, 3, 42
migrant activist students, 188
Miley, Michelle, 145
mission statements, 85, 135
misunderstandings, 59–60
mocking, 91
Moss, Beverly, 19
motivation, 86, 100
multilingual students, 16
mycorrhizae trope, 189–90, 191–92
Myers, Greg, 191

Narragansett Nation, 197
narration, narratives, 4–5, 91; of classroom events, 29, 31–32; teaching assistants, 27–28
narrative methodology, 45–46
narrative theory, 31
National Census of Writing, 67
National Institutes of Health, 119
National Science Foundation, 119
negotiations, 38, 57, 58; seeking advice, 30–31; underlife, 31–32
neoliberalism, 155–56n9, 156n10; teaching in, 152–53
networking, 133
Nicklay, Jennifer, 16
non-senate faculty (NSF), 155n2; excellence review process, 146–47, 148, 151–53; Memorandum of Understanding, 141, 142
non-tenure track (NTT) faculty, 160, 162, 173; collaboration with, 167–68; communication with, 168–69; professional development, 170–72; and writing program administers, 164, 165–66, 176
North Carolina Central University Writing Studio, 206–7
noticing, 26
NSF. See non-senate faculty
NTT. See non-tenure track faculty

observation, 95
Obstfeld, David, "Organizing and the Process of Sensemaking," 25–26, 27
"Off Track and On," 161
Ohio State University Writing Center, 116, 120
Olson, Bobbi, 16
Olsson, Jona, "Detour Spotting for White Antiracists," 70
online protocols, 47; values and goals, 52–55
online training: practice sessions, 55–56; problems with, 50–51; tattling behavior, 49–50; of tutors, 43–44, 48–49
Online Writing Conference: A Guide for Teachers and Tutors, The (Hewett), 44
online writing lab (OWL) protocols, 42, 54
on-the-job training, 44
openness, 18, 19, 95
oppression, emotional relationships, 96
Organizational Assessment: A Framework for Improving Performance (Lusthaus et al.), 113
organizational capacity, 113; measuring, 114–15
organizational chart, UVM Center for Academic Success, 136–37
organizational theory, 4, 5, 113; framework, 111–12
organizations, 4, 112, 116, 184, 195; metaphors within, 12–13; performance, 113–14; stories, 27–28
"Organizing and the Process of Sensemaking" (Weick, Sutcliffe, and Obstfeld), 25–26
Othering, Others, 70, 187
OWL. See online writing lab protocols
Oxford Guide for Writing Tutors, The (Fitzgerald and Ianetta), 21

Palermo, J., 196, 197
Palmeri, Jason, "Letter to a New TA: Affect Addendum," 25
Paradis, James, 191
partnerships, community, 194–95, 196
Patrick, Amy, 46, 47
pedagogy: tutoring, 21; writing, 46; writing center, 12, 45
peer tutors, peer tutoring, 63, 64–65, 74, 76; relationships, 79–80; task and interpersonal conflict in, 77–78
Penny, 28; on student responsibility, 33–34
Penrose, Ann, 160
people of color (POC), 65; antiracist writing, 181–82; policing, 194–95

performance, 88, 151
Peripheral Visions for Writing Center Work (McKinney), 11
Perryman-Clark, Staci M., 185
personal needs, 29, 36–37
plagiarism, 93, 199–200
plagiarism policy, Roger Williams University, 199–200
Pokanoket Nation, 197
police departments, policing, 79; community relations units, 194–95, 196
power, 96, 98, 167, 169, 178n2
practitioners, collaboration, 57–58
praise, 29; teaching assistants, 32–34
prayer, 16
preposition, Latour on, 192–93
privilege, 60, 76, 96
problem solving, community-based, 195–96
professional development, 42, 43, 55, 59; distributed leadership, 170–72
professionalization, 109; individual development plans, 119, 120–21
program-building, emotion, 85–86
Programs that Work (Dickerson, Fulwiler, and Steffens), 129
psychology, of emotion, 86
public safety, 194
punctum, 75
"Punishment and Possibility" (Lerner), 112
Pytlik, Betty P., 23

quality control, 55
quantification, in excellence review process, 152–53

race, 6, 62, 69, 71, 201n2; and antiracist scenarios, 73–74; Four Agreements, 71–72; and tutor interactions, 66–68
"Racial Literacy and the Writing Center" (Johnson), 72
racism, 6, 71, 75, 183; institutional/organizational, 197, 200; police departments, 194–95; in writing programs, 184–85
reflection, 38, 95, 102–3, 129
Reid, E. Shelley, 24; "On Learning to Teach: Letter to a New TA," 25
relationships: hospitality in, 94–95; tutor, 79–80; in writing programs, 96–100
religious discourse, 21; and writing center discourse, 15–16
religious experience: in Jewish Modern Orthodoxy, 17–18; shared identity and, 18–19
research, 146; tutor, 21–22
resiliency, 133; collective, 177–78

resistance, 197; to antiracist conversations, 76–77; student, 92–93
respect, 54, 95
responsibility, 16, 167; student, 33–34
Restaino, Jessica, 23
"Rethinking Our Work with Multilingual Writers: The Ethics and Responsibility of Language Teaching in the Writing Center" (Olson), 21
retreats, faculty writing, 132
rhetorical choices, 16
rhetorical ecology, 46–47; feminist, 161–62
rhetorics, of sensemaking, 28–37
Rhode Island, Indigenous history, 197–98
Robertson, Liane, *Writing Across Contexts*, 187
Roger Williams University, 181; Indigenous Land Acknowledgment Working Group, 196–98; plagiarism policies at, 199–200
Roozen, Kevin, 3
Ruiz, Iris, 184–85
ruling relations, 142, 154; in institutional ethnography, 144–45
Russell, David R., 186
Ryan, Kathleen, feminist rhetorical ecology, 161–62

Saldaña, Johnny, *The Coding Manual for Qualitative Researchers*, 28–29
Sanders, Deion, 207–8
satisfaction surveys, 117
Sauer, Elizabeth, "Letter to a New TA: Affect Addendum," 25
scaffolding, on tutor values, 51
scheduling, emotional responses to, 99
Schell, Eileen, 164
scholars of color, 185, 191
Scott, Tony, 191
self, 29; focus on, 36–37; praise and blame, 32–34
self-doubt, 16
self-identification, 65
sensemaking, 3, 25–26, 27, 129, 80, 81n3, 184; definition of, 4–5; and educational harmony, 47–48; feminist, 177–78; processes, 37–38; rhetorical, 28–37; underlife, 38–39; white privilege and, 63–64
Sensemaking in Organizations (Weick), 4, 47
service work, NTT instructors, 173–74
session notes, 115–16
shame, and silencing, 76
Shulamit, 13, 20; religious metaphors, 14–17, 21
silence, 72, 76

SMART (specific, measurable, achievable, relevant, and time bound) goals, 120
Smith, Dorothy, 142
social contexts, 88, 99
social interaction, 29
social interpretation, 88
Soviet AT, 186
Spinuzzi, Clay, 190
Spivak, Gayatri, "Can the Subaltern Speak?," 210
staff, 42, 62, 62, 69; mentoring, 67–68; relationships among, 96–100
staff development, 22
staff meetings: and tutor interactions, 62–63, 66–69
stakeholders, community, 195
Standard Edited American English proficiency, 183
standards, 56, 58
Standing at the Threshold: Working through Liminality in the Composition and Rhetoric TAship (Macauley), 25
status, and institutional power, 169
Stone, Lynda D., 189
stories, organizational, 27–28
story editing, reflection and, 103–4
storytelling, stories, 4, 12, 64, 133, 197
strategic planning/decisionmaking, 182–83
Strathern, Marilyn, 147
Stretch program, 170–71
Strickland, Donna, 169
string figures, institutional structure, 149–50
structural diversity, 65
student papers, reading of, 94
students, 64, 75, 188, 206; on frustration, 91–92; HBCUs, 207–8; praise and blame, 32–34; resistant, 92–93; and surveys, 117–18; as tutors, 209–10
students of color, identifying, 65
studying up, 145
successes, 100
surveys, 116; design and use of, 118–19; student responses to, 117–18
sustainability, 164
Sutcliffe, Kathleen M., "Organizing and the Process of Sensemaking," 25–26, 27
symmetry, in actor-network theory, 191

tacit knowledge, 122–23
Taczak, Kara, *Writing Across Contexts*, 187
Tagg, John, 72
Tara, 13; community membership, 19–20; lived experience of, 17–18; openness of, 18–19

task conflict, 77–78
tattling, 49–50, 58
Taylor, Breonna, 196
teacherly ethos, 34–36
teachers, and grades, 101–2
teaching, teachers, 30, 91; approaches to, 29, 34–36; composition theory and pedagogy, 206–7; and grades, 101–2; underlife negotiation, 31–32
teaching assistants (TAs), 23; classroom events, 31–32; identity construction, 24, 26–27; narratives, 27–28; praise and blame, 32–34; seeking advice, 29–31; teaching approach, 34–36; work-life balance, 36–37
Tejeda, Carlos, 188
theory building, 43
Third Space, 193; Indigenous Land Acknowledgement Working Group, 297–98; learning in, 188–89
tokenism, 65, 208–9
training, online, 43–45, 48–51
Transforming the Academy (Willie-LeBreton), 69
tricksters, tutors as, 11
truths, honoring, 75
Tuomi-Gröhn, Terttu, *Between School and Work*, 187
tutor columns, in *WLN*, 12
tutors, tutoring, 3, 11, 12, 19, 20; in collaboration, 56–58, 133; education programs, 5–6, 67, 81n4; individualism vs. collaboration of, 78–79; lived experiences, 13–14; misunderstandings, 59–60; online practicing, 55–56; online protocols and values, 51–55; online training, 43–45, 48–49; peer, 64–65; relationships, 79–80; religious metaphors, 14–17; research, 21–22; rhetorical ecology, 46–47; staff meeting interactions, 62–63, 66–68; student, 209–10; tattling behavior, 49–50
tutor-sense, 21
tutor-to-tutor interactions, guidelines, 79–80
Two Hawks, Raymond, 196, 197

undergraduate staff, 14
underlife, 24, 91; negotiating, 31–32; sensemaking, 38–39; teaching assistants, 28, 37–38
union contracts, 141, 155n1; boss text in, 143–45; MOUs in, 147–48
University of California, 155n2; excellence review process, 148–49; non-senate faculty union contract, 141, 143

University of Vermont (UVM): Center for Academic Success, 136–37; collaboration, 132–33; Writing Center at, 137–39; writing program at, 127–32, 133–36
user-experience (UX) research, community-based problem solving, 195–96

values, tutoring, 51–54
value systems, interrogating, 193
venting, 91
Villanueva, Victor, Jr., 72
visibility, of adjuncts, 96–97
voices, student, 64
vulnerability, in antiracist work, 77
Vygotsky, Lev S., 185

Wardle, Elizabeth, 183, 187
WCAs. *See* writing center administrators
WCDs. *See* writing center directors
web designs, community relations, 196
websites, emotion, 85
Weick, Karl E., 165, 182; "Organizing and the Process of Sensemaking," 25–26, 27; *Sensemaking in Organizations*, 4, 47
Welch, Nancy, 191
Wetherell, Margaret, 86, 88, 89, 95
"What Students Write" (Flaherty), 168
whiteness, 185, 192, 195
white privilege, 6, 62, 195; antiracist pedagogy, 65–66; sensemaking, 63–64; and tutor interactions, 66–68
white racial habitus, 66
whites, 70; as allies/accomplices, 181–82
Why We Can't Wait (King), 208
WIDs. *See* writing in the disciplines program
Williams, Roger, 199
Willie-LeBreton, Sarah, *Transforming the Academy*, 69
Wilson, Darren, 194
Winck, Jessica, 91, 92
WLN, tutor columns, 12
Wojahn, Patti, 158
women, married Orthodox Jewish, 18
Woolgar, Steve, 191
work-life balance, 36–37, 40*n18*
workshops, 131; corequisite writing instruction, 175–76
WPAs. *See* writing program administrators
WPE. *See* writing pedagogy education
writers, as community, 19–20
writing, good grammar and, 168; strategies, 54

Writing Across Contexts: Transfer, Composition, and Cultures (Yancey, Robertson, and Taczak), 187
Writing Across the Curriculum (WAC), at University of Vermont, 128, 130–31, 134
Writing Advisory Board, 173
writing center administrators (WCAs), 5, 6–7, 21
writing-center-as-cozy-home metaphor, 11
"Writing Center as Managerial Site, The" (Heckelman), 123
writing center directors (WCDs), 3, 6, 58
"Writing Center Ethics: Sharers and Seclusionists" (Pemberton), 115
writing centers, 6, 12, 47, 62, 65, 74; at all-women's Jewish college, 13–14; as community, 19–20; culture and knowledge, 42–43; documentation, 123–24, 145–46; discourse, 15–16; ecologies, 109–11; individual development plans, 119–21; knowledge, 58–59; organizational performance of, 113–14; University of Vermont, 131–36, 137–39
Writing Centers and the New Racism (Greenfield and Rowan), 70, 71, 72
writing in the disciplines (WID) program, 6, 136; collaboration in, 132–33; at University of Vermont, 127, 129, 131, 134, 135, 137, 138
writing instructors, NTT, 165
writing pedagogy education (WPE), scholarship on, 24–25
writing program administrators (WPAs), 3, 6–7, 42, 148, 155*n7*, 172, 182, 188; antiracist work, 200–201; and non-tenure track faculty, 164, 165–66, 167–68, 176; role and impacts of, 158–59; and teaching assistant underlife, 37–38
writing programs, 159, 160; collaboration in, 166, 167; emotional context of, 90–91, 96–100, 103–4; racism in, 184–85; University of Vermont, 127–28
Writing Steering Committee, 173, 176
Writing Studio (North Carolina Central University), 206
Wutche Wame: A Living Culture Collaborative at Roger Williams University, 198, 201*n4*

Yancey, Kathleen, *Writing Across Contexts*, 187
Young, Vershawn Ashanti, 64

ABOUT THE AUTHORS

Courtney Adams Wooten is an associate chair: WPA and an assistant professor of writing and rhetoric at George Mason University. Her research revolves around writing program administration and feminist rhetorics. She coedited the collections *WPAs in Transition* and *The Things We Carry*, and her previous work has been published in *College English, WPA: Writing Program Administration, Academic Labor: Research and Artistry, Composition Studies, Peitho*, and *Harlot*, as well as several edited collections.

Joseph Cheatle is an assistant professor of English and director of the University Writing Center at the University of Southern Mississippi. He previously worked as the director of the Writing and Media Center at Iowa State University and as an associate director of the Writing Center at Michigan State University. His most recent scholarship focuses on how writing centers connect theory to practice and on creating collaborative approaches to improving services. His work is published in the *Writing Center Journal, The Journal of Writing Analytics*, and *Praxis: A Writing Center Journal*.

Sue Dinitz, senior lecturer emerita at the University of Vermont, directed the Undergraduate Writing Center for more than twenty years.

Andrea Rosso Efthymiou is an associate professor of writing studies and rhetoric and the Writing Center director at Hofstra University. She regularly collaborates with undergraduate tutors and was named the 2022 mentor of the year at Hofstra University. Andrea's research interests include writing centers, undergraduate research, writing program administration, and writing transfer. Andrea currently serves as treasurer of the National Conference on Peer Tutoring in Writing, and her scholarship has appeared in *Praxis: A Writing Center Journal, WLN: A Journal of Writing Center Scholarship, Writing Center Journal*, and various edited collections.

Barbara George teaches at Carnegie Mellon University. She has a background and experience in running writing centers, collaborating with FYW programs, professional and technical writing, and environmental writing. Barbara enjoys exploring "writing ecologies" among her varied interests within the writing world.

Genie Nicole Giaimo is an assistant professor and director of the Writing Center at Middlebury College. Their current research utilizes quantitative and qualitative models to answer a range of questions about behaviors and practices in and around writing centers. Their scholarly and programmatic interest in fair and "well" workplace practices have profoundly influenced their approach to writing administration to be inclusive, intentionally antiracist, and focused on the wellness of both workers and students. The author of over two dozen peer-reviewed articles and chapters, their forthcoming book, *Unwell Writing Centers: Searching for Wellness in Neoliberal Educational Institutions and Beyond*, comes out winter 2023.

Susanmarie Harrington directs the Center for Teaching and Learning and the Writing in the Disciplines program at the University of Vermont, where she is also a professor of English. Her most recent scholarship addresses the intersections of writing in the disciplines, information literacy, and peer learning.

ABOUT THE AUTHORS

Brian Hendrickson is an assistant professor of writing studies, rhetoric, and composition at Roger Williams University. His research areas include writing across difference, writing in STEM, equity-minded teaching and assessment, and community writing. His work has appeared or is forthcoming in *Across the Disciplines, Composition Forum, Composition Studies, Journal of Business and Technical Communication, Kairos,* and *WAC Journal,* as well as several edited collections including *Best of the Journals in Rhetoric and Composition 2018.* Most recently, Brian collaborated with the Providence Cultural Equity Initiative as PI on a grant to develop a racial reconciliation framework for the city of Providence.

Alba Newmann Holmes directs the Writing Associates Program at Swarthmore College, where she is an assistant professor of English. Her scholarship focuses on the operations of race and identity in college writing and writing centers.

Karen Keaton Jackson earned a BS in English secondary education with *summa cum laude* distinction from Hampton University. She then earned her master's and PhD in English/composition studies from Wayne State University in Detroit, Michigan. In May 2015, she received a University of North Carolina Board of Governors Award for teaching excellence. Her current research interests include the importance of the HBCU context when considering issues surrounding literacy, race, and identity for African American students. She has served on the executive boards of the Southeastern Writing Center Association and the Council of Writing Program Administrators. Presently, she serves a as a trustee on the NCTE Foundation Board and is a professor of English and director of the University Honors Program at North Carolina Central University.

Yvonne R. Lee directs the Graduate Writers' Studio at Lehigh University in Bethlehem, Pennsylvania. She earned her PhD in literacy, rhetoric, and social practice from Kent State University. Through genuinely interested in questioning and pushing against assumptions, Yvonne strives, in her everyday work, to help graduate writers make sense of their individual and collective experiences.

Rita Malenczyk is a professor of English and director of the Writing Program and Writing Center at Eastern Connecticut State University. Her scholarly publications include three edited or coedited collections, among them *A Rhetoric for Writing Program Administrators* and, with Susan Miller-Cochran, Elizabeth Wardle, and Kathleen Blake Yancey, *Composition, Rhetoric, and Disciplinarity.* Her work has also appeared in numerous edited collections and journals, including *College Composition and Communication, Writers: Craft and Context, WPA: Writing Program Administration,* and *Writing Center Journal.* She is a past president of the Council of Writing Program Administrators.

With a background in creative writing, technical writing, and writing center work, **Shannon McKeehen**, MFA, PhD, started her career in higher education in 2009. She is currently an assistant professor of composition at Tiffin University in Ohio. Her website can be found at www.shannonmckeehen.com.

Melissa Nicolas is an associate professor of English and director of composition at Washington State University. Her current research focuses on the intersections of disability and composition studies as well as institutional ethnography. Her work has appeared in numerous collections and journals.

Jeanne R. Smith directs the Writing Center at Kent State University, where she teaches in the Writing Program and the Honors College. She is a past president of the East Central Writing Centers Association and a cofounder of the Northeast Ohio Writing Centers Association. She coordinates service-learning experiences, writing center community fieldwork, and individual investigations and directs composition-related theses. Her research interests include tutor learning and reflective practice. She currently studies writer metacognition and self-regulation in the revision process as well as diversity issues in writing centers.

Christy I. Wenger is the author of *Yoga Minds, Writing Bodies: Contemplative Writing Pedagogy* and has published in writing studies on noncognitive factors of learning, feminist rhetorics, and the importance of contemplative pedagogy. Currently, Dr. Wenger continues to research contemplative writing pedagogy and is working on a book-length project on mindful leadership and administration in higher education.

Bronwyn T. Williams is a professor of English and director of the University Writing Center at the University of Louisville. He writes and teaches on issues of literacy, identity, digital media, sustainability, and community engagement. He is currently at work on a book about student experiences during the first two years of the COVID-19 pandemic. His most recent book is *Literacy Practices and Perceptions of Agency: Composing Identities*. Previous books include *New Media Literacies and Participatory Popular Culture Across Borders*, *Shimmering Literacies: Popular Culture and Reading and Writing Online*, and *Identity Papers: Literacy and Power in Higher Education*.

www.ingramcontent.com/pod-product-compliance
Lightning Source LLC
Chambersburg PA
CBHW020526080526
44583CB00013B/752